PENGUIN BOOKS

Eyeliner

Zahra Hankir, a Lebanese British journalist and the editor of *Our Women on the Ground*, writes about the intersection of politics, culture, and society, particularly in the broader Middle East. Her work has appeared in publications including *Condé Nast Traveler*, *The Observer Magazine*, *The Times Literary Supplement*, *BBC News*, *Al Jazeera English*, *Bloomberg Businessweek*, the *Los Angeles Times*, and *The Rumpus*. She was awarded a Jack R. Howard Fellowship in International Journalism to attend the Columbia Journalism School and holds degrees in politics and Middle Eastern studies.

Eyeliner

A Cultural History

ZAHRA HANKIR

PENGUIN BOOKS

PENGUIN BOOKS
An imprint of Penguin Random House LLC
penguinrandomhouse.com

Illustrations by Mercedes deBellard (represented by Folio Art)

Grateful acknowledgment is made to the following for
permission to adapt photographs:

p. xii: copyright © 2022 by Beowulf Sheehan
p. 50: copyright © 2021 by Dave Greenwell
p. 78: Youssef Nabil - *Shirin Neshat, Casablanca 2007*
p. 112: Photo by Leila Ejeilat
p. 136: Photo by Jorge "Big Chuco" Perez, bigchuco@gmail.com
p. 228: Photo by Holly Olmos
p. 249: Photo by Anya Kneez
p. 311: Photo by Fatima Farley Camara

LIBRARY OF CONGRESS CATALOGING-IN-PUBLICATION DATA

Names: Hankir, Zahra, author.
Title: Eyeliner : a cultural history / Zahra Hankir.
Description: New York : Penguin Books, [2023] | Includes bibliographical references.
Identifiers: LCCN 2023015168 (print) | LCCN 2023015169 (ebook) |
ISBN 9780143137092 (hardcover) | ISBN 9780525508601 (ebook)
Subjects: LCSH: Eyeliner. | Cosmetics. | Eye—Care and hygiene. |
Cosmetics industry. | Beauty, Personal.
Classification: LCC GT2340 .H34 2023 (print) |
LCC GT2340 (ebook) | DDC 391.6/3—dc23/eng/20230823
LC record available at https://lccn.loc.gov/2023015168
LC ebook record available at https://lccn.loc.gov/2023015169

Printed in the United States of America
1 3 5 7 9 10 8 6 4 2

Set in Baskerville MT Pro
Designed by Cassandra Garruzzo Mueller

To Teta, Mama, and Yasmin

Contents

Preface

I must've been about seventeen; I can't be sure. But I do remember how insecure I felt. My mother had dragged me to a family engagement party, at which men and women were segregated, per Islamic tradition. We were in my hometown, Sidon, in South Lebanon. Mama had framed her hazel eyes with forest-green eyeliner on the planes of her eyelids and jet-black kohl along her waterlines. She reserved this look for special occasions such as weddings and visits to our home from family friends and potential suitors who wished to ask for my hand in marriage (Mama supported my refusal to engage with said suitors). I often watched her when she applied her makeup, which she did ritualistically, with great care and consideration, as if it weren't merely a beautification process but a moment of transcendence. With six children, a full-time job, and the world's weight on her shoulders—in a country continually teetering on the edge of collapse—she was surrounded by constant chaos. But her hand never wavered when she applied her eyeliner; it was as if the world had come to a standstill. Steadily, and with great precision, she would close one eye and swipe the kohl applicator along her waterlines, allowing both rims to catch the pigment. When she opened her made-up eyes, I marveled at her beauty.

At the engagement party that evening, she took off her floral hijab, volumized her highlighted hair with the tips of her fingers, kicked off her heels, and danced the night away. She encouraged me to get up and join her, extending her manicured hand, but I demurred. The entire guest list was entranced, as though she'd unintentionally upstaged the bride-to-be. I, on the other hand, was seated quietly in a corner, barefaced save my kohl, and dressed somewhat casually. When people greeted us, they commented on how much I resembled my father—which was to say, I had inherited his dark and prominent features, and looked nothing like my mother, nor did I possess her infectious energy. I could only ever dream of being so confident.

Before moving back to South Lebanon following the end of a fifteen-year-long civil war that had all but obliterated the country, my family lived in the UK, where my parents had sought safety and stability and where I was born during the 1980s. As a young girl with Levantine and Egyptian heritage living in a claustrophobic city in northern England, I learned that to "assimilate" or "integrate" with the majority-white community, I had to minimize every aspect of myself. This was perfectly all right with me, in theory; I'd much rather have disappeared into the background than be seen anyway, as I was naturally introverted. But as a family, we couldn't help but stand out, and not just because of how we looked. During assembly, my four brothers and I excused ourselves, as we'd been instructed by our parents to avoid singing Christian hymns; we awkwardly exited the hall daily with the school's few other Muslims and Jehovah's Witnesses. (To ensure we never forgot we were Muslim, my father would sometimes wake us up at the break of dawn to pray with him. I also attended private Qur'an lessons with my Pakistani peers.) We skipped school lunch during Ramadan, and I was rarely allowed to hang out with friends. When we went swimming for our physical education classes, at my parents' request, I wore leotards and cycling shorts to cover my body, prompting stares and giggles. My mispronounced name eventually became my known name. I was once curiously asked to give my class a presentation on Islam and brought along with me a prayer carpet and Qur'an. As I shared the five pillars of the religion, my classmates mostly gawked at me, perplexed.

Even when I made a concerted effort to mingle, I was often taunted and bullied. A larger girl took great pleasure in repeatedly pushing me to the ground during recess. One afternoon when I was eleven, I came home from school with tears streaming down my face; after netball practice, I'd overheard one of my white classmates refer to my brothers and me as "weird" and call us the "P word"—a racist term used to offend people of Pakistani heritage—and two other girls had laughed in agreement. At home, I implored my mother to explain why these girls were so mean to me.

Mama was sympathetic about this predictable reaction to my being othered. But as an immigrant who was fearful for her family's precarious situation back in Lebanon and who had experienced othering herself along with my father in incendiary ways, one of which involved a lawsuit, she also had to contend with more serious matters. She did, however, glean that my early insecurities were exacerbated by the knowledge that I was non-white, Muslim, foreign, and consequently believed to be "strange." I was merely made to feel there was something inherently wrong with me due to the religion I was born into and my heritage, when I should have been taking pride in both, she reassured me.

One of my only genuine friends at the time was May, an Egyptian who wore bell-bottoms and scrunchies and who lived in the same building complex as us. I was twelve, she was fourteen; her parents were less strict than mine, and so she had already started to wear makeup. Unlike me, she was far from timid, but we bonded over our shared heritage and Muslim background. While hanging out after school one afternoon, she was determined to "make me over." With Ace of Base blasting in the background from her stereo, she carefully drew eyeliner onto my lids and curled my lashes with mascara. When I looked into the mirror, I was both pleased and surprised; it was as if I could finally *see* myself, as if I had somehow come into focus.

We returned to Lebanon as a family in the 1990s, as my parents had decided the country was safe enough for us to live in after the end of the war, and partly also because they protectively did not want me to experience my teenage years in England. There, as a young adult whose insecurities had only metamorphosed, I attempted to assert control over my looks, often to my conservative father's dismay. I had the kinks and waves straightened out of my temperamental hair once a week by Fatima, a boisterous Palestinian salon owner who chain-smoked as she fried my strands with tongs. (My eyebrows were thinned out so brutally by this same woman that they've never fully recovered.) I avoided feminine clothing and high heels, for they would mean I'd take up more space in a world that already felt hostile toward me. And I dressed like my four brothers year-round, very much wanting to be a boy, knowing they were afforded certain privileges I was not.

While I wasn't inundated with filtered images of friends and influencers the way that today's teenagers are, I regularly pored over *Teen Vogue* and other Western magazines and catalogs that had made their way into Lebanon. Admittedly, at times, I wished I could look more like the blond white girls who stared back at me from the glossy pages. I once fixated on an advertisement featuring a thin, fair model whose eyes were framed with kohl. As I saw it, she embodied breezy perfection because she was everything I was not: the manifestation of Eurocentric beauty norms. (I'd later learn she was Kate Moss.)

But then, at about fourteen, I encountered her—Queen Nefertiti, *my* queen—for the first time. My father was an avid collector of *National Geographic* magazines, both old and new. Being half-Egyptian, he was also obsessed with all things Egyptology. One of the issues he'd stumbled on, dated 1961, featured a spread on Nefertiti, with an image of her bust, and a white woman peering at it. The left side of the queen's face was visible, and clearly missing an eye, but the eye socket was lined with kohl. I imagined that the queen—whose name, aptly, means "the beautiful one has arrived"—connected me to a larger constellation of beguiling non-Western women. In the years since, I've remained infatuated with her. And in 2022, I finally made a pilgrimage to Berlin to meet her stucco-coated, multicolored bust. She was as exquisite as I'd always presumed her to be, with her mesmerizing kohl-rimmed eyes, chiseled features, and symmetrical face. Years after I first glimpsed her in the magazine, I still see something of myself in the queen.

⁓

I've been likened to Nefertiti at least three times. First, at sixteen, four years after we had relocated to postwar Lebanon. I used to smuggle my eyeliner into school by way of my pencil case, because makeup was forbidden; I'd sometimes hide it in my bra and reapply it in the bathroom. A tall, floppy-haired boy at school who had a mild crush on me said I resembled the queen. Per my dramatic diary, he told me it was the darkness of my eyes, whose lids were weighed down with straight eyelashes and stained with black kohl, that had captivated him.

On reflection, he was most certainly attempting to impress me with his knowledge of ancient Egyptian power women. That said, I was indeed flattered, and, given my insecurities, I appreciated the name-dropping and unsolicited attention before politely rebuffing him. Thanks to my infatuation with Nefertiti, I had already taken an interest in the history of makeup and had come to the understanding that kohl went far beyond prettification. It carried with it stories about my mother, grandmother, great-grandmother, and ancestors before them. I saw kohl as a constant companion for the women in my family, one that protected and empowered my proud lineage.

As my interest in this remarkable product deepened, I searched for its meaning in history. There, I discovered an abundance of figures and cultural practices beyond those I knew from Western music and film. I found eyeliner in the Arab world's deserts and in the savannas of Africa, in the hair salons of Iran, and in the alleyways of Kyoto. I found it on the faces of Indian storytellers, Latin American freedom fighters, and Palestinian activists. Even the Arab pop artists I listened to wielded eyeliner as an empowering tool to express their individuality—I thought Egyptian singer Ruby's darkened eyes were particularly daring, as they deliberately enhanced her seductive aura. And so I started to wear kohl more frequently, all the while worrying my father might notice and forbid me from wearing cosmetics altogether. (It was enough that I'd already pierced my ears—*twice*.)

In the years that followed my troubled time at high school, after I enrolled at the American University of Beirut, my younger, tougher, and only sister, Yasmin, encouraged me to embrace the art of more dramatic eyeliner application by teaching me herself, and later sending me YouTube tutorials. So, I graduated from under-eye kohl to full cat eye—the blacker, the better. I created the look by applying the cheapest Western liquid liner I could find at local drugstores, usually Maybelline, to my upper lids, and kohl imported from Pakistan to Sidon's souks, Hashmi Kajal, along my waterlines. By twenty, my transformation was complete: I had swapped loose clothing for miniskirts, biology textbooks for

Nietzsche and Edward Said, and straightened hair for a bouffant that, at various points, was auburn, jet black, and streaked with blond.

I built two worlds for myself, which I worked hard to ensure wouldn't collide. In South Lebanon, I was my parents' traditional daughter. But in Beirut, I experimented with my looks and beliefs. Occasionally the two worlds seeped into one another: I'd forget to remove my nose piercing when visiting home on weekends, or I'd casually say I believed in civil marriage. By now, I'd rejected Eurocentric beauty norms and embraced eyeliner and kohl as an expression of my identity, also by way of Nefertiti. Wearing eyeliner seemed to lend me a sense of power reminiscent of the queen's authority. My religious mother wasn't too keen on this physical and intellectual transformation: she once stopped talking to me for days after spotting a Facebook photo of me in a bikini (she's since forgiven these transgressions). So committed was I to my eyeliner that I only ever went without it when I returned to Sidon from Beirut on weekends, and when enduring tricky bouts of depression.

During my undergraduate studies, I briefly dated a socialist who asked me what I thought of Syria's military occupation of Lebanon and told me I looked like Nefertiti in the same breath. He was smoking shisha at a café nestled in the Lebanese mountains; we were sitting outdoors. It was a gorgeous late summer evening, the kind of evening Syrian poet Nizar Qabbani wrote about so wistfully. The sun had started to set. The weather was milder than usual, but there was a breeze hinting at the imminent change in seasons, and a nearby jasmine tree made itself known to us with each waft of fragrant air. I'd just removed my oversize sunglasses, which I often hid behind. For a moment, I was worried the socialist would think me disheveled, as my eyeliner had wilted a little in the day's humidity. When he said the queen's name, I smiled coyly, then demanded a drag of the shisha. In truth, my heart was dancing—not because of the person complimenting me, but because of what he was implying: I was not only attractive, but regal. It's a rare moment in time in which I can trace the precise evolution of my confidence. I had, perhaps, finally come of age.

The third time I was likened to Nefertiti was by a British finance bro with whom I shared a corporate elevator in central London. I had left Lebanon for college and my career, and was well into my twenties at this point, though my struggles with confidence weren't too far behind me. "You look exotic," he said boldly. "A bit like Nefertiti." This time around, I bristled at the suggestion. If ever there were an Orientalist compliment, this was it. While his gaze appeared to flatten the queen, my relationship to her reached deep into my roots and identity. Nefertiti seemed a fascinating mirror in this way: what we see in the royal wife reveals more about us than we will ever know about her.

My commitment to kohl has prevailed, to the extent that my mother never fails to ask me if I'm ill when I'm without it. On most days of nationwide lockdowns in the wake of the COVID-19 pandemic, I still donned a full cat eye for video conferences: it helped me maintain the illusion of normalcy. I wear eyeliner to Pilates, to the bodega, and when I'm alone at home. I even wore it during eight days of extreme camping in Chad, where I was re-searching the Wodaabe people for this book. (My eyeliner often reflects the phases of my work: when I wrote the chapter on Amy Winehouse, my wings inadvertently grew larger, until they began to touch the edges of my eyebrows.) I'm rarely if ever without the magical lines adorning my eyes, just as I am never without my culture, my ancestors, or my mother.

It's possible, of course, to assign too much meaning to one's physicality, such that beautifying oneself can become a frivolous and time-wasting mission, an exercise in vanity, or a palpable burden. But my kohl wearing has never merely been about look-ing a particular way (though I can't complain about its aesthetic benefits). Now, I can see my juvenile preoccupation with physical appearance was rooted in my coming to terms with a "strangeness" that was imposed upon me and that I'd internalized as a vulner-able, sensitive girl who grew up in the UK in the late 1980s and early 1990s and, more broadly, as a teenager learning to navigate new worlds.

Because I'd started to encounter Nefertiti's legacy everywhere— in ads on the billboards of Cairo; on the eyes of my Syrian Leba-nese grandmother in Polaroid photos from the 1960s; on Saudi feminists; and on the Lebanese legend Fairuz—I'd also started to internalize the sheer power and reach of "weird" women, and re-sultantly myself. And because kohl originated in the East, I often felt as if I were traversing space and time and conversing with my ancestors while wearing it in the West. Today, kohl is, to my mind, a celebration of my identity and the glorious and profound his-tories swirling around it. When I stencil my eyes with black pigment, I am performing not only an act of self-love, but also one of self-preservation.

The question of where eyeliner fits into one's persona is the driving force of these pages. To minorities and communities of color, kohl transcends aesthetics. It's about identity and one's sense of self; power and gender; spirituality and religiosity; sexuality and coming-of-age; rites of passage; rebellion and resistance; and the relationship between mothers and daughters. Kohl is also a cause for celebration and pride, a tool laden with centuries of layered histories—of empires, queens and kings, poets, writers and nomads. Imagine that? Carrying all that history in a little tube or pencil or pot that fits in pockets and purses.

To wear eyeliner and learn about its origins is to bring not only ourselves, but also some of the world's most fascinating cultures, into focus.

Introduction: Liner Notes

Despite its ubiquity, there's more to eyeliner than meets the eye. This seldom-examined object frames the eyes of women on the New York City subway and Bedouin men in the deserts of the Arabian Peninsula. Instagram influencers experiment with graphic liner designs, and supermodels sport wings on Paris runways. Members of the Taliban smear a form of eyeliner onto their lids to repel the sun, as do Afghan Pashtuns and tribes along the Himalayan and Afghanistan-Pakistan mountain ranges. Per religious tradition, living goddesses in Nepal decorate their eyes with the cosmetic, similar to kathakali storytellers in India, channeling tales both past and present. When they can't access retail liner, some women prisoners in the US make their own with pencil graphite and Vaseline. Fashion-conscious beatniks paired eyeliner with berets, and Russian dancers of Diaghilev's Ballets Russes donned flicks of it while onstage. Vikings wore charcoal to protect their vision during battle; even Mesopotamians may have used kohl, applying it with a stick shaped like a spatula. While they didn't use kohl as prolifically as the ancient Egyptians, ancient Greek women darkened their eyes with a mixture of soot, antimony, and burnt cork. The Prophet Muhammad was said to have worn a form of eyeliner, too, and spoke of its healing properties. There are traces of the cosmetic in the Old Testament, which mentions figures, including Jezebel, with "painted eyes"; two were "harlots," though the use of eye paint was not strictly considered objectionable per the scriptures. A disparate (and not remotely all-encompassing) list of characters and contexts, indeed—such is the reach of this versatile and influential object.

⌒

After the onset of the COVID-19 pandemic, eyeliner sales soared—and lipstick sales plummeted—due to the widespread use of face masks. By 2021, the global eye makeup market had surged to $15.6 billion and was set to swell to $21.4 billion by 2027. The growth trajectory is staggering. It comes as no surprise, however, that eyeliner and eye pencils constitute the largest market segment, edging out mascara and eyeshadow by 5 percent.

Although eyeliner applications have varied over the centuries, cross-culturally, the aesthetic goal has always been the same: to beautify, enhance, or enlarge the eye. The cosmetic can transform faces from exhausted to awake, take an outfit from work appropriate to date appropriate, and elevate an overall look from bare and subdued to adorned and seductive—all with a few swipes. (Commenting on eyeliner's transformative power in her book *I Feel Bad about My Neck*, Nora Ephron wrote: "There are a couple of old boyfriends whom I always worry about bumping into, but there's no chance—if I ever did—that I would recognize either of them. On top of which they live in other cities. But the point is that I still think about them every time I'm tempted to leave the house without eyeliner.") Depending on the day, eyeliner wearers may be sultry or demure, rebellious or clean-cut, low-key or loud. Some are protecting themselves from evil spirits or honoring a god, while others may be treating their eyes for an infection or blocking the sun. Like ink itself, eyeliner helps us deliver messages to the world: we are confident, we belong to a proud subculture, we express ourselves, we are our own creations. There's an eyeliner style and a story for virtually every look.

The art of eyeliner application can be painstakingly precise: experts employ the care and consideration a painter or a calligrapher might use on a blank canvas. The rules are many, though malleable, and the technique can take years to perfect. The applicator must move steadily, to ensure the pigment glides seamlessly onto the eyelid or waterline. Apply too thick a line to the lid, and you risk shrinking the eye; apply lines that bleed, and you may give your eyes an undesirable raccoon effect. Different eye shapes can suit different styles—a black line on the lower waterline can make small eyes look smaller, whereas a single line along the upper lid may make them look bigger. Hinging on the angle of the upturn, wings can widen the eye—or, according to one TikToker, even reveal whether the wearer is a millennial or Gen Z.

The slightest quiver of the wrist can mean entire lines must be redrawn, a time-consuming struggle to which few are immune. Alexandria Ocasio-Cortez, the American politician known aesthetically for her signature dark eyeliner and red lipstick, once posted on Instagram about her botched attempt at a wing: "I just want you all to know that no matter who you are or where you're from, no matter how much you achieve in life, eyeliner will always humble you," she said.

Applicators come in many forms, from fingers and bones to brushes and plastic rods. Some people use their pinkies to fine-tune their imperfect lines, while others use stencils, wipes, or cotton swabs. Color and consistency are important, too. Black eyeliner can be aging, while brown, green, or blue can be more flattering. (Princess Diana famously wore blue eyeliner, likely to echo the blue in her eyes.) Liquid, gel, and cream eyeliners are best used on lids, while pencils and powders work well on waterlines. And then there's the shape and length of the lines; the choices are endless, as Instagrammers and TikTokers have made clear. Your eyeliner can even be "sharp enough to kill a man," declares one popular meme—and cat-eye devotee Taylor Swift.

The effort pays off. Eyeliner, of course, can make a woman appear significantly more attractive, and attractiveness, or "pretty privilege," is meaningfully associated with a disturbingly wide range of positive social and economic outcomes (though often the woman would have to be "conventionally" attractive to benefit from this privilege). Women, especially women of color, are held to high and specific standards when it comes to their appearance at work. In the office, women who wear the right kind of makeup— not too heavy, not too light—are seen as more competent and effective leaders; a pronounced wing may be looked at less favorably than tightlining. When worn well, eyeliner can give the illusion of doe eyes, implying youth. And those with "baby faces" are thought to fare better in life as they're perceived to be more honest, trustworthy, or charismatic than others.

Conversely, some young people wear eyeliner to appear older

or more mature. Twelve-year-olds Alice Craig and Cristina Wilson, grade-school classmates who now attend different Manhattan middle schools, gather in friends' bedrooms on weekends to trade eyeliner techniques gleaned from YouTube tutorials. Among their group, the girls explained, eyeliner is the cosmetic of choice. "It's not about looking 'cute,'" Wilson says. "Eyeliner makes you look cool and bold. It makes you look older, too. It's not like anyone will think you're fifteen. But maybe they'll take you more seriously."

"A lot of girls we know mostly use makeup to cover up things they think are flaws, or they're doing something subtle to look prettier but natural," says Craig. "I think if that makes you feel more confident, go for it. But my friends and I don't find that way of using makeup very interesting. Eyeliner is different. It's basically the opposite of subtle or 'naturally pretty.' Eyeliner shows your personality."

This is eyeliner's sheer power, unmatched by those other items in your makeup bag.

Eyeliner resides comfortably in almost every corner of pop culture, from music and theater to film and art. It's regularly employed as a transformative marker of maturity, drama, seduction, sexuality, strength, or rebelliousness. On Western screens, high-intensity eyeliner has been used to signify madness or transgression. Femme fatales such as Akasha, played by the late Aaliyah in the 2002 film *Queen of the Damned*, and Julie Marsden, played by Bette Davis in the 1938 film *Jezebel*, were made up in eyeliner (Graham

Greene memorably described Davis as having "popping, neurotic eyes, a kind of corrupt and phosphorescent prettiness"). Twisted male protagonists like the late Heath Ledger as the Joker in *The Dark Knight* and Robert Pattinson in *The Batman* wore smudged lines. In the Netflix series *Orange Is the New Black*, several of the rebellious female inmates at a New York prison creatively and consistently trace their eyes with pigment, my favorite look being the long and thin flicks worn by the gutsy Maritza Ramos, played by Diane Guerrero. In *Game of Thrones*, the nomadic group known as the Dothraki wear eyeliner prolifically, particularly its male warriors on horseback. The troubled chess player portrayed by Anya Taylor-Joy in *The Queen's Gambit* draws lines that grow more dramatic as she becomes progressively more unhinged; in an alcohol-induced haze, she paints floating lines a centimeter below her natural lower lashes, producing an uncanny, doll-like effect. And in the HBO show *Euphoria*, the eyeliner worn by actor Alexa Demie's character, Maddy Perez, is distinct and bold, reflecting her tough yet emotionally volatile persona. As depicted in *The Crown*, Princess Diana, prior to being interviewed by the BBC's *Panorama* program about Prince Charles's infidelity, applies black eyeliner heavily to her bottom waterline, giving her eyes a somber, mournful appearance. Eyeliner, incidentally, isn't always used on the eyes. John Waters, the American filmmaker and director, creates his trademark pencil mustache with Maybelline's Expert Wear Velvet Black eyeliner.

Eyeliner has also served practical purposes in the arts. During the 1920s, with the introduction of "movie palaces," films were broadcast in black and white, and directors required that cast members line their eyes to ensure they popped against a mono-chrome backdrop. In theater and opera historically performed against candles or lamplights, eyeliner was applied liberally to performers' faces to help the audience see their expressions more clearly. Some celebrities and artists have had especially intimate relationships to their liner, so much so that it became a trademark that they would be unrecognizable without. Consider, for a mo-ment, Amy Winehouse without her graphic wings, or a barefaced Trixie Mattel.

———

Eyeliner speaks a universal language of transformation. But its roots lie firmly in the East, beginning with ancient Egypt, where the earliest evidence of its use dates to at least 3100 BCE, and where it was used for medicinal, spiritual, and cosmetic purposes. In Africa's ancient Land of Punt, galena was likely used as a source for kohl, as evidenced by trade between the kingdom and ancient Egyptians. People across the continent, from Berbers in Morocco and Oromos in Ethiopia to nomads in Chad, also use kohl to repel the sun and to beautify or medicate their eyes. However one refers to eyeliner in the Global South—kajal, kohl, surma, or sormeh—the cosmetic has been highly influential, and can convey messages about power, religiosity, and a commitment to moral codes.

In the Arab world and spanning swaths of Asia and Africa, some mothers still apply kohl to their newborns' eyes to ward off the evil eye, the superstition that a jealous glance or gaze can cause harm. Across South Asia and Africa, many Muslims don't look at kohl, surma, or kajal as makeup, but rather as an element of their faithfulness and an integral part of preparing for religious holidays including Eid and Ramadan.

Communities of color today also use eyeliner to express themselves and assert their identities in the face of marginalization and white supremacy. Ziwe Fumudoh, an American talk show host who went viral for pressing her interviewees on Black culture and politics, often boasts a signature eyeliner look. "Most hosts are like, 'What's your next project? How can we promote it?' as opposed to 'How many Black friends do you have? What do you like about Black people qualitatively?'" she told *Allure* in September 2020. "I'm asking those questions with my intense eyeliner and pigment on my face. I'm trying to contextualize these products that I have and bring them into conversations about race and class and gender. . . . Nothing exists in a vacuum. I don't exist in a vacuum, the makeup I wear doesn't exist in a vacuum."

New York–based writer Elaine Louie, who's been wearing smudged kohl ever since she was a teenager living in San Francisco, says she's so committed to her look, she sleeps in her lines. "Back in the day, I ruined oodles of white sheets," she says as she shares her kohl memories with me. "Now I have charcoal-gray sheets," which help obscure residue, she adds, joking that she sometimes even reapplies it in the middle of the night.

Jokes aside, Louie, like so many of the figures in this book, and like so many people around the world, myself included, turned to eyeliner as she came of age to help enlarge her eyes, find her personal style, and boost her confidence. "It wasn't just about how you looked," the eighty-year-old writer, who is of Chinese heritage, says. "It was about how you felt. It was about this aura you have. That maybe you were just a little bit exotic." Taking it a step further, Rosana Cipriano, a resident of Rio de Janeiro, says, "Eyeliner can even bring my soul out of my eyes."

This book embarks on a journey through time and across continents to tell just a few of these stories about our enduring obsession with a remarkable substance. Beginning, fittingly, in the East, we'll delve into ancient Egypt to understand the original beauty icon, Queen Nefertiti, and her lasting influence on eyeliner use. Challenging the notion that beauty is an inherently female preoccupation, we'll turn to the Wodaabe people in the savanna region of Chad. To demonstrate how sormeh has been used as a critical instrument for self-expression and political resistance, we'll reflect on the eruption of protests in the wake of the killing of Mahsa Amini in Iran. Next, we'll travel to Petra, Jordan, to illustrate how kohl helps communities maintain and celebrate centuries-old traditions. We'll then get to know Mexican American cholas in California and see how eyeliner can assert cultural pride in the face of racial discrimination and marginalization. Investigating kajal's relationship with the divine and the ethereal, we'll wander over to India to visit Kerala's storytellers. We'll later explore the social implications of the eyes and eye contact in Japan, and meet a millennial geisha in Kyoto.

Back in the West, we'll attend drag shows in New York, exploring the connection between this transformative cosmetic and gender. With a focus on Amy Winehouse, we'll observe the phenomenon of the Western pop star, and witness how the substance can play a significant role in one's physical and psychological development and protection—and even in one's mental health. Finally, we'll meet a few of the influencers both shaping and responding to ever-evolving beauty ideals in the age of social media.

Eurocentric beauty norms have dominated the global beauty discourse in decades past, alternately by suppressing and mocking or fetishizing and cherry-picking unique cultural features and practices found in and founded by so-called exotic societies and groups. This book is a celebration of the innovative contributions of people of color to the beauty industry and the vibrant array of beauty practices around the world.

I ask you, dear reader, to eschew the Western gaze, and to sensitively and thoughtfully expand your understanding of beauty, as well as of the relationship between beauty and power. Though these chapters attest to the rich cultural history of eyeliner, the liner itself is, ultimately, an accessory to a larger story about how we communicate our identities and desires. The story of eyeliner and how it has fascinated us through the centuries is also the story of human ingenuity, resourcefulness, aspiration, and imagination. To open your eyes to the fascinating path that eyeliner has drawn through space and time is to embark on a journey freighted with meaning—if not outright magic.

Glossary

or the purposes of this book, eyeliner will be defined as a cosmetic or medicinal substance whose aesthetic intention is to contour or outline the eyes, with the goal of enlarging or enhancing them. Eyeliner appears in various forms, is made up of different materials, has multiple names, and has been used uniquely across cultures and time periods.

kohl: A generic term denoting eyeliner made with naturally sourced materials, including ground galena or soot. The word *kohl* comes from the Arabic *kuhl*, defined by *A Dictionary of Modern Written Arabic* as a pulverized powder that darkens the edges of the eyelids. Besides its cosmetic use, kohl is used to cleanse or cool the eyes, and to protect them from the sun's rays, the desert sand, and infections. Kohl is widely applied by men, women, and children across swaths of Asia, Africa, and the Middle East. (The origin of the word *alcohol* in English is from the Arabic *al-kuhl*. *Al-kuhl* became how Europeans used to refer to spirits around the seventeenth century because of how kohl was produced.)

kajal: A greasy black kohl traditionally used in South Asia for cosmetic, medicinal, and spiritual purposes. Kajal is made of soot from the burning of ingredients including ghee, castor oil, coconut oil, camphor, aloe vera, or sandalwood paste. While *kajal* is a term spoken colloquially across India, primarily in the Devanagari languages of Hindi and Marathi and also Gujarati, in Bengali it's called kajol; in Malayalam it's called kanmashi; in Kannada it's called kannu kappu; in Telugu it's called kaatuka; and in Tamil it's called kanmai.

ithmid: Considered by some to be the purest form of kohl, ithmid is derived from the mineral galena, or lead sulfide, and is used by Bedouin communities and Muslims across the Middle East and North Africa and other parts of Africa and Asia. The Prophet Muhammad was said to have worn ithmid, which is why it is thought to be sunnah, or the way of the Prophet, by devout Muslims.

Western eyeliner: Eyeliner is worn by people of all genders in the West and beyond to beautify and define the eyes. It comes in several iterations, including powder, pencil, pen, liquid, cream, and gel. Western eyeliner tends to be ultra-processed and is made of a film-forming agent (allowing the eyeliner to be deposited onto the eyelid or waterline), thickeners (enabling the eyeliner to stick to the eyelid or waterline), and pigments (giving the eyeliner its color). Eyeliner often contains ingredients like glycerin, mineral oils, and other chemicals. Western-packaged "kohl" and "kajal" aren't usually made of the materials used in authentic kohl or kajal, and borrow only their names.

GLOSSARY

surma: In Urdu or Bengali, surma is a powdered form of kohl comprised of galena or antimony, though doubt has been cast on the latter. It's commonly sold as a loose powder packed in white paper sheets or in cylindrical bottles. Muslims in South Asian countries decorate their eyes with surma; Muslim men especially can be spotted wearing it, as recommended by the Prophet Muhammad.

sormeh: A loose powder historically used by Persians to enhance the eyes. Traditionally sold in vials or made at home, sormeh is still used in Iran, though not as broadly as it once was. In ancient times, the wearing of black sormeh was believed to ward off evil spirits. A popular form of organic sormeh is made from the soot collected by the burning of nuts including almonds, walnuts, hazelnuts, and pistachios, as well as other materials.

tiro: A black powder mostly extracted from galena and used in Nigeria as a beautifier or to cleanse the eyes. Usually sold in metal containers, tiro is applied to the lower rim of the eye with a small, sticklike applicator and is widely used by the Yoruba ethnic group as a form of facial ornamentation. Tiro is also known as kwali and uhie in Nigeria.

mebari: The Japanese practice of outlining the eyes, often with red pigment, popularized by theater actors, mimicked by townspeople, and adopted by geisha. In addition to serving an aesthetic purpose, mebari with red pigment is thought to protect the eyes from evil spirits.

guyliner: Eyeliner worn by men.

Eyeliner

Chapter One

The Beautiful One Has Arrived

Nefertiti and the Dawn of Kohl

Nefertiti's features are of a frankly exotic order.

—FRANK CROWNINSHIELD, *VOGUE*, 1939

ncient Egyptians were obsessed with their looks. They indulged in intricately designed clothing, jewelry, perfume, and makeup, and put youthfulness on a pedestal. Palettes, pumice stones, hairpins, mirrors, and applicators were likely staples of the ancient Egyptian makeup box, along with red ocher for the face and lips and kohl—in the form of sooty powder—for the eyes. Ancient Egyptian men and women across all social strata wore this early iteration of eyeliner, using it to create thick black lines around their eyes and sometimes to enhance their eyelashes and eyebrows as well.

Beautification in the kingdom was treated as an art and a spiritual or healing ritual. People who wore kohl honored and sought protection from the gods. Ancient Egyptian art on papyrus often features the heavily lined eye of the god Horus, a symbol of prosperity and protection. Ancient Egyptians believed that eyes without kohl may be vulnerable to the evil eye, and that, by wearing it, Horus and the god Ra would guard them against illness. In hieroglyphs, the root of the term *makeup artist* means "to write" or "engrave," while the root of *makeup palette* means "to protect."

When the dead were resurrected, in ancient Egyptian dogma, they were brought back to life as ideal iterations of themselves, not as the fallible beings they were when they passed. The wealthy were often buried with their prized possessions so they could look attractive in the afterlife, too; in their tombs were bags of kohl made of linen or leather alongside other essentials, such as shaving kits and jewelry. "Explicitly linked to physical conception in the tomb, kohl helped an Egyptian to be reborn," according to the Brooklyn Museum. Rebirth required conception, which required a sexual act, which required hotness—which required cosmetics. Cartonnage carvings or "death masks" on ancient Egyptian tombs and coffins boasted younger versions of the departed, all with heavily lined eyes. "It is virtually impossible to find a portrait of an ancient Egyptian whose eyes are not decorated," writes Egyptologist Shokry El-Kantiry.

Kohl had practical applications during the wearer's lifetime as well, shielding vulnerable eyes from the sun, sand, dust, and disease-carrying flies, making it a truly indispensable, multitasking cosmetic in the mostly scorching and arid desert. (Curators at the Brooklyn Museum explain that kohl's use for protection against the sun can be likened to lampblack worn by modern football players.) Kohl was especially useful in the summertime, when locals were susceptible to eye infections from the bacteria in standing waters brought by floods from the Nile—some of which could lead to blindness. Physicians would carry kohl for both themselves and their patients, sometimes in pots with compartments labeled for the different phases of the year: winter, summer, and the "flood season."

Kohl consisted of either malachite, a green ore of copper, or galena, a crystal that is the most important ore of lead. The use of malachite for kohl, known as udju, has been traced back to the earliest predynastic period. Galena preparations known as mesdemet, however, ultimately prevailed as the most widely used basis of eye paint in ancient Egypt. This could be because galena has a low melting point, making it relatively easy to smelt in order to extract its lead.

Science partially validates the ancient belief in kohl's protective powers: In 1888, Kaddour Ben Larbey, an Algerian doctor who studied at the University of Paris's Faculty of Medicine, argued that kohl was an effective treatment for various eye infections. Two advertisements playing up the medicinal benefits of kohl even appeared in the Egyptian newspaper *Al-Ahram*, one in 1901 and another in 1920. In 2010, scientists discovered that the materials ancient Egyptians used in kohl likely *did* kill off bacteria that caused common infections, as intended. That same year, ancient Egyptian makeup samples at the Louvre in Paris were revealed to boost the production of nitric oxide, which provokes an immune response in the body. (That said, the US Food and Drug Administration warns against the use of modern kohl due to "high levels of lead." In 2021, the NYC Department of Health and Mental Hygiene distributed a public service announcement on billboards around New York City and on social media that pictured a South Asian baby whose eyes were heavily lined with kohl, warning against the dangers of lead and advising parents who've used the pigment on their kids to visit doctors for tests. In some Asian countries, lead poisoning from kohl is a serious concern.)

The cosmetic also signaled class distinctions in ancient Egyptian society. While the wealthy were likely to wear higher-quality kohl made of galena, the less privileged used soot from materials including almond shells, sunflowers, and frankincense as a substitute. Per research by Alfred Lucas published in 1930, to make kohl, ancient Egyptians also used substances including antimony, black oxide of copper, carbonate of lead, and brown ocher. Almost a century later, a 2022 study published by *Nature* revealed that inorganic ingredients found in kohl were more diverse than previously thought. Of the eleven kohl samples that were studied, two were lead based, one silicon based, three manganese based, and six carbon based; the study found that a range of inorganic materials used would've also included plant extracts and animal fats.

To complete the kohl-making process, ancient Egyptians would grind the various components with stone or on a palette to create fine powders. The powders formed a black, grayish, deep green, or other dark-colored mixture, depending on the ingredients used. Some believe ancient Egyptians sourced galena at Aswan, a city in southeastern Egypt, and along the banks of the Nile, while malachite was retrieved from the Sinai Peninsula. Hathor, the goddess of love, joy, women, and beauty, had dominion over the area; she was so closely associated with the substance that people also referred to her as the Lady of Malachite.

While materials for kohl in ancient Egypt were likely gathered locally, antimony was not native to the land, and might have been brought over from Asia, Persia, and the Arabian Peninsula. During the Eighteenth Dynasty, Queen Hatshepsut, a ruler of ancient Egypt who had the full powers of a pharaoh, embarked on a famous expedition to the Land of Punt, whose location is a matter of debate but generally thought to be in the Horn of Africa region. Among the merchandise she imported was galena, a sign of its importance in daily life.

Ancient Egyptians used kohl containers made of ceramics, wood, and stone to store makeup, as well as spoons to mix it. Some containers were extravagant and created with glass, ivory, or gold; they were occasionally encrusted with jewels or engraved with hieroglyphs and complex shapes such as palm columns and animals including monkeys, which ancient Egyptians kept as pets. Scores of these pots are scattered in museums around the West.

"A kohl pot's specialized function required a certain shape," according to the Brooklyn Museum. "Broad, low proportions that fit in the palm of the hand; an opening wide enough to allow the insertion of a finger or applicator; and a tight lid to protect the contents from dust, wind, and moisture." The shape of these containers was consistent, the curators note, but craftspeople used colors by turning to different pigments for variety.

Before being applied to the eye, kohl was poured onto the spoon or into the pot, then wetted with saliva, water, water-soluble gum, oil, or animal fat. The concoction would glide onto the eyelid with an instrument, much like modern liquid eyeliner's packaging.

"An ancient Egyptian woman time-traveling to the present would surely find much to puzzle her," writes author Judika Illes, "but hand her a modern kohl container and stick and she would know exactly what to do with it." The pigment formed two lines, one along the upper rim and one along the lower; occasionally, they merged to create a swoosh that traveled parallel to the eyebrows, whose edges were lengthened with makeup. The length of the lines varied—they could end close to the corners of the eyes or stretch as far as the temples.

The applicator, called a "needle" in some Arab cultures, would typically be composed of ivory, stone, wood, bones, silver, bronze, and glass, depending on the person's means. (In the Arab world, if someone asks about a person who's been dead for a while, the respondent says of the deceased that they've been underground for so long, their "bones have become kohl applicators.")

How the lines took their precise shape is unclear. But, in 2009, scientists E. M. Buda-Okreglak and P. Krapiva published a correspondence in the journal *Eye* documenting a unique injury a thirty-one-year-old had sustained after falling from her bed. The "subgaleal haematoma" left her with purple bruising around an eye indistinguishable from the line decorating the Eye of Horus. "The Eye of Horus in a Subgaleal Haematoma: Where Art Imitates Life," the authors titled the paper. The researchers hypothesized ancient Egyptians observed the clinical manifestations of a subgaleal hemorrhage on somebody who'd experienced a similar injury, leading them to imitate the lines with makeup. The observation might explain why the lines were thought to protect the person wearing the kohl from illness. A far-fetched theory, indeed, but to the scientists' credit, the likeness is rather uncanny.

The Elusive Queen

Of all the ancient Egyptians who wore kohl, Queen Nefertiti reigns supreme. But the elusive royal was far more than just a pretty face, and it would be unjust to limit her memory to her physique.

Not much is known about Nefertiti's life, and what is known is often contested. Nevertheless, scattered clues outline an intriguing portrait. Nefertiti served as queen alongside her husband, King Akhenaten, during his seventeen-year tenure in the fourteenth century BCE; she was one of many wives, and the pair likely wed when they were teenagers. It's unclear why Akhenaten married Nefertiti, though her beauty might have played a role. The identity of Nefertiti's parents is unknown, and there are unanswered questions about her racial and ethnic background. Some believe Nefertiti was born outside of ancient Egyptian royalty, and that she may have been a princess from Syria's Mitanni Kingdom. Others speculate she was the daughter of Ay, an adviser who later became pharaoh. In various representations of Nefertiti, the queen appears more prominently than her husband— signaling she had both beauty *and* power. The pharaoh seemed quite keen on his wife, with imagery of the two showing them kissing and frolicking, a departure from the era's typical portraiture. Nefertiti also had certain religious duties and participated in worshipping rituals with her husband. Far from a passive figurehead, she is also depicted in limestone blocks attacking her enemies by pulling their hair or wielding a sword.

Art, architecture, and religion were overhauled during Nefertiti's lifetime. With the queen by his side, the pharaoh tore up every rulebook, abandoned polytheism, and instructed his people to turn to monotheism and devote themselves to Aten, a sun god, in a religious system known as Atenism. A new capital city, Tell el-Amarna, was built and dedicated to Aten. Cliffs surrounded the area, cutting it off from the rest of the empire. Temples were constructed without roofs so sunlight could pour into them. Through it all, Nefertiti remained a source of strength for both Akhenaten and his subjects: "She would live through an unprecedented storm of events that called upon her to become a steadfast and calm leader who could heal the deep wounds inflicted on her people during the strangest, least traditional time Egypt had ever known," writes Egyptologist Kara Cooney in *When Women Ruled the World*. "Nefertiti would receive no credit for this political leadership, even though it was she who started the restoration of a country turned upside down, setting Egypt to rights at its darkest hour."

Historical documentation about the queen ends twelve to fourteen years into Akhenaten's rule. After that, her name was effectively dropped from the record. Some have speculated she ditched Atenism and fell out of Akhenaten's favor, died from a plague or other illness, or took her own life after losing three of her six daughters (among her living daughters was Ankhsenamun, who would become the wife of Tutankhamun). Others say she was deserted as she hadn't borne Akhenaten a son. Either way, Nefertiti apparently vanished. However, following her mysterious disappearance, Akhenaten took on a co-regent who some argue may have been Nefertiti herself. Historian Joyce Tyldesley, author of *Nefertiti's Face*, argues Nefertiti was more likely a deputy, while Cooney posits Nefertiti probably ruled as co-king, "even installing the next king," and that "more than any other Egyptian queen, it is Nefertiti who represents the epitome of true, successful female power."

The changes Nefertiti helped spur would ultimately also vanish into thin air. Akhenaten's imposition of monotheism came to an end when he died; those who disapproved of his upending of tradition reinstated polytheism, and Tell el-Amarna was abandoned.

The remaining clues to Nefertiti's life and the period during which the power couple altered Egyptian faith and art may lie in her tomb, which, at the time of writing, has not yet been found. Egyptologists everywhere continue to deliberate its whereabouts—one of these Egyptologists, Zahi Hawass, tells me he believes the grave is in the West Valley of the Kings and he's hopeful excavators will soon find it. More specifically, British archaeologist Nicholas Reeves has surmised that Nefertiti is buried in a hidden chamber within Tutankhamun's tomb.

Much is still unknown. We can, however, be sure the queen wore kohl purposefully and abundantly. Multiple images of her carved into stone show her large eyes framed with black lines.

And then there's her bust.

The "Most Alive" Egyptian Artwork

When Mohammed el-Senussi was pictured with Nefertiti's bust after it was discovered along the left bank of the upper Nile Valley on a sunny afternoon in December 1912, he appeared to be cradling it like it was a newborn baby. Understandably so—the multicolored limestone sculpture in the foreman's hands hadn't seen the light of day in over three thousand years. The stucco-coated artwork weighed forty-four pounds and was eighteen and a half inches tall. It emerged whole and relatively unblemished from the sands of the Egyptian desert, save a missing left eye and minor damage to its ears and crown.

"Suddenly we had in our hands the most alive Egyptian art-work," wrote Ludwig Borchardt, the mustachioed German archaeologist who led the expedition and later "moved" the bust out of Egypt and into Germany. Words, he declared in his field notes, failed to convey the impression Nefertiti's representation had left on him. And they couldn't possibly capture the sculpture's delicacy. "You cannot describe it," he said. "You must see it."

In this rendering, Nefertiti's face is stunningly symmetrical, with a visage about one and a half times longer than its width. The breadth of her lined, almond-shaped eyes equals the distance between them. And her straight-edged nose is roughly the same length as her forehead. Nefertiti's cheekbones are so pronounced as to appear naturally contoured; they would be the envy of Kim Kardashian herself.

Together, these facial proportions mean Nefertiti's face would score highly if measured against the so-called golden ratio, a proportion thought to be aesthetically optimal. During the European Renaissance, artists used the equation to model sculptures and paintings. And app filters on TikTok today turn to it as a formula to determine, quite unforgivingly, what is hot and what is not.

Celebrities with this particular beauty badge of honor include supermodel Bella Hadid and, unsurprisingly, Beyoncé.

These striking features sit atop a famously slender neck that is commonly described as "swanlike." The queen's slightly pointed chin accentuates her neck's length while softening her robust, square jawline. (A cosmetic procedure known as the "Nefertiti lift" promises the appearance of a longer neck and a more defined jawline. The costly enhancement is made possible by a dozen small Botox injections strategically placed in the face, jaw, and neck area. In 2009, a British woman revealed to the *Daily Mail* that she'd spent a quarter of a million dollars on fifty-one plastic surgeries to mimic Nefertiti's looks. In images of her on the paper's website, she's wearing eyeliner as the queen did.)

Nefertiti's skin tone, per her bust, is terra-cotta with undertones of warm sandstone, suggesting she was quite literally a woman of color. In his excavation diary, Borchardt described the shade as "light red." According to Tyldesley, the color of Nefertiti's skin—as it is shown on her bust—tells us little about her race. Ancient Egyptian portraiture often showed men with red-brown skin and women with yellow-white skin to distinguish the genders. By that logic, the pigment used on Nefertiti's bust was closer to what was typically used to depict men.

The dyes Nefertiti's sculptor used to color her chiseled face point to what may have been in the queen's makeup palette: her Cupid's bow lips were full and painted marsala brown, and her eyebrows were arched, shaped to perfection, and filled with smoky black dye, possibly kohl. The color contrast is stark, yet the queen's overall appearance is seamless. Nefertiti's makeup is, in fact, on trend: there are hundreds of tutorials on YouTube, TikTok, and

Instagram mimicking the queen's face with a great degree of precision.

All features considered, the allure of the queen's eyes—framed with thick black lines—is unparalleled. The lines are perfectly symmetrical, meeting at the edges of the eyes to form her trademark flicks. From a strictly aesthetic perspective, the tracing defines and widens the windows into Nefertiti's soul, lending them a fresh-looking yet sultry appearance.

Mass Consumption of Nefertiti

Nefertiti's portrayal has been replicated, invoked, and tweaked for mass consumption countless times at all corners of the globe for roughly a hundred years. Fans can find her image on postcards, tote bags, posters, jewelry, pocket mirrors, and T-shirts; her kohl-rimmed eyes even appear on sleeping masks. Her looks are carved into our collective memory to an extent that few other works of art can claim.

Before the COVID-19 pandemic, about five hundred thousand admirers visited Nefertiti's bust annually at the Neues Museum in Berlin. When I went to visit the queen myself in October 2022, within one hour, over three hundred people of all ages and ethnicities had shuffled into the majestic room hosting her bust. They peered at her in droves, much like one might marvel at the *Mona Lisa* in the Louvre. (By contrast, a drab-looking bust of her husband, Akhenaten—its most interesting feature being the incomplete lines around one of its eyes—sat somewhat dejectedly with other artifacts in an adjacent room.)

Nefertiti's image is in such high demand that, in 2015, artists Nora al-Badri and Jan Nikolai Nelles said they covertly scanned the sculpture with a mobile device. They used the scans to create a 3D computer-aided design file, which they then shared online for everyone to see, a project they titled "Nefertiti Hack." (Some believed the scans were of such high quality that al-Badri and Nelles likely acquired them by other means.) The artists said they replicated the sculpture to inspire a reassessment of "the colonial notion of possession in Germany." In 2021, British Lebanese artist Nour Hage made a non-fungible token (NFT) of Nefertiti dubbed *Nefertiti: The Revolutionary Queen*, which she posted to Instagram, telling me that she wanted to create a limited series of North African and Middle Eastern female leaders and matriarchs from antiquity.

Adding depth to her aesthetic appeal, the queen sits comfortably at the nexus of beauty, gender, race, and power. "Nefertiti's image is orchestrated to signal the two keys of charisma: receptivity and formidability," says Caroline Keating, a professor at Colgate University who studies facial cues and charisma. In addition, her bust "plays with themes of femininity and power, crossing socially prescribed gender boundaries in many cultures, then and now. Perhaps that is part of the fascination with her—her image violates gender stereotypes, but not too much." That Nefertiti appears bald—with her hair either shaved off or hidden in her high cylindrical crown—gives the queen an androgynous look, depending on which angle you peruse her from.

Nefertiti's eyes, in particular, "feel like front gates," Keating says. "She can let you in, or she can close you out." Meanwhile, she adds, her kohl "seems designed to signal power through nonverbal means. The line along the bottom lends a more powerful, cat-eyed look. Less of a line along the bottom would be a less intimidating look."

Tutmania

Ancient Egyptian or "exotic" women like Nefertiti were fetishized throughout the twentieth century. They were thought to be elusive and attractive yet deemed by some men to be undesirable. This fetishization was more or less an extension of Orientalism, explained by the late, great Palestinian scholar Edward Said as "the basic distinction between East and West as the starting point for elaborate theories, epics, novels, social descriptions, and political accounts concerning the Orient, its people, customs, 'mind,' destiny, and so on."

Before Nefertiti was propelled into the spotlight when her bust was officially unveiled to the public in 1924, *Vogue* had already taken an interest in ancient Egyptian fashion. "The art of makeup, too, is as old as Egypt and played an important part in the feminine toilette. Rouge, kohl, and a powdered green malachite which was used about the eyes were the chief cosmetics," declared a 1921 feature exploring the era's style. "From the Far East comes the true kohl so becoming to brunettes and, in a modified form, to blondes," reads a November 1922 article.

The discovery of Tutankhamun's tomb in 1922 by British archaeologist Howard Carter affected Western popular culture in its own right, spurring what is commonly referred to as Tutmania or Egyptomania, a period of intense Orientalist fascination with ancient Egypt in the West. When the pharaoh's tomb was un-earthed, its chambers offered insight into how the man lived and looked and how his wife, Ankhsenamun—the daughter of Nefertiti—did, too. The reveal sparked a publicity rush and an interest in kohl, the mysterious substance that seemingly pos-sessed magical powers. Tutankhamun garnered more coverage than his partner, but she didn't fall by the wayside—her lined eyes also caught the attention of *Vogue* in 1923.

In "The Kohl Pots of Egypt," Dudley S. Corlett asks readers to join him in "softly" pulling back "the tapestry which hangs be-fore the portal of Ankhsenamun's bedchamber" as the journalist unsettlingly imagines how she prepares for the day. First, he de-scribes a queen with olive skin "stretching her supple body veiled in gossamer garments." After taking a bath and putting on a saf-fron linen robe, Ankhsenamun heads to her vanity to pamper her-self. Before tending to her hair, she calligraphs her eyes with kohl, the only cosmetic she uses. This item of makeup, Corlett writes, "exercise[s] its unabated wiles today, for, above the white veil of Moslem women, daring, kohl-rimmed eyes mock at men and keep them guessing at beauty hidden with discretion from their jealous gaze." Corlett presents kohl and the women who wore it as "exotic" elements of the Orient that exist only to tease men, especially Western men. The looks of such women, he seemed to say, were untouchable—far away, in a remote land, and of a bygone, primi-tive era. (He also speaks of the women's sense of hygiene.)

With the display of Nefertiti's bust in Germany, the world would come to know the queen herself and invite her into discus-sions about beauty, subsequently making way for kohl and eye-liner in their beauty kits. Borchardt's miraculous find triggered a craze when it came not only to Egyptian artifacts but also to "strange" looks in general—and how to gradually come to terms with or even achieve them. The subsequent focus on Nefertiti's physical appearance, particularly her darkened eyes, had a ripple effect on modern beauty standards. In many ways, the sculpture would redefine and refine them. Finally, there was an undeniably beautiful rendering of the enigmatic Nefertiti upon which to fixate. Orientalist images such as headscarf-wearing women, flying carpets, camels, and windswept Arabian deserts were partially eclipsed by a distant, yet somehow relatable, queen.

According to Egyptologist Chris Naughton, the queen's eye makeup played a significant role in our perception of her beauty. "In some ways, it's too good to be true," he tells me. "You wouldn't expect the Eighteenth Dynasty's conception of what it is to be a beautiful woman to be the same as ours, and yet she fits what we understand to be perfectly beautiful. She really was very good-looking, and the kohl certainly helped."

If ever there were an appropriate name, it was Nefertiti's. With the discovery and display of the queen's bust and her elegantly lined eyes, the Beautiful One had, indeed, arrived.

Nefertiti in the Public Eye

Before and after the revelation of her bust at the Egyptian Museum of Berlin in 1924, Nefertiti enjoyed the type of media coverage a newly minted celebrity might experience today—sans Twitter and trolls. "The Ancient Egyptian Type of Beauty: A Pharaoh's Lovely Queen" reported *The Illustrated London News* in 1923, when it published the first available photographs of the sculpture. "This wonderful face, with its dignity and repose, its well-cut features and refined expression, has a haunting attraction surpassing the portraits of Cleopatra, Egypt's famous beauty of a later age, and more nearly akin to the enigmatic smile of Monna [sic] Lisa," the article declared. Also in 1923, a photo of the bust appeared on the front page of the British newspaper *The Sphere*, with the text "one hardly knows what to admire the most." Four years later, *The Illustrated London News* ran another spread on Nefertiti, describing her as "one of the most beautiful women in history."

Across the pond in America, local newspapers from Nebraska to Utah carried stories about or mentioning the queen. The *Wichita Daily Times* published a piece with the headline "The Queen Who Taught Cleopatra How to Charm," which touched on Nefertiti's beauty, including her "black eyes." The article also featured a comparison of a white, Western actress's face with the bust.

Amid this heightened interest in her looks, Nefertiti appeared in *The New York Times* in 1933. A piece titled "The Summer Make-Up Is Natural" called for a not-so-natural method of beautifying the eyes, should a lady be of the "Queen Nefertiti type," with heavy eye makeup and red dye for the lips. However, the writer advised that the face be kept pale, and suntans avoided, implying Nefertiti's appeal was absolute so long as it didn't include her skin color. "Beware of too swarthy a skin," the writer noted. "It is whispered that fairer complexions are going to be in demand."

In 1939, an American *Vogue* feature story—notably written by a man—pointed to new perceptions of attractiveness. "The Strange Face of Beauty" surveyed modern and bizarre conceptions of beauty taking hold in Western society. It explored the "vamp" or "vampire" look, typically involving a heavy outline of the eyes with kohl or an eye pencil. Taken aback by the change, describing this radical and "strange" new form of physical attractiveness, the former editor of *Vanity Fair* and a newly appointed editor at *Vogue*, Frank Crowninshield, wrote that "the somewhat disturbing image that gazes at us so enigmatically across the page is, in reality, the portrait of a beautiful woman. That she dwells, palpably, beyond the familiar surfaces of reality, and more resembles Vespalia, the vampire woman, than the ladies we might hope to woo or wed, are not questions primarily involved." Beauty standards in females, Crowninshield elaborated, could best be understood by "considering all women as completely assembled phenomena."

Nefertiti's beauty was seemingly just "exotic" enough to the West, but, at the same time, not quite European enough. Incidentally, some have suggested Nefertiti's bust was Europeanized by way of plaster surgery, a mechanism sculptors used to make slight tweaks or alterations to their work by covering limestone with plaster. In 2009, CT scans did indeed show Nefertiti's stucco-coated bust had an inner layer and that a sculptor might have shaved her nose and eradicated her eye wrinkles in the outer layers (not unlike today's filters). Even *with* plaster surgery, Nefertiti didn't live up to Crowninshield's standards. The "strangeness of [Nefertiti's] face," he wrote in his piece, was "due, primarily, to the length of the upper lip, the exaggerated austerity of the nose, the great hollows under the cheeks, and her single, almost supernatural eye." And yet, there remained a beguiling, transfixing appeal to her.

Nefertiti's appearance on these pages was noteworthy. *Vogue*'s advertising has, historically, enhanced or altered perceptions of beauty. As it evolved, the magazine, founded in 1892, shifted its focus from reporting solely on society to fashion and makeup. But it still framed the market for cosmetics within broader appetites for particular "looks," including the "exotic" look. The magazine would become the aspirational playbook for women everywhere—from teen glamazons in the Midwest to homemakers in Paris—and spawn generations of readers and imitators. The mere mention of the preferred products of beauty icons in the fashion bible's glossy pages would inevitably spike cosmetics sales.

The makeup industry's spectacular rise following the influenza pandemic of 1918 and the end of the First World War came in tandem with the Western world's fascination with ancient Egypt. The timing of Nefertiti's arrival couldn't have been better; the makeup landscape in the West had never been more fertile. Thus, eyeliner would become omnipresent, a vital tool that the style conscious carry in their makeup bags to the modern day.

It wasn't just her looks women were after, but the power Nefertiti exuded. Speaking of the queen's bust, Keating says Nefertiti's face and makeup seem almost orchestrated to emanate charisma. "Nefertiti's features are enhanced so as to be stylized and refined," she notes. "The effort and resources it takes to obtain this look speak of class, status, and wealth, even today." In centuries past, Keating argues, particularly among women, physical cues and appearances aided by beauty products emerged as vehicles to signal power in understated ways that could be felt, yet were also difficult to define and control.

Women of the Desert

During the Roaring Twenties and the 1930s, an era of mass consumerism, the West seemed susceptible to "exotic" looks, given its cultural norms and perceptions of beauty were in flux. At the same time, women in America started to liberate their bodies from corsets, secured the right to vote, and entered the workforce in unprecedented numbers. Film was popularized, as was jazz. Flappers, who wore dark, heavy eye makeup, naturally embraced eyeliner, using it to cultivate their suggestive looks. Smoky-eyed performers such as Josephine Baker, Louise Brooks, Clara Bow, and Greta Nissen rose to prominence. Nefertiti's bust—with its bold colors and sleek geometric form—fit comfortably into the era's art deco styles, channeling luxury, structure, and sophistication.

Thousands of beauty parlors opened their doors. In the windows of some were replicas of Nefertiti's bust, such was the extent of the West's fascination with her. Women entrepreneurs or smaller cosmetics companies led by women of color or people of lower socioeconomic backgrounds distributed products by mail order, in salons, or via door-to-door sales. Advertisements and features in beauty magazines brought avant-garde makeup looks—including the "exotic" looks of ancient Egyptian queens such as Nefertiti—from the page to the streets of New York, Paris, and London.

"Kohl" wasn't altogether new to the West. Helena Rubinstein launched Egyptian Kohol Jet Grains in 1907 and Guerlain created the Lynx kohl pencil in 1920—an ode to women of the desert. Elizabeth Arden credited itself in advertisements for being first to market the modern use of kohl, defined by the brand as "a superfine powder ancient as the Sphinx, yet new as tomorrow on wide Western Eyes!" And Western actors such as Sarah Bernhardt, Theda Bara, Pola Negri, and Greta Garbo wore kohl or eyeliner, likely by mixing charcoal and Vaseline.

According to the late writer Habeeb Salloum, European crusaders probably became familiar with kohl and its cosmetic and medicinal uses when they invaded the region now known as the Middle East, effectively introducing the product to the West. The tradition was also documented and shared by travelers to the area. Laurent d'Arvieux, a French diplomat who chronicled his time in the Middle East during the 1600s, wrote in his travelogue, *The Chevalier D'Arvieux's Travels in Arabia the Desert*, that Arab women blacken "the edge of their eye-lids with . . . *Kehel*, and draw a line of that black without the corner of the eye, to make the eye look larger; for the chief beauty in general of the eastern woman consists in having great staring full black eyes. The Arabs express a woman's beauty by saying she has the eyes of an antilope."

Maybelline, founded in 1915, grew its offerings to cater to demand. Along with other cosmetics companies, it slowly but surely normalized the practice of enhancing one's natural beauty, leveling up one's looks, and fixing one's perceived flaws. Thomas Lyle Williams, a founder of Maybelline, was "on top of the trends [in eyeliner] even in the 1920s," as he closely tracked developments in Egyptomania, notes Sharrie Williams, his great-niece, in her blog-turned-book, *The Maybelline Story*. The company sold its first-ever eye pencil in 1929 as part of a "multistep eye makeup kit" featuring eyelash darkener and eyeshadow. While Maybelline marketed the product as an eyebrow pencil, Williams said in an interview that women used it to line their eyes throughout the 1930s. And in various timelines of the makeup company's offerings, the product is listed as eyeliner. Having drawn inspiration from Egyptomania, Maybelline was among the first Western cosmetics companies to package what would specifically come to be known as eyeliner.

Later, a 1935 *Vogue* feature titled "Dotting the Eyes" illustrated a Western woman on a ladder in the Egyptian desert, at eye level with a sphinx, a mirror and kohl pencil in hand. "The lady at the right is busy ascertaining the secret of the Sphinx, which is that, if you want the lure of the Orient in your eyes, you should get yourself some kohl," proclaims the story. "It won't hurt your eyes; it soothes them instead. To apply it in true Eastern manner, close your eye and bravely draw the applicator (a little stick or piece of bone or ivory) out from the corners of the eyes between the eyelids. Or, draw a line of kohl just above the lashes inside, on both upper and lower lids."

Get "the Nefertiti Look"

By the dawn of the 1940s, Nefertiti was firmly established in Western minds as a beauty icon—and a symbol of female empowerment. In 1939, the Nefertiti Club, founded by a Nebraskan housewife, garnered media coverage for its unique membership criteria. Some circles believed that Nefertiti suffered from partial blindness, given the left eye on her bust was missing, so the members of the group—all of whom had afflictions in one eye—banded together under the banner of her name to assert their own power and beauty.

"Though most of the members are good-looking, they all possess a defect in one of their eyes," a report in the UK's *Gloucester Citizen* read. "But all, like Nefertiti, refuse to believe that their disability makes them less attractive, and as they go about their daily tasks none of them shows any signs of self-consciousness or embarrassment."

During the Second World War, beautifying oneself in America became a matter of patriotic duty—a way to signal support for the fight against Adolf Hitler in Germany. Beauty companies and advertisers pushed the idea that wearing makeup, and by extension freedom of expression, were essential components of life in a democratic society. Hitler, despite his monstrous obsession with "racial purity" and Aryan "superiority", and his dislike of made-up women—he famously disapproved of red lipstick—once praised Nefertiti, saying he would never relinquish the bust. Some journalists even mocked his supposed infatuation: "Adolf was about 3,000 years too late to pop the question," one reporter wrote in 1946.

Industrial production during the Great Depression lagged amid the economic crisis spurred by the protracted conflict; counterintuitively, cosmetics sales rose. That said, by the 1940s, eyeliner was used only sparingly, sometimes to create a line on the back of women's legs to mimic a stocking seam (nylon stockings were scarce because many raw materials and factories were repurposed for the war effort). Not everyone could afford these luxuries, though, and those who couldn't turned instead to household items to paint their faces (or legs) when their stashes ran out. They used beetroot to stain their lips, chalk powders for foundation (on paler complexions), and everything from boot polish to soot to

darken their eyes—improvising much like poor, resourceful ancient Egyptians once did.

The war again propelled Nefertiti and her beauty into the
headlines. To protect the nation's artifacts, German museums
had moved their valuables, including Nefertiti's bust, into safe-
keeping. "Not all distinguished fugitives from air raids are
people," journalist Emily C. Davis wrote in a 1942 piece titled
"Refugee Relics," referring to the bust. "The most famous and
beautiful treasures from the past are also refugees of war." In
1945, following Germany's defeat by the Allied forces, the queen's
bust was retrieved from the salt mine where it was hidden. The
bust had gone on something of a tour of the country as authorities
attempted to conceal its whereabouts. In 1946, one piece in *The
Post-Standard* referred to Nefertiti as a displaced person who was
"noted for her beauty." The bust's "colors are as bright today as if
the artist had just quit work," the reporter Otto Zausmer wrote.

And so the fascination with the queen's style intensified. That
Nefertiti supposedly painted her toe- and fingernails red made
the headlines, and writers remained hypnotized by her eyes.
"Embellishing the eyes was the greatest beautifier used by Queen
Nefertiti and her ladies," declared a Factographs column in a
1940 issue of a DuBois newspaper. "The under lid was painted
green; the upper lid, lashes, and eyebrows were blackened with
kohl." In 1945, designer Lilly Daché launched a tall hat collection
inspired by the queen. The "modernistic version" of the ancient
crown combined black felt and pink satin and rose to a "new
height."

The coverage was not limited to Nefertiti, though it seemed
that, in the West's estimation, live Egyptian women could not

compare with the ancient queen. A feature on the legendary Egyptian singer Umm Kulthum, in a 1945 *Vogue* collaboration with *Vanity Fair*, described her as "a stocky woman with light copper skin, faintly kohl-tinted eyelids, and ink-black hair. She is distinguished," they wrote, "but not beautiful."

Following the Second World War, the US entered a period of heightened consumerism. Shelves were duly stocked with a range of lipsticks and eye products from dozens of cosmetics companies; pencil eyeliner became a staple product in the makeup kit. Pronounced lines around the upper and lower lashes were firmly in style, meeting at the edges of the eyes with a slight uptick. Cosmetics conglomerates introduced pencils in various shades, including white, gold, and silver.

The 1950s was emphatically a decade of glamour—and eyeliner. Women piled on red lipstick and mastered the art of liner application. Brows were shaped and darkened, and hair was curled. This was also the decade of the doe eye—consider Audrey Hepburn and Sophia Loren, with their famously classic, gentle cat-eye looks. Eyeliner competed with lipstick in popularity, spurred by Hollywood beauties who'd started to wear it. Marilyn Monroe's makeup artist used a brown eye pencil and eyeshadow to elongate the American starlet's lash lines and give her a "bedroom eyes" look, as well as white eyeliner on her lower waterlines for a more "awake" or "bright-eyed" look. In 1955, *Vogue* featured an illustrated piece on "new makeups for larger eyes," writing that kohl was "the ancient eyeliner of the mysterious East—recently made modern . . . by Elizabeth Arden." In a 1957 piece in the magazine titled "The 8-Faced Woman—One Face, Eight Varieties of Makeup," face number one entailed "a dramatic underscoring of eyes and mouth; a look of allure. Eyes widened by pencil eyeliner, deepened by mascara and considerable brushwork." (The era was brought to life once more in 2022 by Olivia Wilde's dystopian psychological thriller, *Don't Worry Darling*. The women in the film live in the fictional, metaverse-esque town of Victory, California, and are entrapped by the expectation that they must perform the role of a pretty, made-up housewife with swooping lines across their lids—primarily to satisfy their husbands' sexual desires.)

Nefertiti continued to inspire this style in the background. In October 1950, the now-defunct makeup company Aziza marketed a new eye pencil. Its advertisement featured a drawing of a "modern" woman superimposed upon a sketch of Nefertiti's bust, her eyes done up like the queen's. On Nefertiti's imposing crown, in place of the partly broken gold band that is shaped like a uraeus (or rearing cobra), lay an Aziza eye pencil. "Let Andre of Aziza, international authority on eye makeup, show you the Nefertiti look!" it read. "It's high fashion's eye enhancement, handed down to us from Ancient Egypt and glamorous Queen Nefertiti, who painted her eyes with kohl!" Jewelry and perfume inspired by Nefertiti were also advertised in magazines. That same year, Maybelline released an advertisement featuring a white woman wearing heavy eye makeup—the appending text read "Achieve the new exotic eye makeup," with the word *exotic* set off from the rest of the tagline in a wonton font.

In a 1955 piece titled "Even Egyptian Lassies Resorted to

Wiles of Art," American actor Anne Baxter reflected on her role in the film *The Ten Commandments*, which was partially based on the 1949 novel *Prince of Egypt* by Dorothy Clarke Wilson. The report in *The Daily Courier* (Connellsville) detailed the queen's beauty secrets, including kohl. "Nefertiti ruled the glamor arena some 3,200 years ago," the actor wrote. "The eye, someone said, is the window of the soul, and the Egyptian beauties seemed to know that it was an extremely lethal weapon. They were experts at dramatizing the eyes." Baxter speculated the ancient Egyptian application of kohl might have been too harsh and out of step with the more muted eyeliner look of the 1950s. "They had terrible mirrors of burnished copper," she wrote. "I wondered if the Egyptian glamor girls overdid things a trifle because they just plain couldn't see enough to be subtle." (Mirrors in ancient Egypt, burnished copper or not, were highly symbolic, as one's physical appearance was closely associated with female sexuality and rebirth.)

By 1960, there had been a full-on "beauty shake-up," per *Vogue*, "a whole new race of women": "smudge-eyed beauties" with swan-like necks and "an aura faintly evocative of midnight departures on the Orient Express."

Nefertiti's "Mysterious Something"

In 1961, *Vogue* ran a feature centered on the idea of "fascination." Helming the splash was a full-page sepia photo of a white woman with a rather long neck posing playfully with a likeness of Nefertiti's bust. Her eyes were lined, and her hair was done up to channel Nefertiti's crown. Both women were adorned with the same bijou earrings. The magazine seemed to be saying that *despite* the fact that one can imitate Nefertiti's beauty, the queen's aura is more elusive—it is one thing to try to copy the "it" factor, but quite another to loyally replicate it. "She had her famous leaning-tower headdress—but that's now being echoed in the new Paris Collections," the story read. "She had beauty, of course—but that too can be managed. Above all, we surmise, she had fascination, the mysterious something that makes someone remembered with delight, with interest, or with love."

After decades of flirting with the idea, magazines and makeup companies began to suggest that the looks of women of color and their darkened and "exotic" eyes were not only desirable and achievable, but also aspirational.

Ironically, that positioning would intensify with the release of the 1963 film *Cleopatra*, in which Elizabeth Taylor, a white woman, became the epitome of borrowed exoticism. (Two years prior, *Queen of the Nile*, a movie exploring Nefertiti's life, was released, though the film did not garner the same attention as *Cleopatra*. Jeanne Crain, another white actor, played the role of the queen.) Cleopatra herself was likely of Macedonian ancestry, per many historians, though there's also speculation that she was of African heritage by way of her mother. Tense discussions over the queen's race and ethnicity were reignited in 2023, when Netflix released *Queen Cleopatra*, a four-part docudrama. The casting choice of Black actor Adele James generated controversy in some Egyptian corners, to which the Persian director of the show, Tina Gharavi, responded in an op-ed for *Variety*, "Why shouldn't Cleopatra be a melanated sister? And why do some people need Cleopatra to be white? Her proximity to whiteness seems to give her value." Meanwhile, scholars have argued that imposing modern conceptions of race onto ancient historical contexts isn't helpful. "To ask whether someone was 'Black' or 'white' is anachronistic and says more about modern political investments than attempting to understand antiquity on its own terms," Rebecca Futo Kennedy, an associate professor of classics at Denison University, said in an interview with *Time*.

Just as Swedish actor Anita Ekberg had when she memorably donned eyeliner in the 1960 film *La dolce vita*, Taylor as Cleopatra helped trigger another eyeliner boom. One columnist in 1962 said it was partly her "exotic eye makeup" that would inspire an "Egyptian look." Prior to the release of the film, Revlon launched Sphinx Eyes. The advertisement featured a woman styled like Taylor in *Cleopatra*, with a black cat and the appending text "If looks can kill, this one will." The actor had begun sporting the look about a year before the film premiered to promote it. (The period was quite a busy one for eyeliner. In 1959, Maybelline began selling a self-sharpening eyeliner. And the company marketed more than one version of the product in 1968 alone—Ultra Liner, a pressed cake eyeliner, and the Frosty Whites collection's Ivory White cake or fluid eyeliner were later followed by an eyeliner brush in 1969.)

For centuries, many have associated the idea of ancient Egyptian beauty with Cleopatra, even though she was potentially not of ancient Egyptian origin, there are few images of her from antiquity, and existing representations of her were a departure from widely accepted beauty ideals. Coinage and sculptures of Cleopatra suggest she had a prominent nose and a protruding chin. The idea of her being beautiful derives less from reality and more from the idea that she'd seduced the Roman statesmen Julius Caesar and Mark Antony, according to Naughton, the Egyptologist. And the descriptions of her penned by Roman writers were far more flattering than how artists and sculptors had portrayed her.

And yet Taylor was cast as an idealized version of the queen, with extravagantly lined eyes and highly pigmented blue eyeshadow, the memorable representation that was essentially made up for the film. While her kohl was probably accurate, historians, including Andrew Hardy, disagree on whether Cleopatra ever wore blue eyeshadow—greens and grays would be more likely due to the composition of the materials at hand, such as galena and malachite. Nevertheless, blue would become Taylor's shade of choice, as it enhanced her violet eyes. (In the 2023 Netflix series, the British actor Adele James is made up in turquoise and gold-glitter lines.)

In 1962, the *San Antonio Express and News*' fashion editor, Mildred Whiteaker, wrote a feature story titled "Echoes of the Nile in Coifs, Makeup." "The Egyptian look is snowballing in the world of fashion and beauty," she argued, mentioning both Nefertiti and Cleopatra. "The Egyptian influence is being reflected in everything from hats to coiffures to makeup to jewelry. Hardly a day goes by that some reference to the seductive costumes and irresistible allure of the queens of ancient Egypt doesn't turn up in my mail." Meanwhile, Ceil Chapman, one of the "giants" of New York's Seventh Avenue, themed her entire spring 1962 collection the "Daughters of the Nile." Similar exhibitions were launched in Europe, with Italian mannequins often sporting heavily lined Nefertiti eyes.

"Exotic Eyeliner"

Despite this ongoing fascination with the exotic looks of women of color, throughout the 1900s, cosmetics conglomerates failed to cater to them meaningfully with their products or to incorporate them sufficiently into their advertisements. As a result, Black entrepreneurs took matters into their own hands, founding businesses to fill the gap.

In 1918, Nile Queen Cosmetics was formed when several Black American investors came together to serve the middle-class Black or brown consumer's beauty needs. "There is just as much real beauty in the colored race as in any people of the world," one of its advertisements read. Madam C. J. Walker, a Black entrepreneur born on a plantation in Louisiana, was a towering figure in this push for diversity. The decades that followed saw similar pioneering efforts focused on Black beauty.

The activism of the civil rights movement in the 1950s and '60s—during which Black women started to make hair and beauty choices that were more Afrocentric—forced mainstream makeup companies to take notice. Beautification and hair began to be seen as tools that allowed marginalized groups to show solidarity with the Black pride and power movements. In tandem, makeup counters were desegregated as part of broader social changes. Black families' incomes rose, increasing demand for a more diverse range of beauty products. Smaller cosmetics companies targeting women of color found themselves up against conglomerates.

In 1959, model Je'Taun M. Taylor was styled in waterproof

liquid eyeliner and diamond jewelry in Maybelline's first advertisement to feature a Black woman. Veteran brands with significant corporate backing, such as Avon and Revlon, followed suit. At the same time, from the end of the Second World War through 1966, the cosmetics industry's value surged fourfold to $2.4 billion.

Concurrently, Egyptian looks were soon declared "in" again—though it's unclear whether they were ever "out"—coinciding with the opening of a Tutankhamun exhibit at the British Museum in London in 1972. Designers such as Robert Goldworm released collections inspired by ancient Egypt, with the season's models in long, slender gowns, high necklines, and kohl-rimmed eyes.

Magazines and newspapers continued to offer tips on how to achieve the "Nefertiti look," which, per a piece in *The Gastonia Gazette* of North Carolina in 1967, had by then included the use of a dark tint foundation that would "go on so much more easily if you have a suntan," a rosy-red lipstick, a rouge blush, and black eyeliner worn with green eyeshadow. Cosmetics companies marketed so many products featuring this "dark" and "exotic" look that one columnist joked "it was back to the Kohl mines" for makeup enthusiasts.

Vogue first featured a Black woman on its cover in March 1966, when Donyale Luna graced the pages of its British edition. Luna, who's thought to be the world's first Black supermodel, wore a lilac-and-gold color-blocked dress designed by Chloé. Her eye makeup was influenced by Picasso's portraits, and her statement earrings were draped and dramatic. The profile shot revealed one almond-shaped eye framed by fishtail-shaped lines; Luna's manicured hand covered the rest of her face. Her index and middle fingers formed a V that directed attention to the made-up eye. (The graphic look was right on trend for the swinging sixties, when bold colors and geometric lines adorned the eyes with architectural precision.) The model's eyeliner became a defining feature of her makeup in this iconic moment—and her overall look evoked Nefertiti. Beatrix Miller, editor of *British Vogue* from 1964 to 1984, described Luna as having "a marvelous shape—angular and immensely tall and strange." "Strange" women were finally being acknowledged as not just curiously beautiful, but potentially enviable.

By 1985, most American women wore eyeliner, and the product had become so popular that some opted to have their lines tattooed onto their eyelids. Dubbed a revolutionary cosmetics breakthrough upon its invention, the twenty- to forty-minute procedure cost $1,000, the equivalent of nearly $3,000 today, and lasted for about two years. (Eyeliner tattooing exists to this day and is gaining popularity, partly as it appears more natural than it did during the 1980s.) "The 1980s woman, unlike Queen Nefertiti, doesn't have the time to apply her makeup," declared *The Evening Telegram* of Herkimer, New York. "It is really exciting that there are so many facets to a woman's life now—family, career, travel, and sports, which makes her just plain busy. Women deserve the convenience of permanently enhanced eyes." Eyeliner had, quite literally, become a permanent fixture in American culture. As another journalist put it, "It's a lasting style—not a fad."

Nefertiti Takes a Throne in Black Culture

While one motif of the cultural awakening driven by Nefertiti was laced with Orientalist attitudes toward ancient Egypt and its "exotic" women, a second was firmly anti-Orientalist and anti-colonial. Amid a celebration of Black African culture in America, these efforts ultimately sought to reclaim Nefertiti as an African queen of color—though her race remains unknown.

In 1963, the American jazz pianist Cecil Taylor dropped an album titled *Nefertiti, the Beautiful One Has Come*; an image of the queen's bust appeared on the album's cover art, her eyeliner extending beyond her eyes, and swirling into bold ancient Egyptian-style patterns across her face and neck. Five years later, in 1968, Miles Davis released his classic jazz album *Nefertiti*, best known for its unique eponymous track. This was Davis's first Africa-related mention; he would go on to make several. The title choice may have tapped into a surge in interest in the queen during the 1960s, wrote researcher Ryan S. McNulty in his thesis about Davis's "imaginings of Africa." In Davis's album opener, "the complexities of the drums, a strong characteristic in much African music, become the focus," according to McNulty. These nods to the queen helped situate the Black American experience within a broader Afrocentric cultural sphere.

Toward the end of the twentieth century and into the twenty-first, Nefertiti took a throne in Black culture. During the 1980s, President Ronald Reagan's policies intensified racial economic disparities, hitting Black American families the hardest. Amid those changes, Afrocentric symbols in the Black community gained a new popularity, by way of clothing, jewelry, music, and dance; the 1980s and 1990s were something of a golden era for Afro imagery in both hip-hop and rap, with artists like De La Soul and A Tribe Called Quest making references to countries on the continent, advocating for a common Pan-African identity among those in the diaspora. (We have more recently seen similar imagery; the short film for "All the Stars," a 2018 song by Kendrick Lamar and SZA on the *Black Panther* soundtrack, sees the performers go on a voyage to Africa.)

The late Tina Turner in 1984 released the song "I Might Have Been Queen," whose autobiographical lyrics were written for the American-born Swiss singer after she revealed that she believed she might have been Pharaoh Hatshepsut in a former life (Turner was fascinated with ancient Egypt and was later styled as Cleopatra by the makeup artist Kevyn Aucoin). In the music video for the 1989 song "Dance for Me," Queen Latifah performs in a commander's uniform, wearing a headdress comparable to Nefertiti's lapis and jade crown. She is made up in eyeliner, whose durability and consistency as a cosmetic had by then improved. Three years later, in 1992, Nefertiti made another appearance in an award-winning song: Michael Jackson's "Remember the Time." In the video, set in a somewhat gimmicky-looking ancient Egypt, Somali supermodel Iman appears unimpressed and irascible as Nefertiti. "I'm bored," she tells her husband, Akhenaten, played by Eddie Murphy. "I want to be entertained. Can my pharaoh find some way to entertain his queen?" Male entertainers are presented to her by the king: one blows fire; another shows the royal wife a magic trick. Still bored, Nefertiti asks that they be executed. (Michael Jackson's life is spared when he delivers his impeccable vocal stylings.) In the video, Iman wears smoky eyeshadow and thick black eyeliner. Jackson, too, wears guyliner.

During the height of her career, the iconic American singer-songwriter Erykah Badu wore her locs high up on her head, wrapping them in a scarf, such that her hair recalled Nefertiti's tall crown. (Badu was a member of the Soulquarians, a rotating collective of Black artists of the 1990s and early 2000s, which included Questlove, J Dilla, D'Angelo, James Poyser, Bilal, and others.) The singer and rapper Ms. Lauryn Hill mentions Nefertiti along with Cleopatra in her 1999 single "Everything Is Everything." Rihanna paid homage to Nefertiti in a 2017 *Vogue Arabia* photo shoot: her eyes were styled with lines and highly pigmented blue eyeshadow. As a literal mark of her love for the queen, Rihanna has a tattoo of Nefertiti's bust on her ribs.

In 2018, Beyoncé became the first Black woman to headline Coachella. She enlisted Olivier Rousteing, the French fashion designer and creative director of the luxury brand Balmain who is of Somali and Ethiopian descent, to help her create five bespoke looks for the historic event, dubbed "Homecoming." Her performance, which centered on reclaiming a lost narrative and evoked symbols of Black power, included a celebration of historically Black colleges and universities in the US.

Balmain modeled Beyoncé's centerpiece look on Nefertiti. During the show, Beyoncé presents herself to the audience in a bodysuit and cape embellished with thousands of gold and black sequins. Embroidered on the back of the cape is an image of the ancient Egyptian queen, clearly presented as a Black woman. Beyoncé's headdress is tall and bejeweled, a look *The Atlantic* described as "Nefertiti chic." Her smoky black eyes complete the outfit.

This wasn't Beyoncé's first nod to the original queen. In 2017, she released images on her website that announced her pregnancy with twins. In one photo, she's posing beside a replica of Nefertiti's statue against a tropical backdrop. And in her 2016 music video for the song "Sorry," she poses like the bust in a way that makes it seem as if she, too, were armless. Her braids are styled to mirror a tall crown, and her eyes, of course, are decorated with eyeliner. The singer also dropped a Nefertiti-inspired line of clothing for her 2018 On the Run II tour, which prompted some Egyptians to call her out on social media for what they believed was cultural appropriation. (In 2023, Egypt banned a team of Dutch archaeologists from excavations at the ancient burial site of the Saqqara Necropolis, due to an afrocentric ancient Egypt exhibition at the Netherlands' National Museum of Antiquities. The show examined the influence of ancient Egypt and Nubia on Black American artists, and included Beyoncé and Rihanna's references to Nefertiti. A leaked email revealed that an official of the Egyptian Antiquities Service accused the curators of "falsifying history" due to the afrocentric lens.)

"I wear my Nefertiti chain every day," a voice narrates in Beyoncé's seminal 2020 audiovisual album, *Black Is King*. The video was released against a backdrop of global racial justice protests following the murder of George Floyd by policeman Derek Chauvin. In these Black culture hat tips to Nefertiti, the queen is established as an icon not only of Black beauty but of Black power and influence.

Nefertiti has also been a source of inspiration for Black-owned beauty brands. In 2016, Juvia's Place was created to "celebrate the rebels, rulers, and queens of the African kingdoms who honored beauty through their innovative and soulful techniques that we still use today." The brand pays homage to Nefertiti, referring to her as "the OG beauty icon," with a Nubian eye palette whose cover features an illustration of Nefertiti's bust. The palette's powder is so highly pigmented, it can be used as eyeliner. Cosmetics company UOMA Beauty, which offers fifty-one shades of foundation, previously sold a "kuul" eyeliner titled Salute to the Sun—Nefertiti in brown, black, and blue. On its website, the brand said it was inspired by Nefertiti to create its "own modern-day version" of her iconic kohl looks.

Whose Nefertiti?

The modern history of Nefertiti—both the person and the artistic rendering—is essentially a dispute over ownership, of the artwork itself and its expansive cultural influence. Perhaps the most dramatic manifestation of this dispute occurred in 2003, when Hungarian artists Bálint Havas and András Gálik filmed Nefertiti's bust being lifted out of her bulletproof glass case. The sculpture was affixed onto a nude-looking bronze torso the men had constructed themselves, creating a bizarre-looking mannequin. The men who moved Nefertiti wore surgical gloves as they manhandled the queen by her long, delicate neck and gave her a body she didn't ask for. Havas and Gálik, known together as Little Warsaw, presented the footage as part of an installation at the fiftieth Venice Biennale, giving it the title *The Body of Nefertiti*.

The eerie "unification process" was recorded on sixteen-millimeter color film; Little Warsaw said on their website that the project was the culmination of their interest in "revitalizing" historical symbols by situating them in contemporary contexts. The bust met the body for only a "short moment," and the event unraveled behind closed doors.

To some, the footage crystallized the tragedy of archaeological plundering: a lack of consent, disrespect for national heritage, an act of violence, and an exercise of entitlement by white men to African artifacts. One wonders how the public might respond to a hijab being superimposed onto the *Mona Lisa*.

What right did these artists have to Nefertiti's image? Why was she given the body of a prepubescent boy? (A female torso at the Louvre that is thought to be hers reveals she likely had a far fuller, pear-shaped figure, with thick hips.) Does it even matter that Nefertiti was fleetingly removed from her case?

It did to Egypt, unsurprisingly. The event sparked uproar in Cairo, with the government claiming Nefertiti wasn't safe in German hands. Her depiction as "nude" was deemed an affront to the country's religious and cultural mores. Farouk Hosni, then Egypt's culture minister, described the "unification" as unethical. An Egyptian newspaper's editors were so furious, they ran the headline "Queen Nefertiti Naked in the Berlin Museum!" In an interview with *The New York Times*, István Barkóczi, one of the project's curators, said he was alarmed by Egypt's response to the artwork and found it "strange."

Germany and Egypt have been quarreling over Nefertiti's bust for almost a century. Numerous repatriation requests from Egypt since 1924 have led nowhere or fallen through at the eleventh hour. Of all the rivalries over archaeological repatriation, this one has been so intense that it has provoked political acrimony at the highest levels, prompting scathing remarks from Hitler and insults from Egyptian kings and heads of state.

The Egyptian city of Samalut attempted its own version of Nefertiti's bust in 2015. Unlike Nefertiti, the stone statue was hideous and white in color—even its kohl-rimmed eyes couldn't redeem the sculpture. Critics likened it to Abdel Fattah el-Sisi, the country's president, and to Frankenstein's monster. Soon after the public outcry, officials ordered its removal.

According to Zahi Hawass, the question of who owns Nefertiti is central to how we perceive her. The Egyptologist heads an office whose remit is to make cases for the repatriation of ancient Egyptian masterpieces, among them Nefertiti, the Rosetta Stone at the British Museum, and the Zodiac of Dendera at the Louvre. Nefertiti is of particular importance; Hawass argues that part of the queen's appeal is that she has kept the interest in Egyptology alive among the youth. He continues to seek her repatriation to this day, his latest effort being a petition calling for her return. "Many museums are talking about the looting during imperialism and how colonialism swept national treasures from their countries," he says. "It's time to return artifacts to Egypt and Africa."

Nefertiti in Modern Egypt

In 2021, Egypt relocated twenty-two of its mummies—eighteen kings and four queens—from the Egyptian Museum to the new National Museum of Egyptian Civilization, located five kilometers away. Dubbed the Pharaohs' Golden Parade, the multimillion-dollar procession was a national spectacle, and an effective way for Sisi to briefly deflect attention from political controversies and human rights abuses. Leading the march were women dressed in white and blue robes with extravagant collars. Their faces were made up in the style of Nefertiti—albeit with thicker lines like those of the Eye of Horus. (Hawass says he asked Germany's former director of the Berlin Museum if Egypt could "borrow" the bust for the opening: that request was predictably denied.)

Nefertiti remains of great cultural importance in Egypt. Women of all generations continue to wear eyeliner and kohl, as Nefertiti did. Similar to ancient Egypt, the type used often depends on the person's financial means, local women tell me—Egyptian brands of kohl on the cheaper end are widely available. That said, many well-to-do Egyptian women instead turn to international brands to decorate their eye. "I grew up believing kohl was a traditional Egyptian practice and that Nefertiti was so beautiful," Maram, an Egyptian woman in her midthirties, says. "When I started using kohl as a teenager, I just thought it looked cool. And I've continued to wear it every day since."

For "The Strong Eyeliner and Nonchalant Beauty of Cairo," a 2015 piece in *The Cut*, photographer Abdallah Sabry snapped images of trendy, young Egyptian women effortlessly displaying their cat eye. Separately, in a "Brooklyn cool girl" tutorial for *Vogue*, millennial Eman Abbas demonstrates to readers how to master "drawing the eye." "I'm inspired by Egyptian art," the Brooklyn-based photographer, who was born to Egyptian parents, told the magazine. "If I look at Nefertiti and I like how she does her eyes, then I want to re-create it."

Eyeliner's cultural significance is also demonstrated in Egypt's entertainment industries, including film, theater, song, and dance, which, combined, contain enough kohl to fill the Nile. During Egypt's Roaring Twenties and the 1930s, feminist icons, activists, and performers wore kohl in abundance, particularly at Cairo's nightclubs and lounges. Singer Mounira al-Mahdiyya regularly darkened her eyes, as did starlets Badia Masabni, Tahia Carioca, Asmahan, Rose al-Youssef, Samia Gamal, and Layla Mourad. Safiya al-Omari and Sawsan Badr, veteran film stars, continue to wear eyeliner prolifically. Indeed, Badr is frequently compared with Nefertiti. Nawal el-Saadawi, the late Egyptian feminist, wore a faint kohl look at various points of her career. In the early 1980s, Saadawi was accused by Egypt of "crimes against the state" and imprisoned, though she continued writing while behind bars—with kohl, on tissue paper. Partly due to her lost eye, Egyptian human rights activist Mahinour el-Masry was likened to Nefertiti in pamphlets demanding her release from prison for allegedly violating Egypt's protest laws. (She was provisionally released in 2021.)

In Egyptian cinema, particularly during its golden age of the 1940s, '50s, and '60s, there seemed to be a correlation between the intensity of the protagonist's story and the dramatic presentation of her kohl, including the messes it made when she wept. In the 1958 Egyptian film *Ana hurra* (I'm free), the lead actor rebels against her religious family and society at large and is never seen without her feline flicks. The film manifests the era's feminism, which challenged prevailing societal norms in the run-up to Gamal Abdel Nasser's tenure as president. In the 1972 film *Khalli balak min Zouzou* (Watch out for Zouzou), a college student conceals her profession as a dancer from her friends, concerned they may judge her. (Singers and dancers were often associated with "loose" social behavior in conservative circles.) Soad Hosny, who plays the young woman, wears thick eyeliner during the performances—she even sleeps in it. Contemporary singers, including Ruby and Sherine, have worn eyeliner looks during rather sensual videos. For example, in Ruby's 2004 music video for her song "Leih bey-dary keda" (Why is he hiding his feelings like this), the stunning singer has her eyes lined while exercising suggestively on a stationary bicycle.

Too Good to Be True

In 2009, a Swiss art historian rocked the world of Egyptology with a shocking claim. In his book *Le buste de Néfertiti: Une imposture de l'égyptologie?* (The bust of Nefertiti: An Egyptology fraud?) Henri Stierlin argued it was improbable the sculpture was 3,400 years old and was most likely a fake. By Stierlin's account, Borchardt had requested the statue so his team could examine how Egyptians used ancient pigments sourced during the Tell el-Amarna expedition, which led to the discovery of the bust. The excavator apparently showed a Prussian prince the fake, and the prince was so taken by the bust's beauty, he assumed it was original. Borchardt then "didn't have the nerve to make his guest look stupid," Stierlin contends.

Besides, he says, Nefertiti's bust is *too* beautiful and refined to be authentic, and her features were made up in the art nouveau style. Some have speculated that Borchardt provided a forger with a photograph of his wife, Emilie, to use as a reference, hence Nefertiti's "Europeanized" features. One convicted forger—who, as an expert in counterfeits, agrees with Stierlin's assessment—told the Smithsonian Channel, "If you look at the bust, you can see a beautiful Edwardian lady done up in Egyptian makeup." All that said, Stierlin's argument hasn't gained much traction among Egyptologists, most of whom consider the bust to be a genuine artifact.

Even if her bust *is* authentic, our understanding of Nefertiti may still, in part, rely on trickery. After all, kohl, too, is a form of deceit. Borchardt acknowledged these limitations in his notes, writing that, as consumers of art, we can see only the artist's perception of Nefertiti—never the real person. "The question of what the artist wanted to depict is easier asked than answered," he wrote. "With the way we present things today, hallucinations are possible. With the Egyptian, the far more frequent, often inevitable, hallucinations . . . occur particularly easily when, as in our case, painter and viewer are separated by thousands of years."

Despite these unanswered questions, we continue to accept Nefertiti's bust as an imprimatur of the queen's beauty. And it's the look of Nefertiti's sculpture that designers, including Christian Dior, Zuhair Murad, Christian Louboutin, and Azzedine Alaïa, have sought to emulate in their work, on Paris runways or otherwise—their models made up in kohl.

Instagram Icon

The preoccupation with Nefertiti's looks in the public imagination remains as vibrant today as it was in the 1920s. There are scores of YouTube videos featuring real-life simulations of her appearance. One of these videos, titled "How Nefertiti Queen of Egypt Looked in Real Life," has over 800,000 views.

Royalty Now, an Instagram account with over 350,000 followers that photoshops "history back to life," re-created Nefertiti in a 2019 post. When founder Becca Saladin digitally rendered the queen's bust, the graphic designer was struck by how immaculate the outcome was. "I know this is going to sound cheesy," she says, "but I genuinely think she's perfect." In the post, Nefertiti appears so natural, so utterly divine, and so eerily familiar, the rendering prompted this viewer to do a double take.

Saladin has studied hundreds of historical icons' faces, from Sejong the Great and Mozart to Marie Antoinette and Anne of Cleves. To generate simulated images of those icons, she scours the internet for pictures of people with similar features and then liquefies them in Photoshop. The features morph to form the figure's likeness from disparate parts: the nose might be that of a contemporary celebrity, for example, and the lips from a stock photo.

But with Nefertiti, Saladin lifted the nose, lips, and eye structure directly from images of the sculpture. She needed only to smooth some cracks and add her hair, derived from a photo of an Asian woman. Saladin sourced the eyes themselves from a photograph of Black British Zimbabwean actor Thandiwe Newton, in which she happened to be wearing kohl. As for the skin tone, Saladin reflected the color of the bust.

In the final image, Nefertiti appears in the re-creation to be a woman of color with contemporary styling and features many young women still view as ideal, with her chiseled nose, full lips, flawless skin, darkened eyes, and high, contoured cheekbones.

"There's a reason why that sculpture is iconic," Saladin says. "At face value, Nefertiti was beautiful. The facial proportions, her cheekbones, her lips, her beautifully lined eyes . . . she's what every Instagram girl is trying to be right now."

One of the post's commenters enthusiastically agrees: "She is stunning both in past and present!!!!"

Chapter Two

People of the Taboo

Worso and the Wodaabe

Here in this vast, dusty stretch of shrubland, just past Dourbali in the Chari-Baguirmi region of Chad, half a dozen young men with kohl-rimmed eyes are gathered after sunset. The temperature is cooler now, though still technically sweltering, even by regional standards. The men of the Wodaabe, a subset of the Fulani ethnic group, are about to practice ritualistic dances known as the Yaake and Gerewol, which will allow them to flaunt their beauty as they perform for potential partners. Tomorrow, they're to take part in the official opening of the annual Worso festival, which coincides with the end of the rainy season. Its traditions—a celebration of Wodaabe identity that features countless hours of dancing, mingling over meals, and the occasional horse race—may date back centuries. Although some elements of the festival might have changed ever so slightly over the years, they're said to have remained largely intact. The Gerewol dance culminates in a courtship ceremony where the women of various nomadic Wodaabe clans pick their preferred men among scores of eager dancers. Gerewol, meaning "to line up," is essentially a glorified beauty contest under the guise of a "war dance"—but in the Worso, it's the women who do the judging. The festival has a strict set of rules, and beyond their appearances, men are assessed on their wealth (by way of the cattle they herd) and their charm. "I'm here to dance and to display my beauty," nineteen-year-old Kai, one of the dancers, says matter-of-factly.

The young men of the Japto clan, primarily teenagers, have been anticipating the festival for months—some for their entire lives. Most of the unwed men and women are spoken for by marriages predetermined by their families as early as their birth. A few are already married to those promised to them. But the Wodaabe are nominally Muslim, so the young men are permitted to wed four women—the festival facilitates these connections. Ultimately, official Gerewol matches will result in new marriages; others will be informal and temporary, not limited to judges and winners. The women are encouraged to pick men of opposing clans to expand the gene pool through marriage and procreation. Partnerships are seen as fluid, and the women of the Wodaabe have the power to leave their husbands if they're unhappy, or avoid marrying their promised partners. And some discreetly take on more than one sexual partner without being shunned by their clan.

Save several torches, the night is pitch black and unblemished by light pollution, such that you can almost make out the Milky Way. Even when it starts to rain, the men continue to dance in a circle to their rhythmic singing and chanting, undeterred by the pitter-patter of droplets and the stubborn refusal of the rainy season to end. They must practice for the coming days, when they are expected to dance their hearts out to impress potential new partners and compete with the Sudosukai, another Wodaabe clan. This evening's dance is known as the Ruume, or "welcome dance." Young children of the group, whose eyes are also framed with kohl, join in, endearingly seeking to emulate and channel the beauty of their older peers. The cheeky kids are soon shooed away by an elder, who, with a cane, smacks the desert ground to motivate the men to work harder and dance better.

The Japto clan signals that the festival season has begun by delivering a transfixing monotone chant to the Sudosukai, who are orbiting the surrounding areas. The declaration is met with a muted acknowledgment, a reciprocal chant. The Japto are made to wait; it will take a full five days for the Sudosukai to arrive. (Given there are tens of thousands of Wodaabe, several Worso festivals take place concurrently in different areas of the stretch of land nestled between the Sahara and the savanna known as the Sahel, and many other clans compete.)

Now practicing the Gerewol dance, the men are standing in line, swaying rhythmically to their tunes. Every few minutes, a dancer or two step forward, commanding the attention of the swelling crowd, which includes dozens of locals from neighboring regions. These men are in a trancelike, psychedelic state; some say they ingest plant stimulants to give them the stamina to dance for hours.

The boys mimic the heron, a long-legged, long-necked bird revered by the Wodaabe for its elegance. They are focused intently on their upper bodies' rapid, jerky movements, tilting their heads upward and flaunting their features as they shuffle in lockstep. To showcase their eyes and teeth, which shine brightly against their painted eyes and lips, part of the dance comprises eye-rolling and teeth baring and chattering. With darting eyes and quivering lips, they signal to the women that the courtship process has commenced. As they look to the starry skies above them, their focus is so intense that they seem possessed by a higher power. Here, among the Wodaabe, there is no stigma around this enthusiastic, colorful display of pride and desire, and there are seemingly no limits to the men's exuberance. (Fittingly, the word *Wodaabe* means "people of the taboo.") The men's preoccupation with their looks is celebrated, not frowned upon. Their beauty is sacred.

"Very often, we think that women are the ones who take care of their beauty and wear makeup," says Elena Dak (Dacome), an Italian anthropologist who's worked closely with the Wodaabe. "In this community, men are the ones that use makeup and wear gorgeous jewels and dance to show how beautiful they are, not women." The trait is so highly valued that unattractive men sometimes request that handsome men in the group impregnate their wives, with their consent, to maintain broader attractiveness levels. To the Wodaabe, being beautiful isn't solely about having certain aesthetic characteristics, but also adhering to the Fulani's ethical and moral code. (Known as the pulaaku, the code emphasizes fortitude, manners, modesty, and dignity.) "Aesthetics are just the base of an essential social strategy for the Wodaabe," Dak says. "Beauty is a social and political value. It's not just a matter of aesthetics but of gaining position in your place in society."

As tonight is a rehearsal, the girls, also mostly teenagers, are observing and not yet making their official preferences known.

From a mere two meters away, they're huddled together, studying the men. The girls giggle as they scrutinize the men's looks and movements in hushed tones. They coyly cover their lined eyes with printed fabrics draped around their necks to conceal their excitement; some of this shyness, however, is understood to be performative and theatrical. The girls are dressed more conservatively than the older women spectators, many of whom are topless, as their breasts are no longer seen as sexual. Occasionally, they flash a light upon the men's faces, indicating that their interest is piqued—or, at the very least, that they approve of the lengths to which the men are going to impress them. The men and women of the Wodaabe mostly pay no mind to the two dozen or so white Western tourists, with their oohs and aahs and large-lensed cameras and "This is Africa!" declarations. Sometimes, though, the Wodaabe flip the script and take their own cell phone pictures of the barefaced tourists, who very likely appear plain to them, and understandably so. The Wodaabe consider themselves among the most attractive people in the world—and the men carry mirrors to keep their looks, especially their kohl, in check.

The following morning, the men wake up at the break of dawn to prepare their festival getups and apply their makeup. They work on their faces for just over three hours, with ample attention lavished upon framing the eyes with kohl. When these men wear kohl, they widen their eyes to appeal to clan women. But they also demonstrate their aesthetic prowess—the lines where light and dark meet are drawn with great concentration. One young man takes more than ten minutes to apply the cosmetic, carefully and skillfully drawing it on his upper and lower lash lines, applicator in one hand and mirror in the other. As he does, his artistry is evident, and his gaze unrelenting. He says he generally applies the cosmetic up to three times a day—once at sunrise, once at noon, and once at sunset—although he tends to top up as needed to keep his lines crisp and kohl's protective properties fresh. For easy access, but also as a matter of pride, he wears a small plastic kohl pot on a necklace. The container is adorned with a cover zigzagged with yellow, red, green, and blue beads. So dear to this young man is his kohl that he wears the pot alongside his protective talisman, a leather tassel pendant, as do many men and women of the Wodaabe.

The Wodaabe have in the past used crushed egret bones, the burnt blood of camels, and other locally sourced materials to make their kohl. But this year, the Japto say they have mainly obtained it from local markets, where they also purchase their kohl pots. Some have walked for up to two hours in the oppressive desert heat to buy small bags of kohl with money earned from selling cow milk; the substance itself has been imported from Saudi Arabia, they say.

Kohl has both a spiritual and practical purpose for the Wodaabe. For beautification, it toys with brightness and contrast—the brighter the eye, and the darker the surrounding skin, the more aesthetically appealing. To the Wodaabe, brightness is an intangible aspect of beauty that supplements its material elements. (This is partly why the group carries mirrors around with them—in addition to using them to ensure their makeup is pristine, they decorate and embroider their clothing with broken pieces of the glass to amplify the brightness of the sun's rays or reflect the light of nighttime fires.) Kohl also protects the wearer's eyes from the sun and foreign particles, much as it did for the ancient Egyptians. "During some seasons, the rain comes. But for many, many months during the year, the season is dry, and the ground is dusty and sandy," says Dak. "These weather conditions are quite dangerous for the eyes. So, kohl, like many other aspects of the culture of nomadic people, is useful and aesthetically appealing at the same time."

While youth is apparently synonymous with beauty, elders are also respected. Soon after their teen years, the older men stop performing in the Worso and become mentors, teaching boys how to dance and groom themselves, including the art of applying kohl. Both men and women wear kohl to different degrees. Older women are committed to wearing kohl in more pronounced but less seamless ways. Given they aren't as preoccupied with appearances—one woman says she wears the substance solely to protect her eyes from the sun's rays—the women smudge the lines along their upper and lower lashes imprecisely, using their fingers to blend. The applicators are shaped like matchsticks, and the pots are often sturdier and larger than those of younger Wodaabe, with a number of them made of clay and protected by leather, their design resembling that of a bong.

As they eagerly but carefully get ready for the event, some men are also applying orange face paint after using the juices of plants as a primer for their skin. Many help each other with the makeup application, their trusted hands decorating their friends' faces. The makeup consists of ocher powder greased with the cow enzyme rennet. The Wodaabe apply the paint with their slender fingers, slowly moving outward, though the consistency remains slightly powdery rather than blended in. The men also use clay and stone to decorate their bodies: mineral and plant-based substances are thought to possess magical properties among the ethnic group. (People in neighboring areas consider the Wodaabe experts in "supernatural medicines.")

Various powders comprising the makeup the Japto are using are available only near a specific mountain in central Niger, with men embarking on a 1,400-kilometer trip to secure them. The color of the face makeup is a matter of choice; some opt to paint their faces red, yellow, or green instead of orange. Red is associated with blood and violence, while shades of yellow signal magic and transformation, and green represents plants and grass used to feed cattle, a sign of abundance or plentifulness. Other Japto men forgo the base altogether, adorning themselves only with white dots that complement their scarification, permanent scars etched onto the face as a form of ornamentation. The white powder is ground so finely and is so highly pigmented that grease isn't required for its application. The men also stain their lips black with coal, though more recently—and dangerously—some have turned to alkaline derived from batteries discarded by tourists along the Sahel. Japto men also color their lips blue to contrast with their orange face paint. To maintain the whiteness of their teeth, several men rub them with the twigs of nearby trees as they walk around casually observing their peers' preparations.

As noon approaches, the dances are in full swing. "I already have a wife," Kai declares when asked if he's seeking a new partner. He gestures at a young woman in the crowd, who smiles back at him. "I'm not interested in finding another."

His friends, who are openly boasting about their chances of finding new partners, chuckle as he speaks. Kai shows off his kohl pot, which dangles from a long, elaborate necklace made with whistles, beads, and plastic cuttings. The man's hat boasts an ostrich plume and pom-poms to maximize his height and mimic the heron. While his wife's hair is plaited, Kai styles his beneath his headdress in pigtails decorated with cowrie shells, which symbolize fertility.

There is something of an androgynous look to the Wodaabe, whose beauty standards demand facial symmetry, a narrow face, a long, thin nose, wide, bright eyes, and pearly white teeth—not a far cry from Nefertiti's "golden ratio" face. Tallness and thinness are also desirable characteristics; Wodaabe men sometimes tiptoe during the Gerewol for this reason. Large foreheads are considered beautiful, and men often shave back their hairlines. The dancers wear beaded headbands and colorful combs wedged into their hair; the beads drape from their hairlines to meet their leather-bag amulet necklaces, which in turn fall to their slender waists. Both men and women are fans of earrings; necklaces, pendants, and chokers are ubiquitous.

The Wodaabe celebrate their identities by way of their theatrics and their style; their bodies and voices are vessels for their culture and legacy. The group marries the modern with the traditional in their flamboyant, dynamic approach to makeup, jewelry, and fashion. For jewelry, the Wodaabe combine discarded and repurposed plastics with traditional beaded designs, shells, precious metals, and wool. (When offered Twizzlers by a Western tourist, one Wodaabe boy understandably assumed the candy was plastic.) Bottles of eyedrops disposed of by tourists become beaded kohl pots. Elastic bracelets are stacked alongside leather bracelets. Necklaces are adorned with copper, brass, and glass trinkets, with even more beads and mirrors. A few of the men wear watches or sunglasses decoratively; they don't use them to shield their eyes from the sun, thanks to their kohl. One has on a pair in the shape of a cactus, another boasts a pair with neon-pink frames. Everywhere, there are pops of color: purple, fuchsia, yellow, and cobalt. For shoes, several are dressed in either socks and sandals or Wellingtons, which they tuck their loose pants into. In this way, disparate items come together to form a gorgeous whole.

Resourcefulness is essential to the Wodaabe; no item of potential aesthetic use is thrown away. Reflective items are sometimes woven into the fabrics: covers of memory cards and empty cigarette lighters are sewn into bodices. Dozens of fluorescent-colored whistles hang from waistcoats and cross-body bags; they jangle to the beat as the men dance. Embroidery is vital, with geometric patterns, buttons, and sequins embellishing materials such as cotton, polyester, leather, and even velvet. Often, the stitches match the designs of their body tattoos. Several men and women wear soccer jerseys (such as those of Barcelona players). One man even sports a top with a picture of Donald Trump on it; another, an American flag. The men's loose tunics, which float in the wind as they shuffle, consist of various prints, including florals, stripes, polka dots, checkers, brocades, gingham, Greek keys, and stars. These explosions of patterns and colors are both dizzying and transfixing. With so many aesthetic options to choose from, each man has his own style. The young dancers are united, however, by the kohl pots that dangle from their necks, and the lines that decorate their eyes.

Several matches are made on the third day of the ceremony. Two girls pick two boys by shyly standing at a short distance from the line of men, before being gently beckoned by a guide to come forward. They then walk quickly toward two of the dancers, poke them, and return to the group of women, who cheer them on. The men drop their heads as soon as the girls make their selections as a sign of respect. (*If only dating in New York were this straightforward*, I thought as I observed the process.) Though the women are the judges in this courtship process, they're sometimes secretive about whom they like—many will send their friends as surrogates to choose the men they desire.

Ali, twenty-eight, has two children, who are being looked after by his wife at home. He says he informally took a temporary wife the previous night and is open to more. Another man is so handsome, he is chosen three times. This man is conscious and proud of the symmetry of his face, the brightness of his kohl-framed eyes, the power of his beauty, and his place within the clan: men who are successful in the Gerewol are hailed and long remembered by the group as heroes.

The origins of the Wodaabe are obscure, though images of people resembling them have been identified in ancient rock paintings across the Sahara, suggesting that their culture may have existed for millennia. Over time, along with their parent group, the

Fulani, they have traveled through a variety of countries and cultures. Some scholars note that the Wodaabe believe themselves to be from the upper Nile Valley in Ethiopia, though the Fulani are thought to have originated in Senegal or even North Africa or the Middle East, before moving southward. More recently, the Wodaabe, guided by the needs of their cattle and the seasons, have moved around Nigeria and Niger and through Cameroon and Chad. Kohl use in the Wodaabe tradition may be as old as the group itself, says Dak. "The daily life of the Wodaabe has been so hard that probably the only way to face it, to cope with such harsh conditions, is to try to wear beauty on your body," Dak says of their commitment to cosmetics. "It's not just a romantic way of considering their life and lifestyle; it's also a useful strategy to survive."

While the Wodaabe community exists apart from modern society in Chad, kohl use is ubiquitous among people of the villages and cities as well. Abba Yahya Osman was born into the Fulani. But when Osman was seven, his father decided to leave for the city to find work, choosing sedentary life over nomadic life. Osman grew up in the city but continues to visit the Wodaabe and Fulani people when he can because he feels that their traditions are a part of his identity. He is loved among them and finds the tradition of the Worso beautiful. He, too, wears kohl, along with his wife and children, though he's now a religious Muslim and prays five times a day. "Kohl unites us all," he says in Arabic, reflecting on its importance in Chadian society. In other regions of Africa, groups including the Hausa, Tuareg, and Wolof peoples also use kohl, as do Muslims along the Sahel and Sahara.

Adam Ismail Rashed, a nineteen-year-old man from the capital,

N'Djamena, who's here to observe the festival, affirms the religious importance of kohl: "It's the way of the Prophet [Muhammad], peace be upon him," he says. But he also applies the product on the advice of his doctor, who prescribed it to treat a persistent eye ailment he has had for the past two years. He's fascinated by kohl's medicinal properties and hopes to one day study in Europe to become a doctor himself, before returning to Chad, where there is a shortage of medical professionals. (It's an added benefit, he admits, that kohl also enhances his looks.)

As the festival draws to a close, the young men of the Japto clan decide to dance until sunrise, which falls at about 5:00 a.m. They take brief breaks for rest and to touch up their makeup but continue performing and chanting until the sun edges up from the horizon. At this hour, their performance seems almost otherworldly. Their clothes remain just as put together as they were on the first morning of the festival, their movements just as coordinated, their body language just as regal, and their kohl just as sharp.

After a long night of dancing and mingling, the men and women plan to rest and then to depart with their cows by noon to find conditions better suited for the cattle as the water in the area has dried up and the grass is scarce. The clan has resigned itself to the idea that the Sudosukai are unlikely to show up to the festival. They are unsurprised; tensions between the two groups have been simmering for two years now, ever since a Japto man bypassed official rules to partner with a Sudosukai woman, drawing the ire of the Sudosukai.

But at the break of dawn, just as the sun's rays scatter into daylight, draping the sky in flecks of pink, a group of Sudosukai sporadically emerge from the bushes like a mirage. They, too, are extravagantly made up and dressed in their finest regalia. With this unannounced, fashionably late arrival, they are clearly here to impress. Almost immediately, in a show of competitive sport, they come together to dance. Realizing their competitors have arrived, the Japto continue to dance instead of packing it in. The energy with which they are performing is, at this point, conspicuous by its presence, given they have been dancing through the night.

Though the Sudosukai are a similarly striking bunch—and they, too, carry their kohl around their necks as a marker of pride—they are aesthetically more daring overall. The men's faces are mostly painted in shades of red, the color of war, compared with the more muted and perhaps more diplomatic yellows and oranges of the Japto. Their makeup is more polished: the face paint is applied seamlessly and blended into their skin, likely due to a finer grinding of the ocher powder, and their kohl is more defined, with not a smudge to be seen, sharp lines meeting soft features. Their eyebrows are filled in with black and brown powders, while the Japto have concealed theirs, opting to draw attention solely to the patterns of their scarification. The Sudosukai make use of white powders, too, with lines drawn from forehead to chin to accentuate their facial symmetry. They lack scarification, but still adorn their faces with the powders in intricate designs such as circles and flowers, rather than just dots and lines.

The clothing of the Sudosukai is also more elaborate—they wear tall, bejeweled hats and turbans, similar to the crown of

Queen Nefertiti, topped with ostrich feathers. Most of their skirts are embroidered; some are made of leather. They carry straw fans and swords. Their Technicolor bodices are bolder and more sparkly—one man even wears a black velvet waistcoat embellished with gold sequins. Unlike the Japto, they show plenty of skin. While they, too, imitate the heron, they sway more gently and slowly, and though their claps are louder, their chanting is more subdued. Altogether, they give the impression that their movements are not the focal point; they prefer to let their looks speak for themselves.

Separately, and at a comfortable distance, the two clans continue to dance, outperforming each other, as they compete to attract women's attention from opposing sides. Eventually, though, they stop to exchange greetings, and finally form one long line in the shape of a semicircle to dance. This is at once a hello and a good-bye dance, an expression of solidarity and singularity, with the two clans competing as one group with no clear winner (though I'd have voted for the Japto). In the face of recent tensions, the unification isn't to be taken lightly.

Two older women, both wives of one of the minders, dance around the group, unencumbered by the pressures of youth. They wail in joy as they do, encouraging the men as they hop around. They are beautiful in every way imaginable, their silk scarves floating in the morning breeze, their kohl smudged imperfectly onto their eyelids. The men lower their heads for them. The women's eyes appear brighter than ever. The energy is electric; even the cows seem entranced. Soon, one Japto woman chooses one Sudosukai man, and one Sudosukai woman chooses one Japto man. Equilibrium is restored.

"We hope to continue coming together in this way," Jodi Laamido, chief of the Japto Shibo clan, reflects, "to express the beauty of our people. We value beauty because it's sacred." As he speaks, he gestures at his lined eyes, and the kohl pot around his neck, referencing the significance of the cosmetic in the prettification process.

At this point of the festivities, after various clan chiefs lecture the children on the Worso's importance, the Japto men begin to retreat, while the Sudosukai, who dance with an air of victory about them, keep performing, eager for their bit of fun.

The Japto remove their face makeup with splashes of water. They change into more comfortable clothing and fall into heaps on the ground, where they will nap in the open air beneath the acacia trees. They will soon return to their regular daily activities, such as milking their cows, searching for water, and taking care of their children.

Tomorrow will look vastly different from today. Their kohl, however, will remain.

Chapter Three

Eye Paint as Resistance

Sormeh in Iran

*I*n the photo, twenty-two-year-old Mahsa Amini is clearly done up. Her lips and nails are painted burgundy, her eyelashes are curled, and her cheekbones are contoured. Eyeshadow and eyeliner accentuate the Kurdish Iranian woman's smoky eyes. And her hijab is arranged loosely around her face, exposing her neck, and revealing a dark head of hair and the tip of a French braid. While this is the image that was displayed on posters around the world in a series of 2022 protests—from Tehran and Beirut to Rome and Los Angeles—in another less widely shared photo, Amini is seen wishing on a dandelion and blowing off the seeds, her lips stained crimson and her hair side-parted under a chiffon scarf. In the picture, her eyes are also lined.

According to sources close to her, as reported by Reuters, Amini was reserved, avoided politics, and didn't outwardly challenge Iran's strict Islamic dress code. Known also as Jina, her

Kurdish name, she kept to herself, and had hoped to live a "normal and happy life." She'd just started a job at a shop in her hometown, the northwestern Kurdish city of Saqez, with dreams of finishing university, getting married, and having kids. Though Amini dressed conservatively, covering the outlines of her body and her hair, as required by Iranian law, her aesthetic had its own special flair and demonstrated a sense of individuality.

But on September 13, 2022, Amini paid the highest price for the simple act of how she chose to dress that day: a black robe, a black headscarf, and black pants. Amini had just arrived in Iran's capital city from her hometown; she was there to visit family. As she stepped off the subway with her brother, she was arrested by Iran's so-called morality police and accused of breaching the dress code (the precise nature of the violation remains unclear). Amini and her brother said they weren't familiar with the city's rules and pleaded with the police to let her go. Those pleas were ignored.

Eyewitnesses said Amini was severely beaten while in custody after she was picked up by a van and transferred to a detention center for "reeducation"; she subsequently fell into a coma and died within days. Police denied all allegations of misconduct and claimed she had a preexisting medical condition and died of a heart attack. Amini's death sparked months of protests across the Islamic Republic and its Kurdish region, led mostly by women. It was the biggest show of opposition to the country's clerical establishment since demonstrations in 2009, known as the Green Movement. Those protests began in the wake of Mahmoud Ahmadinejad declaring victory in the presidential election despite reported irregularities, but they were eventually quashed after a government crackdown.

The 2022 demonstrations were met with lethal force as security personnel used bullets and batons—at the time of writing, hundreds had been killed and thousands detained. Despite that force, videos online showed women taking to the streets without the hijab and dancing in protest, with some cutting their hair or shaving their heads and throwing their headscarves into bonfires. One particularly moving video features a woman seated on a chair in the middle of an Iranian backstreet, removing her hijab, and brushing her hair.

Demonstrations included people of all generations and classes, especially Gen Z, who are keenly aware that for life to change, matters must be taken into their own hands. Schoolgirls and university students joined the battle cry, ripping pictures of Iran's supreme leader, Ali Khamenei, off walls and shouting slogans of defiance. Days into the uprising, sixteen-year-old Nika Shakarami, who was seen on video protesting and burning her hijab, went missing and was later found dead. Her mother accused security forces of murdering her, a claim officials denied. In the picture of Shakarami that also went viral after her death, she's wearing eyeliner with distinct, sharp wings, her hair fully exposed and cut into a bob, with multiple gold chains around her neck.

Sarina Esmailzadeh, another sixteen-year-old who was killed by police while she was protesting, was active on social media, regularly posting vlogs about life as a young woman living under Iran's restrictions. "What are the needs of a sixteen-year-old?" she asks in one video. "Giving love, receiving love, being loved, and being in love. We are in need of joy and recreation, good spirit, good vibes, good energy. In order to have these, we need freedom. This is where the conversation gets a bit dark. Because of some of the restrictions which are specifically put in place for women, such as the mandatory hijab."

Amini's image is now synonymous with the struggle not only for women's rights in Iran but also for social and economic justice for all Iranians. Her killing and its aftermath have thrown into the spotlight once more how the appearance of Iranian women is heavily policed in the Islamic Republic—and how their sartorial choices can become a matter of life or death.

Restrictions and Resistance

To understand the relationship between women and their appearance in Iran today and, by extension, how they view makeup and eyeliner, we must first look at the Islamic Revolution of 1979. The revolution—spurred by a backlash against the constitutional monarchy of Shah Mohammad Reza Pahlavi, which had pushed for an aggressive modernization of the country—hit women hard.

Iranian women had, since the late nineteenth century, demanded expanded rights, and continued to do so at various points throughout the 1900s. In 1935, before Pahlavi came into power, a decree barred women from wearing the veil, a different form of control. And while some rights had improved under Pahlavi, not everyone approved of his rule.

The 1979 overthrow, which saw the religious leader Ayatollah

Khomeini topple Pahlavi and reverse his policies, affected the freedom of movement for women and how they dressed. "The state set out deliberately and consciously to reconstruct and redefine the place of women," writes Haleh Esfandiari in her book *Reconstructed Lives*. While many women participated in the revolution and were a force behind it, she wrote, "the vast majority of women expected the revolution to lead to an expansion, not a contraction, of their rights and opportunities." And they certainly didn't expect forced segregation or the loss of control over what makeup or clothing they could wear.

Following the end of the revolution, Khomeini declared Iran an Islamic state, effectively making it a theocratic, totalitarian regime, with leadership quelling Western influence—political, economic, and cultural. The government scrapped personal and family laws offering women limited freedoms. The hijab and full-body coverings were soon made compulsory, women weren't allowed to mix freely with men, and authorities restricted their access to work and education. In this new world, women were prohibited from beautifying themselves with cosmetics, whether taking lipstick to their lips or an applicator to their eyelids. After the hijab ruling, tens of thousands of Iranian women took to the streets to protest the changes, to no avail. Despite their resistance, women had no choice but to become overly self-conscious under the state's scrutiny.

Before the revolution, bold eyeliner was popular, and women were more likely to wear noticeable makeup publicly, according to Dr. Mansoureh Ettehadieh, an eighty-five-year-old historian, publisher, and former professor at the University of Tehran.

Women were influenced by the styles of Western and Iranian movie and theater stars and modeled their hairdos and makeup on magazine photos of them, she reflects. From the 1950s through the 1970s, iconic Iranian celebrities, including Vida Ghahremani and Hamideh Kheirabadi, adorned their lids with thick black lines, using either eyeliner or sormeh, a deep black powder.

In the aftermath of the revolution, the Iran-Iraq War—which saw scores of women participate in military and relief efforts—left over one million Iranians dead. During the conflict, divisions between public and private life intensified: "It was you inside the house and your sphere, and then outside you had to decide whether you were going to carry that private bit of you [including the wearing of eye makeup] into public and then confront costs for that," academic and author Azadeh Moaveni said on a 2019 episode of the BBC World Service podcast *The Documentary* that explores the history of sormeh and is hosted by journalist Nassim Hatam.

After the revolution and the end of the war with Iraq, women— especially young women—who chafed at the regime's authoritarian restrictions viewed their appearances in public as opportunities for civil disobedience, Moaveni tells me. Some would go as far as to show a "puff of hair," known as a kakol, under their scarves, wear lipstick, manicure their nails, flaunt bright colors, and dress in shorter chadors (robes) than what was required by law. Beneath the chadors, many of which were even bejeweled or embroidered, others wore dresses or Western-style suits that were occasionally exposed. At universities, women sometimes styled their veils so loosely that they revealed the tips of ponytails or bangs.

Today, the way women wear their makeup remains a "symbol

of women's resistance," Esfandiari cites one interviewee as saying, though each woman must weigh her desire for self-expression against her assessment of risk. Zahra, a twenty-five-year-old woman living in Tehran, is careful and deliberate in her eyeliner application: "I don't wear makeup to the extent that it attracts attention. I only wear a reasonable amount." Shabnam, a thirty-year-old nail artist, says she tries "to avoid places where there are restrictions on makeup," and also chooses not to wear conspicuous cosmetics, including heavy eyeliner.

Ketayoun Nejad Tahari, a sixty-one-year-old hairdresser who's been in the salon business for thirty-eight years and runs a parlor in Tehran, has lived with the stark contrasts between private and public arenas for most of her life. She recalls that, after the revolution, though heavy eyeliner use in public was rare, "in private circles, at home, and at parties and weddings, it didn't change. As much as we used to wear makeup at parties before the revolution [in those spaces], we did so after the revolution."

"Limitations and Etiquette"

While remaining relatively restricted, prior to Amini's death, the situation for women in Iran seemed to have improved slightly, due in part to their pushes for change. In 2017, under former president Hassan Rouhani's leadership, Tehran police chief Brig. Gen. Hossein Rahimi said the morality police would alter its approach to enforcing Islamic values on women, essentially implying officers would become more flexible or less strict when monitoring them. (The police force had for decades fined, detained, and lashed women for wearing nail polish and heavy makeup, or for loosely tying their headscarves.)

Despite police continuing to roam the streets to crack down on these sartorial choices, women in and around the country's urban centers could be spotted in intricate makeup styles and lined eyes. Veils became looser, colors brighter, and hair more exposed. Outside the workplace, more women wore noticeable makeup publicly. In some areas, hijab laws were enforced selectively, with women being shielded by ties to the regime or their economic status—while upper-class women enjoyed certain privileges, middle-class women like Amini did not.

"Especially at parties, the use of makeup [including eyeliner] has increased a lot compared to the first years of the revolution," says Ettehadieh. "And today, women do many things to beautify themselves." (This isn't so much the case for women with public-facing jobs, particularly women who work in government offices, the judiciary, the post office, and universities, she adds, as most of the time these employees are told to wear "uniforms" and "very little makeup.")

While women are seemingly freer to wear makeup publicly today compared with the 1980s, like those of the younger generation, Tahari understands that applying eyeliner or sormeh still has its limitations and etiquette. "Every place has its own [type of] makeup"—a wedding has its makeup, while going shopping has its makeup, she says. "So makeup depends on where we want to go. I have limits for myself, and I know where I should wear elaborate makeup and where I should wear less makeup."

When Ebrahim Raisi, an ultraconservative, came into power,

he reinforced religious rules governing women with a heavy hand. The hard-line president demanded that the imposition of the hijab be ramped up as violations were "promoting corruption" and damaging Iran's purported values. In the month before Amini's death, videos on social media showed police dragging and detaining women.

To many observers, his crackdown has felt particularly out of step with the critical role women who were born before or around the revolution have played in public life, despite restrictions—not to mention the boldness of Gen Z. The literacy rate among women aged fifteen to twenty-four stands at 98 percent. About 19 percent of women are in the workforce, up from 11 percent in 1990; women are authors, directors, journalists, and members of parliament. Compared with the time preceding the 1979 revolution, they are also getting married later and having fewer children, and by 2018, roughly twenty times more women had completed higher education.

"Countless videos and memes in the Persian language social media sphere compare the youth of the 1980s to the youth of today. Many posts highlight Iranian girls' dress codes, particularly how girls dressed very conservatively in the obligatory all black and were expected to have obedient and meek personalities 30 years ago," Holly Dagres, a senior fellow at the Atlantic Council who specializes in Iran, writes for *Foreign Policy*. "Those images are contrasted with the more revealing, colorful clothes Iranian girls wear today, daring to show their curves and hair. Not surprisingly, these young women are more outspoken against authority in general."

"Caught between Cultures and Spaces"

Shirin Neshat is concerned and cautiously optimistic at once. Sitting on the patio of her Bushwick home in Brooklyn on this crisp late September afternoon in 2022, she's surrounded by geraniums, butterfly bushes, gardenias, hibiscuses, and Brazilian jasmines. But the sixty-five-year-old visual artist and filmmaker is preoccupied. Her mind isn't here, in New York. It's firmly in Iran, her motherland. It's focused on the women of her birthplace: on her mother, on her sisters, on her friends, on Mahsa Amini.

The protests against the killing of Amini had by then entered their second week. "We're all wondering, is it possible this could be the real thing? How long can young people stay on the streets while being attacked with gunshots, while being brutalized and killed?" She pauses for a few moments, as if to catch her breath. "All I can do is just keep supporting them from here," she says. The artist is currently living in self-imposed exile, and hasn't returned home since 1996, but is committed to making a difference from afar.

Neshat is a beautiful, petite woman, known as much for her bold aesthetic as she is for her art, which borrows from both aspects of her identity, blending the Orient with the Occident, extravagance with simplicity, and modernity with antiquity. Today, she's wearing a pair of sneakers, dark blue skinny jeans, and a navy athleisure top (she's about to head to a dance class), but she more or less dresses casually all the time. Her jet-black hair is tied into a low bun with a large scrunchie; not a strand is out of place.

It would be a minimalist "Western" look indeed, had it not been for her ornate jewelry: she wears chandelier earrings from Morocco, a gold collar necklace, and a statement silver ring. She has drawers filled with tribal and traditional necklaces and bracelets she's collected from all over the world, "ordinary people's" jewelry, she says.

And then, there's her larger-than-life eyeliner. It's the stuff of icons, the stuff of ancient Egyptian queens and kings—Nefertiti herself would be proud. It begs questions, it demands answers. The lines around Neshat's deep brown eyes are concentrated more on her bottom rims than on her eyelids. The heavy, precisely drawn swooshes start at the inner corners of her eyes, stretch across her lower waterlines, and extend past her outer corners before finally resting a few millimeters away from the edges of her eyebrows. It takes her just two minutes to apply the makeup; she uses either MAC or Lancôme pencils as they don't smear, and turns to their liquid variations for more dramatic evening looks, though she says she's not purposefully loyal to any particular brand.

Neshat's liner is so eye-catching, she's often on the receiving end of quizzical looks, even on the subway. Occasionally she's questioned about it outright. Once, when she was in a public restroom in Morocco, two women stopped her while she was on her way out to tell her "something was wrong with her eyes." When she explained that the look was intended, they were incredulous and laughed—and Neshat laughed with them.

When first asked about how she cultivated her trademark eyeliner look, Neshat smiles, and says even she isn't sure; she wonders if she was subconsciously influenced by ancient Egypt's gods and goddesses. "I once went on a beautiful boat trip along the Nile in Egypt. When we visited the temples, and I saw these images of goddesses like Queen Nefertiti, I thought, 'Oh my God! Yes, that's where my eyeliner comes from!'" she says. More seriously, she feels her eyeliner aesthetic isn't solely the result of her being Iranian, but isn't independent of it, either. Rather, it has to do with her being caught in between Iran and the West: she says she takes some influences from her native culture and others from her adopted one.

Neshat has had a complicated relationship with Iran for most of her life. She was born in 1957, twenty-two years before the revolution, to an upper-class family in the town of Qazvin, known as Iran's calligraphy capital. Her father, a physician who embraced Western values, encouraged her and her four siblings to pursue higher education. At his behest, Neshat left the country at just seventeen to move to California, where she briefly attended high school before studying art at the University of California, Berkeley. "It was like a rug had been pulled out from under my feet. I was alone and devastated to be away from home, from everything I knew," she says. "I was lost. Those were the hardest years of my life, I'm lucky I survived the situation. At the same time, I grew up. I'd reached the end of my adolescence and was becoming a woman, just without my mother."

Neshat was reserved and insecure, lacking money and family, and channeled her energies into survival. Her looks were an afterthought. But at college, she met Lauren, a half-Black, half–Native

American woman who quickly became one of her best friends. "She was very conscious of being a minority, and it impacted her style and makeup. I found that beautiful," Neshat says. "Being another female minority and seeing how through her aesthetics, she defined her own identity, that inspired me."

Slowly, Neshat began paying attention to her own style as an Iranian woman and immigrant, and started wearing eyeliner more prominently. She was in her early twenties, and instead of drawing thin lines, as she'd done when she lived in Iran, she drew them thicker, and thicker, until finally they seemed just about right to her. "I remember, suddenly, I felt beautiful, even though it was a very tough time," she says.

Though Neshat insists she borrows from both cultures, it's clear the earliest explorations of her looks were influenced by her teenage years in Iran, where she was surrounded by sisters and a mother who lined their eyes with sormeh, back when the Islamic Revolution had yet to unfold. The way she presented herself to the world then developed in part as a reaction to living away from Iran, in exile, during and after the 1979 revolution.

One of her older sisters in Iran, in particular, was blessed with an effortless beauty and confidence. "She wasn't only beautiful, she was obsessed with being beautiful," Neshat says, while the artist, by contrast, was timid. "While I looked very plain and was always the good girl, she spent time separating her eyelashes with a pin and darkening her eyes. She was always the naughty one, secretly seeing boys." Her sisters sometimes made their own sormeh by burning almonds and moistening their ashes—they applied the pigment on the insides of their waterlines, a look Neshat mimicked for some time. Black-and-white pictures of the artist in Iran show a young girl with subtly lined eyes shyly looking at the camera.

She was also greatly influenced by her mother. "Iranian people are inspired by Western looks, and so they were always very glamorous," she says. "But my mother's eye makeup was very Oriental, very Asian, in a way that didn't resemble any European fashion. It was thick." Neshat carried that aesthetic in her subconscious mind, until it gradually started to seep into her own style as she found her footing in California.

"I gravitated toward Western and non-Western styles. With this idea of being caught between cultures and spaces, as someone who spent most of their adult life here, but is still rooted in Iran, I developed a hybrid style," she says. "The combination of the two really represents who I am—my own identity. There's an ancient past behind me and there are roots behind me that I still belong to. Yet I'm here, and I'm with you, and I'm modern."

Neshat understands deeply that her ability to experiment with her style and eyeliner with no limitations is, by comparison with her people in Iran, a privilege, and the guilt she carries because of this and other privileges is palpable. "As much as you want to cut loose this cord, you just can't," she says. "I'm not unique. There are a lot of people who have been through the same."

Enlighten My Eyes

The prevalence of sormeh in Iran is in part due to its use being halal, or permissible, in Islam. In other majority Muslim countries, including the United Arab Emirates and Saudi Arabia, kohl is also worn by both women and men. Iraqi cleric and militia leader Muqtada al-Sadr has been spotted with darkened lower lashes, presumably achieved with the help of kohl or ithmid, and members of the Taliban also line their eyes. This is likely because per hadith (Islamic sayings), the Prophet Muhammad wore ithmid, a form of kohl or sormeh made of antimony or galena, to protect his eyes. According to these sayings, he wore the substance at night to clear or brighten his vision and make his eyelashes grow, and advised others to use it medicinally. The Prophet used sormeh so frequently, the reference *Mesbah al-Zayer* notes it was among five essentials he carried with him during his travels, along with mirrors, forks, toothbrushes, and combs. Some narrations say that he used truffles as sormeh or kohl to prevent conjunctivitis. Per an Abu Hurairah narration, those who enter paradise will be gifted with eternal youth, no body hair, clothes that do not wear out, and kohl for their eyelids.

Imam Jafar al-Sadiq, an eighth-century Shia Muslim scholar and jurist, narrated that applying sormeh at night is good for the eyes' health, while using it during the day is a form of ornamentation. According to a separate hadith from Imam Sadiq, sormeh has four main benefits: it assists with eyelash growth, it prevents the excessive shedding of tears, it polishes the eyes, and it even sweetens one's breath. And in another hadith narrated by Imam Muhammad al-Baqir, the fifth imam in Shia Islam, sormeh is said to make the lashes firm.

While applying sormeh was considered halal, narrations offered best practices around its use. For one, it was recommended that kohl wearers ensure the sky is clear of clouds before the substance is applied—otherwise, the eyes risk being "stained." The Prophet was said to apply sormeh to his right eyelid four times and to his left three times before sleeping. Using the cosmetic in odd numbers is therefore believed to be sunnah; some hadith offer different numbers, such as five or three, the commonality being the odd number. (In Islam, odd numbers hold great significance, as they are seen as a reminder of the oneness of Allah.)

Various hadith recommended Muslims recite a prayer prior to applying sormeh. Imam Ali Reza, the eighth imam in Twelver Shia Islam, advises the pious to invoke Allah's name first, and to apply it with their right hand. He also asks Muslims to recite the following prayer before using it: "May Allah enlighten my eyes with sormeh and put light in my eyes (not only can material things be seen through it, but I can see truth with it). Allah, guide me to the path of truth and guide the way to growth. Allah, enlighten my world and the hereafter."

There are also special requirements for using sormeh during ihram, the "sacred state" Muslims enter before performing the holy pilgrimage in Mecca. According to Imami jurists, men and women alike weren't allowed to wear "fragrant" sormeh during this period. (The Prophet forbade the wearing of perfume for the occasion.) Imam Sadiq banned the use of sormeh mixed with saffron, which gave it a distinct scent, for example. Some jurists argue non-fragrant kohl is forbidden if used by women for beauty.

Interestingly, and by sharp contrast, in the Jahiliya (age of ignorance) era, referred to as such by religious Muslims to denote the period before the advent of Islam, kohl—at least as it was written about in poetry and elsewhere—was viewed as feminine. "What's become of you that you let the king rape your brides," wrote Afira bint Abbad in the third century CE. "If you're not moved by this outrage, you might as well bathe in scent and kohl your eyes and wear the bridal dress." Academics Mohammad Abu Rumman and Hassan Abu Hanieh wrote in their book *Infatuated with Martyrdom: Female Jihadism from Al-Qaeda to the 'Islamic State'* that later "the women of the *mushrikeen* 'pre-Islamic polytheists of Mecca' at the Battle of Uhud '3 AH' . . . would enter the battlefield carrying *kohl* eyeliners. Every time a man would retreat or hesitate, one of these women would hand him an eyeliner, saying, 'Are you a woman?'"

Sormeh is defined in the Persian-language *Farhang-e Ānandrāj* dictionary as "a glossy stone that shines and benefits the eyes." According to the dictionary, it's also the name of an Iranian village "where a lot of sormeh was extracted, and it's a kind of wine in Turkestan." Hasan Amid's dictionary, the *Farhang-e Amid,* describes sormeh as a material made of leaded soil and black powder obtained from ferrous sulfur or lead sulfur that is used to darken eyelashes and eyelids; substances applied to the eyes for medical treatment are also called sormeh. Similar to the many colors eyeliner can be found in today's, which have made way for graphic liner trends, the sormeh colors have varied over the centuries. Mowaffaq Heravi, the author of the oldest Persian medical treatise, writes about purple, pink, and even white sormeh.

The terms *sormeh* and *kohl* are often used interchangeably, and the substances are similar in appearance, composition, and purpose. Sormeh is extracted from mines containing kohl materials, Iran being home to some of the world's most important, according to analyses published decades apart by physicist Eilhard Ernst G. Wiedemann and historian James W. Allan. This assertion is backed up by early tenth- and eleventh-century Muslim travelers Abu al-Qasim Muhammad Ibn Hawqal, Abu Ishaq Ibrahim al-Istakhri, and the unknown author of the *Hudud al-Alam*. The travelers note in their works that there were famous mines for sormeh ingredients in Khorasan, Sari, Anarak, and Isfahan. The mines in Isfahan, particularly those in the mountains, were celebrated.

Various Persian sources reveal several types of kohl or sormeh: *Asmad* means black kohl, while *tutia* means white kohl. *Kohl asfar* (yellow kohl) is a medicine for the eyes made of saffron and camphor, while *kohl Isfahani* (kohl from Isfahan) is composed of antimony sulfide (though recent studies have cast doubt on this formulation) and has primarily been used to darken the eyes. *Kohl al-aghbar* was used as a less potent option for children. Perhaps most alluring among these sormeh varieties was *kohl al-basr*, comprised of uncut pearls ground and mixed with other jewels; the powder was used to brighten the eyes. A mixture of turquoise stones with kohl was also touted as beneficial for the eyes and thought to sharpen and polish them. (A book of minerology from the ninth century CE mentions that some turquoise stones were mixed with gold and copper, making a fine sormeh powder.) But the crème de la crème of all sormeh types was the "kohl of seven jewels," which consisted of crushed and powdered gold, silver, diamonds, rubies, emeralds, and two types of pearls.

"My Sormeh Is a Magnet"

Sormeh recipes date back at least two millennia; wearing the powder in ancient Persia was a cultural norm for men and women. "Archaeological evidence tells us a lot about the remains of kohl pots," Lloyd Llewellyn-Jones, an ancient history professor at Cardiff University, says in Hatam's BBC News podcast episode (pots that, I may add, should be in their national museums as opposed to the museums of colonial and imperial powers). Sormeh's use in the ancient Persian context made sense for medical purposes due to harsh weather conditions, including strong sunlight, but also for aesthetic purposes, to enhance the eyes, he says.

"If you look back at very early [ancient kingdom of] Elamite sculptures, they all have enormous eyes, much bigger than is proportional to the sculpture, with kohl lines drawn very carefully around them," the historian explains. "Throughout Iran's history, there's a play on sight and seeing. Rebellion was punished by the blinding of individuals and the gauging out of eyes. There's this sense, therefore, that to have eyes is to be able to see and to be able to judge. So, there's something about sight, seeing, and the beauty of the eye which is really endemic or indigenous to the idea of rulership in Iran." (Incidentally, in February 2023, various media reported that the Iranian regime had been targeting the eyes of women protesters amid the broader crackdown.)

Similar to how kajal is present in Indian literature and poetry, and kohl is present in Arab literature and poetry, there are multiple references to sormeh in Persian literature and poetry and its myths and legends. Sormeh also takes on magical and spiritual meaning in these texts—in one tale, "Soleimani's sormeh" was said to give its wearers the power to discover the world's secrets. Meanwhile, "stealth sormeh" allegedly made its wearers invisible. By contrast, "Khosrow Parviz sormeh" or the "khakbin" gave kings extraordinary vision, allowing them to see the depths of the earth, its secrets, and its treasures. In 1641, an earthquake shook Tabriz, a city in northwest Iran—the event was so catastrophic, a poet wrote "the color of sormeh spilled from the eyes of the idols."

Sormeh has been used as a symbol to express devotion to a beloved. In one poem, a lover believes the soil of their significant other's feet is sormeh and stares at it to illuminate their eyes. In another, a poet asks his partner to "paint [her] cute eyes with sormeh again" to "double the taste of madness and the enthusiasm of the lyricist." When lining their eyes, women were advised to sing a song to their husbands, which included the words "My sormeh is black sormeh. My sormeh is a magnet. He laughs when I apply it." The proverb "Sormeh should be removed from the eye" alludes to the skill required to steal (given it's difficult to wipe off the substance). And if events have "burned an individual like sormeh in mortar," they have left the person more experienced.

The transformative power of sormeh and eyeliner is also conveyed in Iranian cinema. In the 2014 short film *Sormeh*, directed by Azadeh Ghochagh, the cosmetic acts as the plot's catalyst. An Iranian couple plans to attend a wedding amid protests unfolding during the 1979 revolution. While she gets ready, the wife joyfully heats her sormeh applicator using the steam of a kettle, to help moisten the little powder she has left; she hums until she's jolted by a loud noise from outside and realizes she's run out of the pigment. Instead of hunkering down, she decides to pick up some sormeh from her friend. With just one eye made up, she rushes out, only to encounter a runaway rebel fleeing from guards; as she assists the rebel, ushering him into a storage room, she finds herself inadvertently embroiled in new and terrifying political realities. In the closing scene, having failed to retrieve sormeh from her friend, she's teary-eyed, with one eye still bare, the weight of the country's political developments finally hitting her.

In a scene of the 2014 film *A Girl Walks Home Alone at Night*, a Persian protagonist, played by the actor Sheila Vand, dances to the seductive hum of an electronic track. As the music lingers, she regards her reflection with contempt. Though her eyes are already lined, something must be done to this tabula rasa of a face; a transformation beckons. The woman grips her eyeliner pencil and draws not one but four thick lines around her large doe eyes. Eyes now sufficiently darkened, she stains her lips with red. After throwing on a black chador, the transformation is complete; the protagonist is now her alter ego, a vampire who roams around an Iranian town referred to as "the Bad City."

In the blanket of darkness, she searches for her next victim. Most susceptible to her attacks are the men of the town who disrespect women—the pimps, the misfits, the criminals, and even the older man who you might suspect is harmless. The vampire isn't the villain, filmmaker Ana Lily Amirpour seems to be telling us; she's committed to protecting sex workers and attacking the scum of society. Despite these rough edges, and what she's up against, the character embraces her femininity, propelled by her costume and makeup.

Sormeh was traditionally used on special occasions in Persia, including weddings. In Khorasan, women wore sormeh on their wedding days. Upon giving birth, they applied it to their own eyes and those of their babies. Historically, the preparation of sormeh involved the grinding of assorted stones, with the soft powder being poured into a container shortly afterward. A sormeh "stick" or applicator would then be soaked with rose water or another liquid and dipped into the container to catch the powder. Finally, starting at the inner corner of the eye, the applicator was dragged gently across the lower waterline, on the eyebrows, and over the eyelashes. (By closing the eye and using a similar motion, the wearer simultaneously applied the sormeh to the upper eyelid.) This technique is still used by many today.

While sormeh was often made from stones, like kohl, it was also procured from the soot of other materials such as butter, tallow, and various animal and plant fats—even from the brains of cows and the blood of hoopoe birds. (As tallow sormeh was said to be cooler than most forms of the pigment, it was worn when the eyes were "burning" or hot; hoopoe-derived sormeh was thought to beckon happiness.) Similar to how kohl is made in the Arab world, the substances were burned in a double-layered furnace, creating soot at the top, which was later scraped off and mixed with fats to create a smooth texture. Persians applied sormeh made from almond oils for the "strength and beauty of the eyes."

Just as commoners and royalty in ancient Egypt wore kohl, so too did people of all classes in ancient Persia. Both religious and tribal leaders recommended sormeh, beyond the days of the Prophet. Muhammad Baqir Majlisi, a Shia scholar and thinker of the Safavid era, mentions its benefits in the book *Hilyat al-Muttaqin*. In *Borhan-e Qate*, a Persian dictionary compiled in the seventeenth century, sormeh is also cited as one of seven substances, including henna, that should adorn women. The term *haft ghalam* (seven pens) refers to these cosmetics—it's still used metaphorically today. Adib al-Mamalek Farahani, a writer of the Qajar dynasty, makes note of these beautifiers in his poetry.

As it does in the modern era, wearing sormeh carried class connotations. Wealthier women lined their eyes with it, sending servants to buy preprepared powder from markets instead of making the journey themselves. Those who were less affluent made sormeh at home and used silver or wooden applicators; the former were believed to help boost one's eyesight. Materials used would depend on those available. For example, in Meybod, a city in the Yazd Province, women burned hazelnuts, almonds, or walnuts to make sormeh. In Bijar in Kurdistan, soot was obtained from burning cow parts. Inspired by new makeup trends in Babylon, Nineveh, Damascus, and Tyre, the women of the Persian Jewish community beautified themselves with sormeh on their eyes and magenta on their cheeks after coming into wealth; they also wore luxurious clothing and expensive jewelry.

A primary reason sormeh was worn in Iran throughout history, whether the wearers were nomads, tribe members, or women of the city, was for beautification. During the Qajar period, court women incorporated sormeh into their self-care routines. After taking long baths and resting, they applied henna to their nails and sormeh along their eyelashes. (Replace henna with nail polish, and this routine sounds like my Sunday nights.) Gaspard Drouville, a French officer who lived in Iran from 1812 to 1813, describes the darkened eyes of Iranian women as being central to their beauty: "Some Iranian women who think their eyes are not big enough apply sormeh to their eyes several times a day," he writes. French Orientalist and painter Eugène Flandin also details the women in the harem of the famed Persian artist Prince Malik Qasim, one of the sons of Fath Ali Shah, the second shah of Qajar Iran: "Of the Iranian women I saw in the harem, they all had small mouths, beautiful teeth, charming faces, sweet and large eyes. Iranian women are accustomed to adorning their eyes with black objects with a sharp bar."

On the other hand, the poet Saeb Tabrizi points out that naturally beautiful eyes shouldn't require sormeh: "What is the use of rubbing your eyes with sormeh? Shorten this trailing excuse." Women were also said to wear sormeh because the eyes and eye movements convey one's inner thoughts and feelings—similar to how the eyes of kathakali dancers in India convey their emotions.

But, in line with the sayings of the Prophet, sormeh was also worn for medicinal, therapeutic, and ceremonial purposes, depending on the materials used. Persian philosopher al-Ghazali noted in "On the Manners Relating to Eating," the eleventh chapter of his book *The Revival of the Religious Sciences*, that it was good form for hosts to offer guests kohl for their eyes and oil for their skin. He also listed the use of kohl while asleep as one of four practices that strengthen the eyesight along with "sitting in the direction of the *qibla* [direction of the holy site of Islam in Mecca] . . . looking at greenery, and the cleansing of garments."

During the Safavid period, Iranian men and women applied sormeh to their eyes and eyebrows daily, according to John Chardin, a French traveler who documented his experiences there. "They believe that sormeh increases the eyesight," he observed, echoing al-Ghazali. Poet and mathematician Omar Khayyam writes in *Nowruznameh* that if you apply sormeh on your eyes with "golden desire," you'll be safe from night blindness, in addition to helping hydrate the eyes and boost one's vision.

The wearing of sormeh, in some instances, also carried a practical purpose. Cyrus the Great, who founded the first Persian Empire, was described by Xenophon, the Greek philosopher, as emulating his grandfather's appearance: "Cyrus saw that his grandfather adorned himself, painted his eyes with sormeh, adorned his face, and had bare hair." (The king would later confirm the importance of sormeh use as a beautifier.)

Tahari, the hairstylist, says she applied sormeh when she was younger to strengthen her eyelashes, one of the reasons the Prophet was believed to have worn ithmid and advised others to. She traces her first memory of wearing the powder to when she was fifteen—after applying it, she studied herself for a long while in the mirror. "I'd changed a lot. I liked myself a lot; I'll never forget that I thought I had become beautiful," she reflects. During her youth, other girls wore less makeup than she did, Tahari remembers, but seeing as her family "wasn't too fanatical," she and her siblings were allowed to. Her mother used to line the corners of her eyes, and now Tahari's daughter wears eyeliner, too—such is its staying power. But as she grew older, Tahari ditched sormeh for eyeliner. When she became a hairdresser and makeup artist, patrons expected more modern styles of eyeliner application to be on offer, and so she started wearing it, too, to boost her business.

Tahari is so committed to her look that she has had her eyeliner tattooed; she exaggerates it in private spaces with an eyebrow pencil or liquid eyeliner. (Tattooed makeup is permissible in Iran; tattoos are not.) Despite choosing to wear less makeup today than she used to, given that she's older, eyeliner is one of two makeup items Tahari turns to daily, the second being lipstick. The hairdresser says beauty, not male attention, is her goal: in gatherings, "we use eyeliner to look more beautiful and to look impressive."

The former professor Ettehadieh says she rarely wears eyeliner, given her age. But, like Tahari, she recalls the joys associated with using it as a younger woman, especially when attending parties. She first tried a pencil at the relatively late age of twenty-two, but "couldn't use it well," she says. "My hand was shaking, and I couldn't draw the eyeliner carefully." Ettehadieh had watched her friend steadily apply her eyeliner and hoped she could achieve the same result before realizing that how one applies eyeliner is as unique as the outcome, which often depends on the eye shape. "For me, eyeliner is a symbol of nothing but beauty," she says. While Ettehadieh and her mother used eyeliner, her grandmother wore sormeh—she sourced it from local markets that used natural materials, including hazelnuts and almonds, like Neshat's relatives.

To Moaveni, who lives in the diaspora, sormeh symbolizes "Persian womanhood as a distinct cultural and aesthetic identity. I remember sitting in the bathroom watching my mother get ready before parties. I'd hold the sormeh container, velvet with sequins, and it seemed such a theatrical and glamorous ritual," she says. "Her bathroom was lined with European face creams and other Western products, but when it came to eyes, out came this prop, almost, that she drew with the long spike."

For the UK-based journalist Hatam, the story of sormeh begins with her grandmother. "Like most grandmothers, she was full of fascinating and mysterious stories," she says in her BBC podcast episode, "My Personal History of Sormeh." One of the things her grandmother passed on was "this mysterious black kohl powder kept in a beautiful, intricate pouch," Hatam says, adding that she told her "sormeh gave the woman who wore it a certain allure and added mystery" to her eyes. And so Hatam wears sormeh herself, sourcing it for her friends and relatives from Iran, as she feels it connects her to her identity and ancestors. "Sormeh has been bonding us for millennia: it has been protecting and healing our eyes, it has been used by the ancient kings and pharaohs, and it has been a tool for female empowerment and civil disobedience in Iran," she says. "It has been a way for me to connect to my Iranian roots."

Mystical Allure

As women in Iran aren't allowed to expose their bodies in public—and likely won't be permitted to anytime soon—their faces continue to take on outsize importance, with makeup acting as a vehicle to elevate desires and ambitions. The preoccupation with facial beauty or improvement, in the face of restrictions, is as such far reaching. The proverb "Kill me but make me beautiful" is popular in the country, with women sometimes going to costly measures to level themselves up. Iran has the highest rate of nose surgeries in the Middle East, with many women also opting for lip fillers and Botox. Some also turn to permanent makeup application methods. Iranian women do not "perceive beauty as a common good but as a necessary evil," write academics led by Ladan Rahbari in a paper titled after the proverb. Perhaps unsurprisingly, Iran has been ranked the second-biggest cosmetics consumer in the Middle East after Saudi Arabia.

"The majority of Iranian women's self-expression is right here on their faces, because most of the rest of their body is covered," Neshat says. "So they treat their faces very differently than a woman in any other part of the world. And your identity is defined right here in your eyes, your lips, your skin, and your gaze."

Tahari says makeup application in general in Iran has become more "elaborate," as women have become more daring (she notes that, by comparison, European women "barely wear makeup"). However, she adds, Iranian women tend to overdo it to the point of obscuring their natural beauty, "when they can make their face look more beautiful with simple and light makeup."

This commitment to beautification also comes despite crippling economic sanctions and repeated financial crises. In 2019, when inflation in Iran was among the world's highest, the *Financial Times* ran a feature exploring how women were still committed to buying cosmetics. "The last thing I need now is to look miserable," the newspaper quoted a thirty-eight-year-old mother as saying. Her husband had been forced to shut down his restaurant business due to the country's economic situation; as a result, she had to cut back on mascara, turning instead to her trusty eyeliner—which she couldn't dispense of—even more.

Sormeh is little used today by the younger generation as compared with the past—kohl was sold in abundance in Iranian markets until at least the mid-1800s—but its mystical allure lives on. Containers have been passed down from generation to generation, and older rural women continue to tightline their eyes like they once did as young women.

Sormeh's consumption has declined for various reasons, among them the addition of impure materials to the cosmetic's composition, which negatively affected its healing properties, to the extent that they were all but lost. The entry of new eye cosmetics into the market also diminished sormeh's appeal. Women began turning to Western products, including those by Maybelline and Revlon, which were easier to apply but harder to acquire. "Many middle- and upper-class Iranian women no longer rely on sormeh because it's seen as traditional and not trendy and modern like liquid or pencil eyeliner," Dagres of the Atlantic Council tells me. "Additionally, if someone were to compliment an Iranian woman on her eye makeup, she can pull out her liner and share the name and place she bought it."

Zahra, the twenty-five-year-old, used sormeh for many years before turning to eyeliner. From twelve through nineteen, she bought it from local markets, as it was helpful for beauty and eyelash enhancement, wearing it on the weekends. Meanwhile, Shabnam, the nail artist, says eyeliner helps elongate her eyes (she uses the Bell brand for wings rather than tightlining). Though once or twice as a younger woman she tried the sormeh her grandmother made from bitter almonds, she uses liquid eyeliner today. But she recognizes the allure of sormeh in that she says it injected soul into "a soulless state" while also strengthening her eyes medicinally. The beauty of an Iranian woman whose face is "intact and without surgery," she says, is in her "black and beautiful eyes"— so these must be decorated and protected.

Sepideh Pourmehdi, thirty-four, says she's so used to wearing eyeliner that if she doesn't, she also looks "soulless." The physical education coach uses the local Violet brand and has been lining her eyes blue since she started university. "My friend drew eyeliner for me with a dark blue pencil, and I fell in love with it from that day," she says. Pourmehdi uses just two makeup items, blush and eyeliner, as she likes to keep her look minimal (for special occasions, she adds lipstick). The millennial says she doesn't feel restricted when wearing eyeliner publicly because—like the other young women interviewed—she avoids wearing it heavily, and applies only thin lines to her upper lids. She says she's put off by plastic surgeries and defines beauty as a "completely natural face." "I don't like these manipulated faces," she explains. "That's why I don't see Iranian girls' faces as beautiful anymore."

Though they may be careful about where and when they apply their eyeliner, younger women in Iran today are inspired by celebrities who flaunt skillfully drawn makeup, including Golshifteh Farahani, Niki Karimi, and Leila Hatami. But many also look at the trends set by Western starlets. For example, as a university student, Pourmehdi says she mimicked the "punk" look of Pink, but today, she's drawn to the more low-key and natural look of Jennifer Lopez. Similarly, Shabnam copies the sleek styles of Rihanna and Selena Gomez.

In pharmacies and retailers across major Iranian cities,

including Tehran and Shiraz, makeup is displayed under glass tops, featuring eyeliner from international brands such as L'Oréal and Bourjois Paris. Sormeh, along with eyeliner, both counterfeit and genuine, is sold at bazaars, small shops, markets, and malls. While you're more likely to see local eyeliner brands on these shelves, women like Tahari and Ettehadieh often opt for international products, which aren't always authentic. This is due in part to the government regulations and restrictions on banking that hinder major cosmetics companies from doing business in Iran, not to mention the political, financial, and logistical messiness associated with selling products to a country slapped with Western sanctions and a trade embargo.

"No one has quite cracked the market, but it has immense potential," says Esfandyar Batmanghelidj, the founder and chief executive officer of the Bourse & Bazaar Foundation. "The sheer market size and the enthusiasm of Iranian women for cosmetics make Iran one of the great untapped markets for global cosmetics brands."

Domestic makeup producers have become more sophisticated as they cater to local tastes and fill the gap left by global firms. These businesses have benefited from Iranian policies designed to bolster local cosmetics firms such as My Cosmetics over Western imports. "The potential for growth in the cosmetics market in Iran is best illustrated by the sharp rise of local brands creating high-quality cosmetics often inspired by traditional makeup and ingredients," says Batmanghelidj.

The void created by international cosmetics companies has also made way for unofficial distributors and bootleggers, which control about 60 percent of the market and sell illegally imported makeup. (According to research conducted in 2017 by ISNA, the Iranian Students' News Agency, about $1.7 billion worth of cosmetics are contraband or fake, $390 million worth are imported legally, and $722 million worth are produced in the country.)

The appeal of global brands is unmistakable, with sellers circumventing traditional or legal methods to cater to demand, whether via social media, a third country such as the UAE, wholesalers, or affiliates. An Instagram account named Kylie Cosmetics Iran, for instance, claims to offer the American brand's products. "Now that there's bootleg MAC, Kylie Cosmetics, Urban Decay, and other big-name brands pouring in from Asia to countries like the US and Thailand, it wouldn't surprise me if they've also made their way to Iran," says Dagres.

The cosmetics section of Digikala, Iran's version of Amazon, sells eyeliner from US brands such as Maybelline and Rimmel. A quick search for eyeliner turns up products from local and international companies, sometimes fake and sometimes authentic, including MAC's Real Pen eyeliner (a dupe) and Turkish brand Golden Rose's liquid eyeliner. Maybelline eyeliner is available on the site at the cost of 230,000 tomans, the equivalent of 2.3 million rials or about US$6, similar to its price on Amazon. That said, the per capita income of the average Iranian in purchasing power parity terms is about one fifth that of an American, so internationally branded eyeliner is, by comparison, expensive.

The demand for international cosmetics in spite of their steep costs attests to trend-conscious Iranian women's commitment to wearing high-quality makeup regardless of the economic, political, and social difficulties associated with it. "The combination of greater convenience and the desire to appear socially modern and economically upwardly mobile is probably driving the adoption [of international cosmetics]," Batmanghelidj explains. "Here the demand is more important than the supply. The foreign cosmetics are imported because that's what Iranian women want."

Ideal Self

In a 2016 study, researcher Nazanin Ghafaryanshirazi explored how and why Iranian women often turn to cosmetic surgery and makeup. Female bodies are employed "as a means of sociopolitical nonconformity . . . as a sign of their existence in the society and as a tool to protest against sociopolitical restrictions," Ghafaryanshirazi writes. The author argues further that there's "a link between the use of makeup and self-expression among citizens in oppressive regimes." While some beauty perceptions rely on Western ideals, the motivations go beyond mere prettification. However minor and of no consequence in other parts of the world, the decision to apply eye-catching eye makeup takes on a new meaning in this unique Iranian sociopolitical environment.

On the other hand, and as noted by Ghafaryanshirazi, some academics argue that even though Iranian women's aesthetics have been interpreted as a battleground for identity negotiations, their use of makeup and, by extension, eyeliner just isn't that profound. Instead, Iranian women may simply be immersing themselves in the world of cosmetics to lift their spirits, boost their confidence, or fill their time.

Zahra, for example, says she uses eyeliner to create her ideal self—to add some depth to her face due to what she describes as her pale skin tone. "When I leave the house, and I want to go somewhere, I must wear makeup," she says. "But if I'm very bored or I want to go to a friend's house or if I want to go to a very special place, I also put on makeup. When I think of Iranian beauty, the first thing that comes to mind is the beautiful eyes of Iranian girls."

Specifically looking at sormeh, Moaveni argues the cosmetic may "sit outside politics and contestations because it's seen as quintessentially Iranian. Persians record their history and civilization through their poetry, and eyes are a recurring metaphor—the beauty of the eye, the way it's drawn. Chadori women [women who cover themselves head to toe, with one large covering] have always lined their eyes after marriage—so in a way, that's also a rite of womanhood." (In Persian religious and customary culture, makeup was reserved for married women. The makeup of the eyes and eyebrows was a feature distinguishing unmarried girls from married women. Historically, women couldn't even buy sormeh containers from local markets until they were married, and had to use handmade ones instead.)

The wearing of sormeh isn't necessarily "rebellious," Moaveni elaborates. "Wearing less makeup is something of a class distinction in Iran. The old upper-middle class wears less, the new post-1979 middle class, which is the former culturally working class, wears loads. So, this dynamic also muddles the notion of makeup as disobedience or resistance, or perhaps is another layer of it?"

The cosmetic also isn't seen by authorities as "super sexualized" in the way lipstick is, she posits. "When the authorities were overbearing in the 1990s and aughts and hassled women for their appearance, especially going into universities or government

offices, they fixated on nail polish and lipstick and often demanded it be wiped off. The lining of the eyes is somehow just
perennially halal."

With this distinction in mind, it's important to note that the
wearing of sormeh is more subtle and less detectable from afar, as
compared with eyeliner, with the pigment usually lining the eye's
waterlines rather than the eyelids.

While Neshat was at college in California and the 1979 revolution
shook Iran, she felt increasingly homesick but couldn't fully fathom
the transformation imposed upon women in Iranian society from
afar. It wasn't until she returned for a visit over a decade later, in
1990, that the depth of the changes became apparent to her. "It
was like day and night. Similar to today, there were terrifying
things about a new reality that showed how fanaticism had rooted
itself in society and how it had really transformed the country and
the situation for women, even on the visual level," she says. "At
the beginning, the morality police were more forceful in terms of
not just the wearing of the headscarf, but the full hijab. I was
shocked, because before the revolution, it was entirely different.
There were women in miniskirts and heavy makeup," including
heavy eyeliner or sormeh.

Neshat felt distant from her Iranian counterparts, partly because of her bold aesthetic. "I had created this other identity on
my own, and I had this distinct look away from Iran that was
maybe louder than what I had expected or wanted it to be and

definitely louder than what people had expected from me or what the norm was," she says.

As a member of the diaspora, Neshat feels her distinct style of eyeliner has helped ground her, reminding her of her roots. "My eyeliner gives me this feeling of security that goes beyond beauty, it's psychological," she says. "As a young woman, with so many things changing around me at once, I felt vulnerable and anxious about having to face new realities. That feeling is probably more intense for immigrants or people who feel uprooted and are in constant transition. There were certain things I needed to keep consistent, to feel grounded, safe, secure, and in control. My eyeliner has been part of that sense of security."

Neshat's eyeliner and appearance are—like Frida Kahlo's and Louise Nevelson's—an extension of her art, in that they tell a story. That story reached its climax in the East Village of New York, where Neshat had moved after college to explore a career in art. It was the 1980s, and NYC's underground bohemian culture had taken off. She started dating a graffiti artist; she attended gallery openings, parties, and exhibits; she encountered radicals and anarchists. This was the era of Madonna, Blondie, and Jean-Michel Basquiat—the city was teeming with possibility, while her homeland seemed to be stifled by war and the revolution's aftermath.

"My aesthetic and style just crystallized," she says. "I found my match because everybody was improvising, too. There were crazy hairdos, secondhand clothes, lots of eyeliner, everywhere. That's really when I blossomed. I was still in my early twenties, but I really felt beautiful, like I was part of a bigger artistic community." In this vibrant context, toward her thirties, Neshat's lines became even more pronounced. Her signature look was now appreciated as being part of her Iranian identity, and so she grew even more daring.

"I realized I was looking more for a sense of individuality in this bigger, competitive, Western male–dominated atmosphere," she says. "Here I was, a Middle Eastern woman living in exile in New York. I was becoming successful, and people also respected that I looked different. I had finally found myself, and my eyeliner was part of that journey. It's to the point where I don't even walk the dog without my eyeliner on, and I don't do video calls without it on, either. I wouldn't even recognize myself without it."

Today, Neshat refrains from using sormeh as she says it smears easily and sometimes itches her eyes. But she wore it for years as a young woman in Iran, and still has some in her arsenal of makeup products—a nostalgic reminder of her aesthetic roots.

"Women's Revolution"

While Neshat was—and remains—disturbed and enraged by developments that have led the women of her home country to this precarious point, she also finds hope in their courage and their efforts to demand an end to their repression. And she admires how creative they've been with their appearances in the face of severe restrictions.

"If you look at the style of Iranian women, especially young women over the past ten to fifteen years, and how they transformed the hijab into something so beautiful and so chic, you'll realize how sophisticated, elegant, and fashionable they are," says

Neshat. "It's not at all borrowing from the Western culture, as their mothers' generation often did. Instead, they are pioneering, they are improvising."

The women of Iran—women like Amini—are, according to Neshat, the Iranian government's biggest problem, because they're a force to be reckoned with. Even if this current wave of protests is crushed, she predicts their efforts will continue, and eventually effect greater change. The gutsiness of these women taking their veils off and burning them, dancing, and cutting their hair in public is almost unfathomable considering what they are up against, she says.

"It's hard to explain to Westerners that how you style yourself in Iran can be a weapon, or a point of resistance, or a form of protest. And I don't mean that in a simplistic, superficial way. These women don't simply put makeup on their faces. They don't casually show some of their hair under their hijab. They're choosing to perform acts that are strictly forbidden by the state," Neshat says of their fortitude. "So, by doing these things, things that are taken for granted in the West, they're challenging the government. And to me, that's beautiful. There's nothing more inspiring than seeing a beautiful woman who's also highly intelligent. Their body and their looks are their weapon."

Neshat, like people the world over, is particularly moved by the popular Kurdish protest slogan "Woman, life, freedom." Women bring life to this world, she says, and ultimately—even if they must fight for it—women will also usher in freedom. (The artist was commissioned by the Cultural Institute of Radical Contemporary Arts to create artwork featuring the slogan, which was displayed in protests held in London and LA.)

"They say you can't wear nail polish; they wear nail polish. They say you can't wear heavy makeup; they wear heavy makeup. They say you can't show hair; they show hair," she says. "That's probably why the government refuses to let go of the hijab to this day. The minute you see a woman without a hijab walking around in Iran, that will be the end of the Islamic Republic of Iran. This is a women's revolution."

Neshat's work has been inspired in part by these political developments in Iran and by her experiences as an outsider in the US. Her photography series during the 1990s dealt with the question of Iranian women confronting Islamic fundamentalism—it featured Persian calligraphy interspersed with arms, legs, hands, feet, and faces with lined eyes. Her latest film, *Land of Dreams*, starring Sheila Vand, is about an Iranian immigrant who works for the US Census Bureau as a "dream catcher," experiencing and exposing deep racial divides in the country. Vand, who also starred in *A Girl Walks Home Alone at Night*, has her eyes lined heavily in the movie. Neshat and Vand collaborated again for a short 2022 video and 2023 photo exhibit titled *The Fury*, about female political activists in Iran who have endured sexual assault during detention, sometimes taking their own lives as a result.

"A lot of these women never become whole again," Neshat says. "They really break down." In *The Fury*, the protagonist, played by Vand, lives freely in America, but is still shackled and haunted by memories of the past. After experiencing a flashback of her detention in Iran from the safety of her new home in New York, she runs into the streets, naked. "There comes a point of affinity and a dance of rage," Neshat says, as passersby from multiple communities and social classes join the protagonist in support. "It's like when Mahsa Amini died, and her death forced people onto the streets."

Vand is fully unclothed in the scene. All she wears is her dramatic eyeliner, which evokes Neshat's in its extremity. The lines are a manifestation of her mental state, but also of her freedom of choice. "She was driven to insanity, and she's not recovered from past traumas," Neshat says. "But she's also free, and she's not alone."

Chapter Four

Pirates of Petra

*Kohl in the Hashemite
Kingdom of Jordan*

he juniper tree towers six feet above us, offering shade in the dry heat. Its branches, shrouded in dense, prickly leaves, resemble tangled limbs reaching across the clear desert sky. The coniferous tree stands lonely in the desert land—it has proven tougher than its peers, surviving the scorching sun. The juniper, known as arar in Arabic, boasts the ability to self-prune, disposing of branches to prevent unnecessary drains on required nutrients. These are intelligent trees that desperately want to flourish and impress. And to do so, they guard underground taproots that spread like tentacles over a distance of about twenty-five feet in every direction, scouring the dry earth for water. They can live for a millennium—and this particular tree, which is said by locals to be five hundred years old, has witnessed much in its lifetime.

"The tree is nature, and nature gives us life," says Sleiman, a forty-five-year-old Bedouin man who works in tourism, as he observes the juniper. (The Bedouin are nomadic peoples who have historically inhabited the deserts of the Arabian Peninsula and Middle East and Northern Africa.) "Nature has taught us how to sustain ourselves. It gives us samegh (bark extract), which we need to make kohl."

The juniper tree is a reliable source of both aesthetic and medicinal products. Its berries and sap are used to treat everything from digestion problems and skin infections to snakebites and bronchitis. When dried, the berries are also used for bracelets and necklaces, while the tree bark's extract is used in cosmetics, including foundation, bubble bath, and body lotion. In Umm Sayhoun, a small village on the northeastern edge of the archeological reserve of Petra, where Sleiman hails from, it's widely used for kohl making among the Bdoul community.

Usually, the Bedouin group source their kohl from the sap of the farsetia, a flowering plant that is native to the Arabian Peninsula, North Africa, and Iraq. Like the juniper tree, its bright white extract can be used as the basis for kohl when burned. But the foliage's ideal conditions are met only in July, a month the locals refer to as shahr al-kohl, or the "month of kohl." During the month of kohl, the farsetia can grow up to a meter high. However, with changing weather precipitated by climate change and prolonged droughts, the Bdoul have had to rely more heavily on juniper trees, says Sleiman. "Farsetia and juniper are for top-tier kohl. Anything else just doesn't cut it."

With his hands, Sleiman chips away at the fibrous strands of tree bark till the extract emerges, looking like yellow crystals as they sparkle in the sun. After rolling the sap in his fingers, its consistency becomes a gummy sort of gel. Next, Sleiman painstakingly surveys the tree for more extract; it takes about twenty minutes to gather a handful, roughly two grams. He predicts these two grams will create enough kohl to fill a pot (locals can sell one pot for twenty Jordanian dinars, approximately twenty-eight US dollars).

Back at his humble home in Umm Sayhoun, about two miles from the juniper, Sleiman prepares to make the kohl. First, he pulls out a lighter, the lid of an iron pot, and an aluminum baking tray—aluminum is vital, he says, to withstand the heat. After removing the substance from a plastic wrapper, he sets it alight until it catches fire and starts to emit thick black smoke. Once it does, he places the baking tray over the extract to trap the smoke. Next, he leaves a two-centimeter space between the tray and the marble surface by resting it on the pot lid. "There needs to be enough air for the extract to breathe, but not so much that it will interfere with the process," he explains.

I wait for several minutes, during which Sleiman periodically lifts the tray to ensure the flame is not extinguished. As we wait, Sleiman recalls his earliest memories of kohl: his mother used to apply the pigment to his eyes, and he'd smudge it, he says earnestly. When he flips the tray over and puts the flame out, the bottom of the pan is covered in black soot—the kohl. Using the cardboard tab of a Lipton tea bag, Sleiman then scratches at the tray's surface, gathering the kohl in a corner. It's a delicate process: he doesn't want any product to go to waste. Finally, Sleiman transfers the substance to a brass pot, one of many he has readily available in his home.

He dips a small applicator moistened with saliva into the pot before applying the kohl gracefully to his lower lash line. When he blinks, the upper lash line catches some of the pigment. With his now-darkened eyes, Sleiman, who wears a traditional red-and-white shemagh scarf on his head, and is dressed in a khaki robe, looks strikingly handsome. "And now, I'm mkahhal [made up in kohl]," he says, seeming to enjoy his glow up. "But I don't use kohl to appear more handsome, and if I do appear more handsome, well . . . I can't help getting attention either way," he chuckles.

Sleiman's wife, Azizah, who owns a cosmetics shop and has kohl on herself, teases him for his vanity. "No, really!" he exclaims. "I use it to protect my eyes from the sun and dust when I work outdoors." Incredulous, Azizah gives him the side-eye before clapping her hands loudly as she breaks into laughter.

Kohl is ubiquitous across the twenty-two-nation Arab world, particularly in villages and among Bedouin and rural communities. Both women and men use it to beautify themselves and for medicinal, spiritual, and religious purposes. Residents of these communities often make their kohl at home from natural elements, including tree sap and stone—imparting the traditions from one generation to the next. In cities, many turn to imported Western or South Asian eyeliner brands for practical reasons. But kohl is king (or queen). Once the materials are sourced, they are burned to ashes in an iron pot, melted, or crushed into powders with a mortar and pestle. The ashes are then mixed with olive oil or saliva and applied to the lower and upper lash lines, as Sleiman demonstrated.

"Arabian kohl" first appeared in the pre-Islamic era in the

form of antimony stone in what is now considered Saudi Arabia. One ancient method of preparation involved placing the stone on burning coal until it burst. The remaining gravel would then be soaked in water and Arabic coffee for forty days before being ground into powder, which was sifted through a cloth and packaged for use and distribution. In another method, the mixture was composed of water and henna leaves, and in yet another, the concoction was composed of rose water and either saffron or water.

Different villages, regions, and tribes use various methods and materials to create kohl: shepherds in Palestine have used olives, and Emiratis have used date seeds, for example. (In centuries past, Emirati women believed kohl was among three essentials to be taken to the afterlife upon burial, along with jewelry and pottery.) In the Basta neighborhood of Beirut, an apothecary sells hyena gallbladder as a kohl ingredient right off the shelf. "The bile in a hyena's gallbladder should be mixed with cedar honey, then applied as a kohl around the eyes," the store owner told *The National* newspaper in 2022. "It improves eyesight, repels glaucoma, and it lengthens eyelashes." Antimony stones are sold in the souks of Tripoli, Lebanon, and in the markets and mosques of Yemen, where men congregate to apply kohl during the holy month of Ramadan. In addition to practical and religious purposes, some Saudi Arabian men wear kohl to preserve the traditions of their tribal ancestors (the Saudi "flower men" of the Qahtan tribe decorate their heads with wreaths of flowers and wear sandals made of palm leaves, along with their kohl); in France, many young Algerian men flaunt kohl to honor their Indigenous heritage.

Like those belonging to the ancient Egyptians, the region's kohl pots and containers have been quite ornate. One multicolored, double-barreled kohl pouch from Palestine, when it was under the British Mandate in the early 1900s, features Syrian silk satin at the front and dyed cotton at the back. It's also stuffed and padded with cotton and wool and is decorated with velvet and silk tassels, plastic, and glass beads, as well as silver coins. The container, on display at the British Museum, has an applicator that is made of carved wood. Another kohl pot at the museum that dates from the late nineteenth to early twentieth century and was found in Tripoli, Lebanon, is made of brass, with a leaf-shaped applicator, and inscribed with the Arabic text "ya nur al 'ayn," or "oh, light of the eye!"—a phrase used regionally to express admiration.

Abu Ali, a seventy-one-year-old Bedouin who's lived in different areas of Petra his entire life, has twenty-four children and seventy-four grandchildren. Both generations had kohl applied to their eyes when they were newborns, he says, noting it helped "strengthen their eyesight." Kohl is so commonly worn in the Middle East and North Africa that girls are sometimes named or nicknamed Kahla by their parents or friends, roughly meaning "the girl who appears to have kohl around her eyes." The symbol of the lined Eye of Horus and nazar, an eye-shaped amulet, are also worn as jewelry by women and men across the region and in Asia to protect against the evil eye.

Kohl is a feature of many millennia-old myths, rituals, and legends. Zarqaa al-Yamama (Blue Dove), a heroine of pre-Islamic folklore, was famed for her intuition and ability to predict the future. She was also known for the strength of her eyesight, which was credited to her use of kohl. It's thought that Zarqaa was among the first Arabs—if not *the* first—to apply the substance. According to the myth, Zarqaa could see as far as the distance traveled over a three-day journey. During a war between kingdoms, enemies hid behind branches of trees that they had carried with them as they advanced toward Zarqaa's tribe. With her incredible eyesight, Zarqaa spotted them from afar and warned her people, but they didn't believe her. Upon arrival, the enemy killed its opponents, destroyed their dwellings, and poked out Zarqaa's eye. In various accounts of her death, her eye socket was said to be filled with a black stone she would grind to make kohl, and kohl pigment was found in all the veins of her eyes. Following her death, Zarqaa's vision was remembered as being so sharp that if someone had good eyesight, onlookers would say the person had "vision stronger than that of Zarqaa al-Yamama."

Bdoul women wear kohl at home and on special occasions such as weddings or engagements, though they turn to it less frequently overall than Bdoul men. That said, given many Bdoul work in tourism in Petra, kohl is worn by most for sun protection. Raeda, thirty-one, says, "Some women use kohl for medicinal purposes. But women are comfortable with saying it's to make themselves prettier, too, whereas men hesitate to even though they're aware they're more handsome with it on." Aminah, a forty-five-year-old Bdoul woman, says she doesn't use foundation, eyeshadow, or even lipstick. "Kohl is all I need. Without it, I feel like something's missing," she says. "I like how I look when I have it on." Umm Lafi, a woman in her fifties, used to show off pronounced lines as a young girl, but stopped after she got married. She says she misses kohl as an older woman, so she sometimes pinches some from her daughters. And Umm Firas, who lives be-tween a cave in Petra and a home in the village, recalls making herself up with kohl as a single woman. "When I went to parties, I'd wear it, flirt, and be flirted with," she says. "Whenever I had free time from work and being a mother, I'd go to the trees for more."

In Middle Eastern and North African folklore, literature, song, and dance, kohl is ever present. In Arab poetry, Middle Eastern and Arab women are portrayed as being staggeringly beautiful in part due to their 'oyoun kaheela (kohl-rimmed eyes) and 'oyoun al sood (black eyes). An Arab woman's charm is thus seen as incomplete without kohl. Arab women may give up all kinds of makeup, but not kohl, whose use has persisted for centu-ries despite the growing popularity and practicality of Western products and colored pencils.

Indeed, Nizar Qabbani writes in the poem "You Want" that his lover desires "fans of feathers," kohl, and fragrance, as all women do. Meanwhile, the Sudanese poet Muhammad al-Mahdi al-Majdhub wrote in his second collection of poems, *Al-sharafa wa al-hijra* (1973), "the lights of her kohl / memories are candles burn-ing in a tomb." In Petra, it's said that after husbands returned to their homes following long journeys, they would check the vanity area in which their wives applied their kohl to see if they could find visible remnants of it. The scattered pigment would indicate to the husband that the wife had cried in his absence, and hence that she loved him.

In one of her songs, the prolific late Lebanese singer Sabah—along with her entire village—notes the welcome arrival of a loved one with "kohl-rimmed" eyes who'd been absent for some time. The Lebanese novelist Hanan al-Shaykh wrote about her mother's eyes being stained with black pigment in her book *The Locust and the Bird: My Mother's Story*. After meeting someone whose eyes were lined with green and not black, al-Shaykh reflected: "They were the first eyes I'd seen that weren't black. . . . Mother had black eyes—she ground black stones and used the grinds to line her eyes." The description added to the character's portrayal as a strong and stubborn woman committed to tradition while breaking from it simultaneously. (In an interview with al-Shaykh, reflecting on her own use of kohl, she tells me, "I first used black eyeliner when I was fifteen years old, and it changed my look and therefore my life for the better!")

Western films about the region and its peoples, including *Lawrence of Arabia* (1962), *The Message* (1976), and *Kingdom of Heaven* (2005), feature actors such as Anthony Quinn and Peter O'Toole on horseback in the desert donning robes, headdresses, and, of course, kohl. A shepherd poem written in Nablus, Palestine, which was initially addressed to the British Mandate but repurposed for Israeli occupiers, states: "There will be two kinds of eyeliner to wear / The second is his ground bones."

Many religious Bdoul see kohl use as sunnah—a manifestation of their religiosity. "The Prophet didn't allow for physical adornment, but he did allow kohl and wore it himself," says Mohammad, thirty, of Umm Sayhoun. "Kohl isn't makeup. Kohl is the way of the Prophet. I wear it on Fridays to show my devotion to sunnah." To Abu Awad, who's forty-five and used kohl in his youth, the neeyeh, or intention, is most important. "What's in your heart matters," he says. "My whole life I wore it without bad intentions. But either way, God is beautiful, and God loves beauty."

Despite kohl being considered sunnah per hadith, there have been debates over whether it's permissible for women to utilize it solely for the purposes of beautification. So powerful is kohl's ability to elevate one's attractiveness when applied well that, in 2010, the UAE's General Authority of Islamic Affairs and Endowments issued a fatwa that declared the cosmetic was allowed for women—only if they used it absent the intent of attracting male attention.

On a mild Friday afternoon in mid-October in Umm Sayhoun, a group of young Bdoul men sit together on a curb: it's their day off. Most of them work in tourism in Petra, selling souvenirs or serving as guides escorting tourists on mules or donkeys. (A few have joined the Jordanian army, and those who have leave their kohl at home.) After Friday prayers, this is a time for them to unwind and catch up over casual conversation and gossip about passersby. Their persistent chatter and laughs, the humming of car engines, and the Qur'anic verses recited by muezzins from nearby mosques fill the air. Each young man has his own aesthetic: cigarette in hand, one has a head of untamed curls and wears a gray hoodie over a printed T-shirt with faded blue jeans, ripped at the knees; another covers his thick, dark hair with a brown scarf and has paired black sweatpants with leather sandals; and another has gelled his wavy hair back into a low ponytail and is wearing a deep red shawl draped over a gray thobe. But all of them are made up in kohl.

"Kohl is as old as time. It started with the pharaohs, who wore it to protect their eyes, and we use it for the same reason," says Omar, twenty-one. "We, too, use it to treat eye redness and eye infections. We don't just use it for our physical appearance." Omar says he was drawn to kohl at sixteen; his brother, whom he looked up to, had started applying it, so he wanted to do the same. The siblings would go on trips to retrieve the materials required for the kohl from the farsetia or juniper tree, and their grandmother would make it for them at home.

With schoolboy humor, Omar's friends make fun of him for this formal explanation, noting they all really use kohl for "nisbah," a word used to denote a desire to enter a relationship with a woman. But then they return to seriousness, assuring me that kohl does have beneficial properties and the different reasons for wearing it need not be mutually exclusive. Omar says the decision to make oneself up in kohl can depend on one's mood, the weather, the day of the week, or the occasion. Shy or introverted men sometimes forgo it altogether or draw their lines in as subtle a manner as possible. All the men say they turn to kohl to repel the sun's rays when working; they add that they don't even own sunglasses, as the black pigment gives them protection from the sun's ultraviolet rays.

Siding with Omar, Mohammad says, "God forbid I put kohl on for women! I'm married! And do you think the Prophet wore kohl for women?" Mohammad is one of the few village men who prefer imported kohl from Pakistan, due to his allergy to natural kohl; he buys it for 2 dinars (roughly US$2.80) from his local grocery store (Umm Sayhoun doesn't have pharmacies or large retail chains). The other young men say they only resort to the pen when they run out of natural kohl, in between seasons.

In this community, kohl is a rite of passage, a sign of coming-of-age, and even a symbol of belonging. "We're like one family here in Umm Sayhoun," says Mohammad. "If one of us does something, others will, too." The cosmetic is also a marker of youthful vitality: it's rare to see men use kohl past age thirty-five, locals say, and teens usually start experimenting with it at age fifteen. Rizk, thirty-three, says that, while he still wears kohl, his lines aren't as obvious as they used to be, given that he's now slightly older; from a distance, they are somewhat thinner and less discernible than those of his friends. Men commonly stop applying it once they're married as a sign of respect to their partners, he explains. Others refrain from wearing it if they leave Umm Sayhoun for Amman, Jordan's capital, to help them blend in—though some, like Rizk, do precisely the opposite, to ensure they are seen as Bedouin rather than city boys. Rizk says he takes his kohl pot with him wherever he goes.

In some Arab cities, kohl use among men is frowned upon. For example, in more conservative areas of Lebanon, such as Bab el-Tabbaneh in the North, men use kohl to imitate the Prophet Muhammad. But according to *Vice Arabia*, Lebanese men have faced stigma for wearing kohl elsewhere, as the product is associated with queer or—ironically—satanic subcultures, and deemed a form of rebellion against established gender or religious norms. Ahmed el-Sayed, an artist, was kidnapped by "extremist youths" and beaten because of how he dressed and his kohl, as he was accused of being a devil worshipper. "I almost lost my life because of kohl," he told *Vice*.

While most make their kohl at home after visits to the juniper trees or farsetia, others buy it from sellers who specialize in the product, including two infamous women named Sabah and Thuraya. These sellers will often go on daylong expeditions to source the tree extract from areas other locals don't frequent. As a result, the kohl costs about ten dinars (fourteen US dollars) a pot, compared with two to four dinars for pens imported from Pakistan. "Sometimes, if people run out of natural kohl, they'll buy imported kohl. However, most on demand is natural kohl," as people believe it is safer and performs better, says Azizah, Sleiman's wife, whose shop sells both. "There is simply no comparison."

Kohl is deeply embedded in Bdoul customs and traditions. The Bdoul have traditionally survived by growing wheat and barley and herding and raising cattle, including goats and cows. They connect deeply with animals—to such an extent that they refer to mares, leopardesses, and tigresses as kuhaylah, denoting a female with darkened eyes. "It was once believed that if you eat an animal's meat, you'll take some of the animal's properties," says Sleiman. "The Bedouin men and women who used to eat camel meat were even said to develop naturally dark eyes." As the Bedouin admire the eyes of camels, they wore kohl to imitate them, says Habu, thirty-eight.

One man in Umm Sayhoun is affectionately referred to by villagers as Abu Kohla (the father of kohl), not because he darkens his eyes with kohl himself, but because they appear naturally lined. Some villagers believe the pigmentation may have occurred because kohl was applied to his eyes repeatedly when he was a newborn, dyeing their rims in the same way a tattoo might, or because his mother wore kohl so much that he inherited her dark eyes. (Similar discussions have been had over the actor Nestor Carbonell's eyes, which appear to be unnaturally lined—Carbonell denies that he uses eyeliner.)

But the widespread practice of kohl use among Jordan's Bedouin, at least today, appears to be specific to the Bdoul. On a mid-October's day at an annual horse race held in Petra, dozens of locals gathered to compete and socialize. While the young men of Jordan's other Bedouin communities in the area were bare eyed, the Bdoul wore generous amounts of kohl.

"Kohl grabs people's attention," Rizk says. "But wearing it is also about retaining the Bedouin culture and taking pride in it. We are a proud, welcoming people. Kohl is among our customs and traditions. Things have changed for us since the 1980s, yes, but we try to hold on to these customs and traditions. We don't look at kohl as makeup; it's far more than that." Omar agrees. "Kohl is part of our ancestors' traditions and customs," he says. "We wear it to preserve these traditions." There may be a performative element to kohl use, too, says Sleiman. "If you don't put kohl on, it's as if something is missing, like you're not fulfilling the idea of a Bedouin."

In Jordan, the number of Bedouin inhabiting the desert over the past century has dwindled, as many have joined the urban population. But those who now live in cities and nearby villages still fight to preserve their culture and tribal traditions, including poetry, music, and sword dancing.

Umm Sayhoun was built across two square kilometers, on a cliff wedged between valleys. Though a 2015 survey put the village population at just over two thousand people, locals say it's now home to four to five thousand members of the Bdoul community, which has shared influence with other groups in the area. The lives of the Bedouin began to shift irreversibly during the 1980s when Petra was designated a World Heritage site by UNESCO. Hundreds of families were resettled from Petra to the newly built village in 1985 at the behest of the Jordanian government following the recommendation of the United States Agency for International Development (USAID) to safeguard the site. Some say the resettlement was welcome due to the village's facilities, while others viewed the move as deportation, as their lives and heritage were upended.

The Bdoul, long accustomed to open spaces in the caves, were suddenly forced to settle into small apartments in cramped concrete buildings. As families have expanded over the decades, the problem has intensified. According to the independent Jordanian news website *7iber*, several Bedouin have chosen to return to the caves of Petra due to overcrowding, poor infrastructure, and a lack of government assistance in Umm Sayhoun. Many have also stopped or reduced raising livestock, as they've been cordoned off from their land, reports *7iber*.

From an economic perspective, the surge in tourism following the UNESCO designation was a boon for the community. In addition to their work as guides and souvenir sellers, the Bdoul provide visitors with food, drinks, and accommodations. Western tourists had been visiting the area for well over a century by the time it was declared a World Heritage site—it was "revealed" to the West by a Swiss archaeologist in 1812. Petra's sandstone cliffs today draw tens of thousands of tourists to Jordan every month. (Numbers have varied, often depending on geopolitical and other global developments: they shot up following a peace deal with Israel, then dwindled after the outbreak of Syria's civil war and the COVID-19 pandemic, though they have since somewhat recovered.)

Kohl is especially useful for the men and women of Umm Sayhoun working in tourism and those who remain in the caves at the foot of the mountains. They spend hours in the sun and sand, selling souvenirs and guiding foreigners across the ruins. "It's also helpful not to wear sunglasses when speaking to tourists, as we can see them eye to eye," says Rizk. "We show the person respect this way, and we can earn their trust."

According to locals, before the surge in tourism, Bedouin also likely wore kohl as they worked as guides for pilgrims on their way to the Hejaz before the construction of the Hejaz Railway and the opening of the Suez Canal. The former capital of the Nabataean Empire had offered a home to nomadic groups for centuries, stretching back to at least the 1500s. Locals say that alongside the resettlement of Bedouin communities in small villages near or adjacent to Petra, social norms have shifted—though Mohammad Samaheen Abu Abdallah, seventy-five, says people can't completely divorce themselves from the culture of the caves, even in villages and cities. When the community lived on the archaeological site, people "used to be much more open to visiting and socializing," he says. Men and women mingle less freely now as political Islam has gained traction across the broader region, sending shock waves into even remote communities. But kohl has withstood these changes due to its presence in hadith—even the most religious young men use or have used it.

Despite this context, some of the young men of the village will admit to appreciating kohl because they are aware that women, mainly white tourists, may find them more attractive that way. These men seem to intentionally play into the stereotype of the "exotic-looking" Arab man of the desert in order to appeal to Western and non-Arab visitors. Raed, nineteen, says tourists, especially women tourists, will often tell him he looks like Jack Sparrow, the character portrayed by Johnny Depp in the *Pirates of the Caribbean* film franchise. (Depp has said that Keith Richards of the Rolling Stones was his inspiration for the character, who is a fan of heavy eye makeup.) Playfully, Raed retorts, "Do I look like Jack Sparrow, or does Jack Sparrow look like me?"

Raed takes pride in what he calls the "Bedouin style," which consists of stringy or braided hair, the shemagh scarf, and, crucially, kohl. While he works from Petra, he checks his kohl with a compact mirror to ensure it's intact and hasn't smudged. Given the cosmetic's potency—one application can last for days, and he usually applies the black pigment before he sleeps for religious purposes—he rarely needs to touch it up.

Firas, twenty-nine, who works in the ruins, says he used to don the full Bedouin "style," knowing tourists would compare him with Jack Sparrow, too. But once he met his wife, Natalie, an American tourist who settled in Petra, he stopped wearing kohl daily and cut his hair. "I'm taken now," he chuckles. "There's no need for the kohl anymore."

Natalie observes us quietly as we speak. Dressed in a black thobe, she's a stunning woman with blue-green eyes and a shiny mane of long, straight blond hair that reaches her lower back. "I was attracted to him because of how he looked when we met; how could I not be?" she says. "He had kohl on and long hair." Natalie now has kohl-rimmed eyes, too—Firas taught her how to use it.

⌒

In the touristic heart of Petra, steps away from the al-Khazneh building, known as the Treasury, thirty-six-year-old Mahmoud lists all the ways the "Arabian kohl" he sells is by far superior to Western brands of eyeliner. "How can you apply something so close to your eyes without knowing its ingredients?" he says when I tell him I often opt for NYX liquid eyeliner. "Would you put something metal or plastic in your eye?"

Mahmoud is known in Petra as a kohl aficionado—the king of kohl, in fact. He started selling kohl at eighteen and has been wearing it for more than half of his life; his mother applied it to his eyelids during his first forty days on earth. (Forty is a significant number in Islam, as the Prophet Muhammad is said to have received the first message of the religion from the angel Gabriel at the age of forty; it is also significant because the Prophet Moses received the Ten Commandments at Mount Sinai over a period of forty days.) To prove his hypothesis, he pours imported, impure kohl powder onto a buyer's hand, alongside pure kohl powder made from the farsetia plant. He then hovers the magnet over both mounds of kohl powder: it sucks almost all the imported powder off the woman's skin. "When we say kohl is medicine for the eyes, we only mean the original, pure kohl from stone or trees, not this imported stuff," he tells me. "Any processed formula, including Western eyeliner formulas, won't have medicinal properties."

This little performance isn't Mahmoud's first rodeo; he offers it to all foreign tourists who visit his shop. He says that once they convert to kohl, they rarely go back. (Mahmoud's shop attracts tourists with large banners at its entrance marked with the text TRY THE REAL ARABIAN KOHEL, ITS FREE TO TRY above a picture of an Arab woman with heavily lined eyes, long, thick eyelashes, and impeccably shaped eyebrows—not a rogue hair in sight. The kohl seller's offerings are so popular, he's set up an online shop on Facebook for repeat buyers, called Lion Love Shop. He says sales are stable and that at least 70 percent of the tourists who try his kohl put in regular orders, particularly those from South America, Italy, and Spain.)

In the absence of farsetia extract, Mahmoud has resorted to importing kohl from Yemen, which he says has the highest-quality kohl in the region, along with ithmid from Saudi Arabia (which is pricier, at about US$150 for one gram). "I've personally seen the benefits of kohl," he says, sharing that he had an eye allergy as a child that could be cured only with kohl. Initially, as a boy, Mahmoud put the kohl on at night and then removed it in the morning with olive oil before heading to school. But as the product worked its magic on him—and as he noticed a favorable change in his appearance—he started applying it in the daytime and never stopped. His friends soon began copying him. "I want to share these benefits with people," he says. "Kohl isn't a product; it's a cultural institution."

One of his pots lasts for an entire year, he says, because one application per week should suffice, even with repeated soapy face washes; olive oil can be used to remove it sooner if need be. The imported pens, by contrast, often need to be reapplied multiple times a day. Though he touts kohl's medicinal benefits above all, he also notes that the jamal (beauty) it imparts is an undeniable bonus. "If you saw one of my eyes with kohl and another without it, you'd be shocked," he says. "It'd be like I'm two entirely different people." (Though Mahmoud has reached the age when most men would ordinarily ditch the kohl, he finds it permissible to continue, as he is single.) Mahmoud has high hopes for his business; under ideal conditions, he'd be able to source enough farsetia extract to make about four hundred pots per year (at 10 dinars or about US$14 a pot, US$5,600 seems a decent turnover).

While his brick-and-mortar shop also sells trinkets, jewelry, and clay pots, an entire corner is devoted to kohl. There are dozens of brass, copper, and glass pots out for display, a section filled with Yemen- and farsetia-sourced powdered kohl in small plastic bags, and imported kohl pencils from Pakistan, mainly of the popular Hashmi Kajal brand, which is manufactured in Karachi but distributed throughout the Arab world. Hovering over this display with watchful lined eyes is a giant brass statue of Queen Nefertiti. "Nefertiti was the real queen of kohl," Mahmoud says.

Abu Ali has a plain white shemagh on his head, held together at its top by two circular black cords, known in Arabic as iqal. The lined face of the seventy-one-year-old Bedouin shop owner tells countless stories of his long life in Petra and its surrounding areas. While his eyes aren't kohl rimmed today—due to his age, he says—he recalls kohl fondly, as he associates it with his boyhood and early manhood. Abu Ali fingers his rosary beads as he speaks, recounting his memories of a bright and hopeful youth, transporting us to another era in which he and his family still lived in the caves. When the Bedouin would herd cattle in the sweltering sun, they protected themselves from the heat and desert rays by wearing long, primarily white thobes, headdresses—and kohl, he recounts.

"We loved kohl. We had no shame back then in saying we wore it to attract women," he says. "While we knew it had practical and medicinal properties, it was widely understood that wearing kohl meant that you were single and looking for a partner." The beauty of Bedouin men and women, to Abu Ali, is their kohl-stenciled, wide eyes, their dark hair, their height, and their slender physiques. "If I saw two women, one with kohl and another without it, I'd be attracted to the one wearing it," he says. "And it was the same with me. Women would find me more attractive with kohl on."

Abu Ali and his wife wore kohl at their wedding, whose festivities lasted fifteen days (traditional Bedouin weddings can last longer than a week). He says he used the cosmetic proudly from ages twenty to thirty-five (he married more than once), noting that if Bedouin "didn't have kohl on back then, whether you were a man or a woman, it was like you were invisible." Like the young men of Umm Sayhoun do today, Abu Ali gathered kohl's ingredients from the juniper tree or farsetia while he was out tilling the fields. "I miss those days," he says. "People cared about and took pride in their looks and work."

In the evenings, neighbors would visit one another, he recalls, sometimes ten to twenty families at a time. They would sing, dance, eat, and drink. The caves were open to all, and people were abundantly generous and welcoming. Tarab was commonplace, a word that has no definition in English but can be best described as a transcendental emotional state, such as rapture or ecstasy, brought about while experiencing intensely moving music.

Given the weather was more predictable back then, Abu Ali says he had more cattle to herd and raise, and wheat and barley were plentiful. As a young Bedouin man, he spent all his time in nature before his father moved the family to the village. While working to support his family, Abu Ali experienced the practical benefits of kohl, given it protected his eyes. "It was about caring about one's looks *and* one's health," he says, before pausing for a long while.

"I often think of the freedom associated with the days we wore kohl. The mingling, the mixing, the singing, and the sharing of stories." Abu Ali finds it reassuring that young Bdoul men today continue to wear kohl, no matter their personal reasons for doing so. "Our traditions live on. And that's what matters."

Chapter Five

Not a Costume

Cat Eye in Chola Culture

Cholas have always presented what I term a beautiful contradiction—women who have always strived to possess a femininity that is traditional and steeped within Mexican-American culture and one that can be seen as progressive and abrasive at the same time. Cholas are often spoken about as a subculture that in today's society is both maligned and mined for aspects of its style but they are much more. Cholas are young women who like their pachuca forebears have been able to carve out an identity deeply rooted in culture and customs as a means of maintaining their Mexican-American identity in the face of persecution and oppression.

—WENDY HACKSHAW, WRITER

In the grainy photograph, two-year-old Winnonah Perez is nestled snugly in her mother's lap, looking up at her in awe and amazement. It is 1978, and the young mother is radiant. Her blown-out shoulder-length hair is lush and fluffy, blending into her burgundy tie-up top. Her eyes are delicately lined and adorned with long, curled false lashes. She's sitting on the floor, crisscross applesauce, peering at her daughter and grinning ear to ear. "This is me, looking back at my mom, and realizing eyeliner and lashes are life," Perez says of the image, one of very few she still has of her mother. "I can't say with confidence what I must've been thinking, but it sure does look like I saw her eyeliner and false lashes and fell in love!"

It's impossible to tell in this precious photo that Perez's mother, Jennifer, was struggling with mental illness and addiction. She'd been trying to battle these demons while being a doting mother to her baby girl, though she was still very much a girl herself (Jennifer and her partner, Miguel, had Perez together when they were both seventeen). But at twenty, within one year of the photo being taken, she died by suicide, and Perez's life was forever altered.

Today, forty-seven-year-old Perez wears wings to honor her mom and to channel her legacy—her chola aesthetic. Eyeliner, she says, connects her to her mother, who was particularly proud of her Mexican identity and heritage. Like Jennifer, Perez wears eyeliner daily in homage to her ancestors. She refers to it as her "magic," the visual vehicle through which she communicates her "inner strength and power."

Perez's wings are drawn heavily and expertly, with both the upper and lower lines stretching well beyond the corners of her eyes, extended by the centimeter, not the millimeter. "The thicker, the better," she says of her lines. "I liked extreme liner right out of the gate. I wanted to take the lines as far as they could go." The stylish Chicana wears large gold hoop earrings that catch the sunlight; her lips are lined and filled in. Her hair, the same deep brown color as Jennifer's, is voluminous. And on her hands, she wears chola bands—black jelly hand bracelets.

Perez has many tattoos that speak to her family history and identity. One arm boasts the image of a chola with lined eyes, much like her own. Her other ink includes her lowrider car and the lyrics of "I Stand Alone" by Calif Malibus, which she describes as her life's theme song. On her sleeve, she wears a peacock, a nod to the peacocks that roamed around the Santa Clara County jail campus where she lived. Perez was in and out of jail for five years, and the peacocks there came to symbolize "brown folks becoming products of their environment, victims of society," she reflects. "One day, I was sitting there realizing I had succumbed to what society expected of me. And that's the moment I changed. I took that realization and made the decision to use the campus as a positive motivator to do whatever was in my power to never call that place my residence again."

Perez's chola aesthetic turns heads in her hometown of San Jose, California, and not always in a good way. Sometimes, when doing things as innocuous as picking up groceries, she's followed. In professional spaces, Perez has had to contend with judging eyes—she works as a production planner at an aerospace manufacturing company. When people stare at her or make rude comments about her appearance, she says she uses the moment as an "opportunity to engage and educate. . . . I know my look creates conversation. But I get to break stereotypes [about the chola aesthetic] because people get to know me and how proud I am." In that vein, her look speaks to her deep-rooted sense of identity. "I don't dress chola as a costume," she says. "It's who I am, and it empowers me. I haven't changed in thirty-five years. I'm older, yes. But my hair, my makeup, and my clothes are still the same."

Perez's positive attitude belies a profound pain. Her parents' families had immigrated to the US from Mexico three or four generations ago, she says, seeking prosperity and better lives for themselves and their children. But difficulties trickled down, from generation to generation, and Perez's father, Miguel, faced discrimination and economic hardship. "He settled at jobs for lesser wages even though the work was physically harder," Perez says. After his partner's suicide, Miguel fought to be a good parent to Perez, bonding with her by taking her to neighborhood lowrider shows (in which members of the community gathered with modified versions of their cars, including lowered suspensions, usually to express their identities). Despite those efforts, he continued to fight through his emotional obstacles in secret, struggling with depression that was exacerbated by the loss of his partner. Twenty-five years after Jennifer took her life, so too did he—on the anniversary of her death, when Perez was just shy of thirty.

"I became determined to live out the happiness they couldn't grasp here for themselves," Perez says. "Part of the way I do that is carrying on with their estilo [style]. Keeping it alive is important to me because it was important to them. My mom's chola looks and my dad's love for lowriding . . . I keep both of these things alive."

> Her eyeliner was all
> messed up because she'd been crying.

—SON OF MELISSA LUCIO, WHO WAS GRANTED A
STAY OF EXECUTION IN 2022, FROM THE HULU
DOCUMENTARY *THE STATE OF TEXAS VS. MELISSA*

The roots of the chola aesthetic can be found in the history of the Mexican immigrant community in the US and its protracted struggle for equality. Amid the earliest waves of their immigration into the country, Mexicans were discriminated against and deemed undesirable in part due to their "Indian features," according to the late scholar F. Arturo Rosales, who researched and wrote about the Mexican experience in America. During the Mexican

Repatriation in the early twentieth century, the US government forcefully exiled almost two million Mexicans from the country, deepening tensions amid the Great Depression. Against this ongoing backdrop of discrimination came the gradual formation and development of the Mexican American civil rights movement, later known as the Chicano movement. The group was characterized by struggles over land, farming, education, labor rights, and the preservation of culture and language.

Mexicans were described or portrayed as violent and dangerous; their physical attributes or identifiers often signaled an "outsider" status, making them vulnerable targets. While "extreme ethnic differences separating Mexicans from Anglo-Americans exacerbated prejudice," those differences also led to the ethos that "brown is beautiful" within the group, argues Rosales. The allegiance encouraged mobilization, both politically and aesthetically, with the two elements becoming intertwined.

During the Second World War, as patriotism surged among Anglo-Americans, Latino youths in LA started taking to the streets in zoot suits—colorful long coats and high-waisted trousers. The flashy style was known as the pachuco look, and it became a symbol of rebellion against assimilation and Anglo-American hegemony among Chicanos. The feminine or "pachuca" iteration of the look—with its cardigans, pleated skirts, fishnet stockings, platform heels or sandals, dark lipstick, beehives, heavy makeup, tight sweaters, and slacks—was, by extension, also nonconformist, and was met with fearmongering by the mainstream. "The media of the time played an important part in portraying the *Pachuca* as a physically excessive, dark, provocative, and dangerous woman," scholar Amaia Ibarraran-Bigalondo writes in *Mexican American*

Women, Dress, and Gender. It deepened discrimination and the per-petuation of stereotypes, with one news article depicting the women as "dark-eyed 'cholitas' packing razors in the tops of their black mesh stockings," according to the author.

Zoot-suiters, though largely Mexican, included other minorities, among them Black Americans (the style also had origins in Harlem in the 1930s, where it was popularized by jazz performers). The Black civil rights and Chicano movements had experienced similar struggles over racism, police brutality, and economic deprivation, and sometimes mobilized. And similar to the rise of Afrocentrism, being Chicano, or "brown," became a fundamental source of pride and activism during the 1960s and 1970s. The term Chicano was originally a slur used to refer to working-class people of Mexican descent, and was reclaimed by Mexican Americans at the time to express ethnic pride—especially Indigenous pride—and anti-assimilationist sentiments.

The chola aesthetic evolved out of the pachuca style and atti-tude, becoming in some ways more defiant and feminine—while continuing to embrace a masculine edge. The look entailed a combination of cat eye, pencil-thin eyebrows, a dark shade of lip liner (so dark that sometimes black eyeliner was used), slicked-back baby hairs, oversize hoop earrings, acrylic nails, and gold nameplate necklaces. The distinct style originated in the 1960s in Southern California among first- and second-generation Mexi-can American women and girls who'd endured discrimination, poverty, and educational disenfranchisement.

Some elements of chola style have been shared among women in the Black and Mexican American communities, particularly the hoops, lipliner, and eyeliner. "Their conscious particular use of clothing and physical appearance turned them and their male counterparts into part of a subcultural movement that was understood by many as an affront to mainstream society," according to Ibarraran-Bigalondo.

Chola style has also been appropriated as a costume by many celebrities, performers, and designers. Consider Gwen Stefani in the video for her song "Luxurious," with her cat eye, thinned-out eyebrows, nameplate necklace, and lined lips; Lana Del Rey's *Tropico*; and Givenchy's fall 2015 "chola Victorian–themed" runway show. And this appropriation didn't occur just on television sets and in magazines, but also in schools, where white girls "performed" chola culture, using makeup as a tool to appear more "tough," scholar Julie Bettie explains.

Clothing, hairstyles, makeup, and body language among California's Mexican Americans were indeed political tools; traditions were passed down and along, from mother to daughter, cousin to cousin, and friend to friend against the backdrop of a politically charged environment. While these women were expected to "assimilate," they chose instead to wear provocative hair and makeup styles and to put their agency to good aesthetic use. Eyeliner was not just eyeliner for cholas and the broader female Mexican American community: it was an expressive and transgressive act, delivering the message to Anglo-Americans that they were proud Mexicans, while also indicating belonging to a particular gang (sometimes acting as a form of communication between those gangs).

The pachucas, Chicanas, and cholas also used their physicality to deviate from what was expected of them as women within the group, writes Ibarraran-Bigalondo. Chola women and women who wore the chola style were boundary breakers—religiously, socially, aesthetically, and otherwise. Getting dressed often entailed deviance; the women were battling gender norms that sometimes required that they remain docile and submissive, and that they focus on childbearing and rearing. Whereas at various points in the Mexican American community's history women steered clear of makeup to protest these gender norms, they would later embrace it in chola culture, turning daily to eyeliner.

While the chola aesthetic can be tomboyish, it also flirts with hyperfemininity, aided in part by the heterogeneous styles and consumerism of the 1980s and 1990s. By the 1990s, Southern California had become a hub for the chola look, with judiciously applied eyeliner being a visible marker easily recognizable by others. There were also class elements to wearing and performing chola culture at school, argues Bettie, who notes that cholas' "perfect hair and makeup represented an effort to defy the color/poverty link at the same time that it refused white middle-class norms by rejecting the prep version."

The young women who channeled the chola aesthetic were commonly typecast as violence-prone girl gang members. But being a chola and dressing like one weren't the same; one could certainly exist without the other, though the media and pop culture would conflate the two.

"The chola look boasts generational ties and cultural roots and pays homage to a unique geographic subculture," says Stephanie Montes, a thirty-two-year-old Mexican entrepreneur, fashion and beauty editor, and former fashion designer. "It's a look people have adopted from their parents, older siblings, and cousins. It's no different than any country's traditional garb. It's unfortunate that it's only associated with gang culture. It's more than just a fashion statement, it carries a broader significance while telling a story about a person's upbringing." (Montes embraces elements of this look herself and is an expert at cat eye. She's so good at it, she can apply it while she's in a moving car, and even once filmed a tutorial in the back of an Uber.)

In a sensationalist news report from the 1990s, Diane Sawyer of ABC News spoke with trepidation about girl gangs dressed in the chola aesthetic, their eyes heavily lined, while glossing over the socioeconomic and racial backdrop that likely precipitated these events. "If these women continue to break with tradition, the children they raise face a future of violence and so do the rest of us," she said in the report. Prejudice at school, life on the sidelines, and the desire to attain and sustain empowerment, friendship, and emotional support among like-minded and like-blooded individuals were not major factors in the report.

There were few films about the Mexican American female experience; those that rose to prominence, such as *Mi vida loca* (1993), tended to portray young Chicanas and cholas as being preoccupied with boys and drugs (and, as a consequence, premature motherhood). Latina women had "either frivolity (as exemplified by tropical-music confection Carmen Miranda) or mysterious sensuality," writes academic Amanda Martinez Morrison on the phenomenon. They were depicted as fiery, sexy, and passionate; in the 1997 film *Selena*, starring Jennifer Lopez, the late singer's "voluptuous body becomes an overdetermined metonym for numerous social conflicts, desires, and anxieties about Chicana/o and Anglo/a relations." Selena, known for her distinct and sensual style, which included wings, was firmly placed "on the 'virgin' end of the virgin-whore binary." Mexican women in these depictions were, therefore, props, or the "forbidden other," and rarely fully formed.

Meanwhile, as they enjoyed the benefits of being born with Eurocentric features, many white American women relished in the freedom to explore their aesthetics. "The excessive cat eyeliner on Elizabeth Taylor in the 1960s started a craze, with fans clamoring to see more of her and copy her makeup to capture the sexuality she exuded," writes Rae Nudson in her book *All Made Up*. "But the heavy eyeliner worn by Mexican American girls in the 1940s—after Mexican Repatriation, the mass deportation of Mexicans and Mexican Americans between 1929 and 1936— added to white people's prejudices and was seen by many whites as evidence of delinquency and prostitution."

Chicana activists worked hard to dismantle these stereotypes, and chola women did their part, too, to an extent, by continuing to brandish their eyeliner.

If you want to know
who is a chola, just look
for eyeliner.

—EXCERPT FROM A STUDY BY
ANTHROPOLOGIST NORMA MENDOZA-DENTON

Mexican women have had a long-standing love affair with winged eyeliner. During the golden era of Mexican cinema, celebrities including María Félix showed off prominent wings on the silver screen. As makeup trends have evolved over the years, winged eyeliner has enjoyed a constant presence.

According to forty-one-year-old Regina Merson, the Texas-based founder of Latina makeup brand Reina Rebelde (meaning "rebel queen" in Spanish), women in Mexico use eyeliner as a tool to control how they present themselves to the world. "A Mexican woman in eyeliner is a woman in power," she says. Merson moved to the US from Guadalajara at age ten; her love for makeup was cultivated by her mother, whom she watched get ready to go to discotheques, applying blue eyeliner and volumizing her hair. But Merson also took inspiration from Mexican telenovelas, and their "overly rad love stories," in which the women with exaggerated liner cried dramatically—she appreciated their hyperfemininity. "It might be a paternalistic culture, but women run the show" in Mexico, she says. "That notion of beauty as a strength and putting yourself together well as a self-confidence builder, it stuck with me."

As a law student in America, Merson would show up to school in her wings and receive quizzical looks from her peers, "as if a woman couldn't be brainy and care about makeup at the same time," she recalled. "In Mexico, people don't have any issue reconciling these two things." Realizing makeup was an assertion of her identity—not just a fleeting "look"—Regina decided to leave law altogether to build a makeup brand that would specifically celebrate and honor Latina women.

Today, Reina Rebelde offers its clients Zapatista eyeliner, which pays homage to revolutionary fighters in southern Mexico. The Indigenous group, some of whose land has been appropriated by the Mexican government, doesn't consider itself Mexican. The women cover themselves for anonymity, but their lined eyes are left exposed; Merson observed several during a research trip to the region in 2015. "A lot of them always had on black eyeliner, and it was the wing that caught my eye," she says. "I loved how fierce and powerful they looked."

"Chola winged eye is a hybrid of two cultures," the look boasted by women in classic Mexican cinema during its golden era, and 1960s trends in American beauty, Nydia Cisneros, founder and creative director of cosmetics brand Cholas x Chulas, told *Nylon* in 2020.

According to a 2017 Pew report, whether people with Hispanic ancestry in the US choose to identify as Hispanic has a lot to do with how long their families have been in the country. "The closer they are to their immigrant roots, the more likely Americans with Hispanic ancestry are to identify as Hispanic," but the further they are, the less likely, the report says. In the context of Hispanic identity fading "across generations as immigration connections fall away," many second- and third-generation immigrants, such as Perez, aspire to preserve their cultural identity, and aesthetics play an important role in their efforts.

"The eyeliner look, to me, is an iteration of that immigrant story, the desire to retain a sense of home," Merson says. "It's impossible to divorce yourself from your culture of origin. The chola look has the same eyeliner look women were using in Mexico in the 1920s. It's the same extended wing; the same opaque black.

The pencil eyebrows, the lips, and the hair give it more of the chola urban vibe. But the eyeliner hasn't changed."

Jennifer Torres, a twenty-five-year-old model, producer, and stylist from South Central LA, says that when she frames her hazel eyes with eyeliner, she channels decades of her Mexican family's history. Her parents were immigrants who moved to the US from Zacatecas, Mexico, during the 1980s and have had to contend with multiple challenges along the way; she and her sister grew up watching their mom and aunties put eyeliner on amid these struggles, until they started wearing it themselves, at fourteen and fifteen. "Being Chicana is an identity that holds a lot of weight, a lot of history, and a lot of pain," she says. "My parents literally put their lives in danger coming here; they sacrificed so much for us. They have always instilled in us that we shouldn't be ashamed of where we come from.

"When I wear my makeup and I have my eyeliner on, I feel powerful. I feel like it's my armor. It holds so much history. Eyeliner shows strength, it shows power, it shows femininity," she says, batting her eyelashes and joking that occasionally the lines take on a life of their own—sometimes they're identical twins, other times they're merely cousins. "I think of my mother and my aunties, about how they used this tool to transform themselves into these beautiful brown women, and I feel like a beautiful brown woman myself." Beautiful, she most certainly is.

Perez, now a mother of five and a grandmother of three, has passed her mother's legacy on to her daughter, who at fifteen started wearing eyeliner. Winged eyeliner in some ways in Mexican culture is a rite of passage, particularly after the quinceañera, or the celebration of a girl's fifteenth birthday. In the coming-of-age event, women are given jewelry and are allowed to officially start wearing makeup, including eyeliner, and mothers and daughters bond over makeup application techniques.

In the absence of a cohesive nuclear family history she could turn to, Perez instead gravitated toward cultural history, meshing that with the precious scattered memories she has of her mother. "Growing up, I had no idea who I was. I didn't have any examples of what I was supposed to be doing as a maturing girl, or what that even looked like. So, I used my mother's images as my strength," she says. "My family suffered—extending down the whole family tree—with alcoholism and drug addiction. But my mother was my role model, a woman I was going to grow to be. In all the pictures I've seen of her, her power comes through when she has her eyeliner on. And I wanted that; I wanted to be a representation of that and to pass that down to my kids."

Perez started applying eyeliner at fourteen, during the 1990s. Back then, she says, few brown people on American television rocked a thick winged liner look, and there were no YouTube tutorials for her to look up to learn the craft of eyeliner application. She didn't know what makeup to purchase, let alone how to apply it. So, she learned from observing her older cousins, whose children she'd babysit on Friday nights, as they prepared to go out.

"Their hair was perfectly feathered, and for it to last all night, they plastered Aqua Net hairspray all over it to ensure not one strand gets out of place. The wall behind the mirror in the bathroom was stained a dingy yellow from all the overspray, it was hilarious!" she recalls, fondly. "Eyeliner extended to the temple, looking as sharp as their creased Ben Davis pants. Crop tops and tube tops were big back in those days, always exposing that beautiful brown skin. My cousin always wore her Raiders jersey crop top with a white tube top underneath. Big hoops, chola bands, and Mary Jane shoes to complete the Friday night look."

Eventually, Perez bought the cheapest eyeliner she could find at a local store and began to experiment, using a heavy hand when applying her wings. "I was a hot mess for years," she says. "My lines were uneven and messy and super garbled." Her cousins would try to redo her makeup with cute little wings, but she wasn't having any of it. "I wanted extreme," she says. "Refined technique came way later."

As she tried desperately to find her feet, Perez struggled to fit in at school, particularly among her white peers. But she says she also struggled among her Mexican peers, as she's lighter skinned, being half-Italian. "I didn't ever feel like I fit in with any certain crowd. I was the odd one out. And that's what inspired me to create my own lane," she says, noting that while she was certainly seen, she was rarely heard. "Back in those days, holding on to your culture—and being proud of it—was frowned upon. We were taught to blend in, and I was most opposed to that. I didn't want to blend in. And I didn't fit in, so I just made my way." Eyeliner was part of that journey. Its starkness set her apart, but also made her feel like she belonged to something bigger than herself, and reminded her of her mother and other proud cholas.

Two weeks into her freshman year—at just fifteen—Perez fell

into serious trouble. She'd gotten caught up with the wrong people, she says, and ended up embroiled in turf wars, which culminated in a court trial. The trial involved one of the earliest cases of gang enhancements, which add punishment time to people charged with felonies who commit crimes in association with street gangs. Perez says the severity of the situation was compounded by racial profiling. "It's like they turned a blind eye [to socioeconomic factors] and lumped all of us into one group," she says of the experience. "In actuality, we were stuck in this rut that we couldn't get out of and doing the best we could to get out." When Perez showed up to court, she still wore her statement eyeliner. "I wear my war paint in all battles proudly. On the streets and in the courtroom alike," she says. That said, she "never thought of it as defiance, more so protection."

It's a moody March day in Venice, LA, just past lunchtime. But by the time the dozen or so classic rides pull up, the rain has cleared, and the California sun is out. Scores of neighborhood locals congregate to catch up and observe one another and their cars' bouncing hydraulics before setting off for a long cruise along the highway and to the beach. The women are decked out in their best. Melina, who's a member of the Dogtown Devils Car Club, wears wings, lip liner, hoops, and a plaid shirt over a black tank top—staple items in the chola wardrobe. Her tied-up stick-straight hair flows down her back, and she presides over her wagon (the only one here) with an unmistakable sense of tenacity. She says she's here to celebrate "the classic lifestyle and classic cars," but also "for the community, friends, and family; we bring out our cars, we put in our work, and it's just a lovely art form to bond over." For Melina, wearing her eyeliner reminds her of the glamour years of her grandmother, and allows her to share elements of her identity—to be a proud Mexican American. "Eyeliner is part of the beauty of our Mexican culture; we were brought up in this culture, and we've passed this beauty on, from generation to generation," she says.

Celia, who also wears cat eye, is dressed in a slightly more feminine getup, with a white A-line minidress and Ferrari-red acrylic nails; her baby hairs are sideswept. "My mom would rock the eyeliner. It was just something that I loved during the '80s," she says. "I'd feel naked if I didn't wear my eyeliner. I wear it every single day. I even go to the beach in it. It's one of my favorite things!" Celia says she's passed the "eyeliner tradition" on to her twenty-one- and twenty-three-year-old daughters, who usually accompany her to lowrider shows.

Both women have adopted different aspects of the chola appearance, without explicitly identifying as cholas. But they are united by the way they wear their eyeliner in the lowriding community and beyond, and the fierceness with which they claim space in a predominantly male setting. Women in lowrider culture are "beautiful but so fierce . . . classic but modern—my interpretation of lowrider culture is that it embodies so many of these exact dualities," Merson told *The Zoe Report* in 2021. The entrepreneur spent months studying aesthetics in the subculture, later using that research to inform her brand.

Perez also took inspiration from women in the lowriding scene as she cultivated her chola style. Around the same time she started wearing eyeliner, she began driving a '79 Cadillac Eldorado Biarritz—before she even had a driver's license. The Chicana and her father would go cruising together in his '67 Chevy Impala to join others in the neighborhood. People would ceremoniously parade their cars, talk shop, and catch up, Perez recalls. They'd stop to eat at Wienerschnitzel, the iconic hot dog chain, and hang out at the park, pulling up chairs on breaks to prevent their cars from overheating, and watching people drift along. Everyone would be dressed to the nines, with clean shoes, creased pants, ironed shirts, and sharp wings. "Lowriders are an extension of our pride in ourselves," she says. "Our cars are an extension of us, so the more flashy, the better. You want to stand out, not only with your car, but also how you look, and your wings."

Drawn to the art form thanks to her father, Perez would walk miles on Saturday nights to watch the old-school cars with their glitzy designs cruise by on Santa Clara Street. There, she was captivated by Mary, one of the only women with a lowrider in the area. "Back then, cruising was more of a machismo thing. The guys had all the cars, and the girls were the eye candy, sitting next to them. The girls couldn't have their cars, they couldn't have a job, they were expected to stay at home and raise kids. They needed to be accounted for," she says. "But Mary was a force. She had the car and the look; she had the thick wings. I was in awe, and I wanted to be her. She influenced me to go overboard on the whole look and to own it."

Perez appreciated Mary's representation of the SoCal style, with the trademark heavy wings topped with white eyeshadow—a "raccoon" look, so to speak (in Northern California, the eyeliner isn't as thick, she notes). It's a look she often opts for today. "I was like, 'This is who I want to be when I grow up. I want to be the only female out there with her own lowrider doing her own thing and looking this way,'" she says. "And, somehow, that's who I became."

Perez found freedom and confidence in lowriding. But, soon enough, her community was targeted by the San Jose Police Department, which banned the activity from its streets altogether in the late 1980s (the ban has since been lifted). It wasn't safe to cruise on Sundays or even to go to the grocery store without being profiled, Perez recalls. People driving in old-school cars were pulled over, questioned, and ticketed. Embracing the look, including eyeliner, had become even riskier. But Perez never stopped wearing her wings; in fact, she was emboldened. And though the lowriding scene lost some popularity during the late 1980s due to the ban, before fading throughout the '90s, she continued to ride when she could.

For the past fifteen years, thanks to a younger generation of Mexican Americans, lowriding has made a roaring comeback, says Perez—and she and her friends have urged them on. "Folks are starting to take more pride in wearing their eyeliner, and wearing the chola aesthetic at lowrider shows, showing where they're from and being proud of it," says Torres, whose partner is a lowrider. "The scene is really a melting pot of Black and brown folks just coming together to express solidarity and pride. We are the blueprint. It just shows that we created our own beauty standards. There's so much beauty and art in our communities."

Inspired by the courage of Mary, the memory of her mother, and her father's hobbies, Perez continues to set an example for other

Mexican American women, by way of her presence in the lowriding community and by being a proud chola at work, at home, on the streets, and even online (she has nearly 130,000 followers on TikTok).

Today, Perez drives a 1951 Chevy Styleline Deluxe. She treats her car like she treats her face—with care, emphasizing and celebrating its unique cultural features. In the California lowriding community, there are now several female lowriders and lowriding groups who cruise alongside one another, including the Dueñas Car Club, the Vintage Ladies Car Club, and the Varrio Vamps Car Club. In 2022, LA-based concert promoter Angela Romero opened Hello Stranger, a lowrider-themed restaurant and bar, to pay respect to the culture, while honoring her late brother, who died from pneumonia in 2014, and highlighting work by women artists. "I want people to know that a female opened this space," she told the *Los Angeles Times*. In a series of photos for the story, Romero is boldly wearing eyeliner.

Perez's children and grandchildren now also partake in weekly lowrider shows—and her daughter, too, wears cat eye to the weekly events. "Sunday cruising is our family tradition. No phones, no distractions, just family time. There's just no greater feeling. That sense of pride and community," she says. "With lowriding, I had to find my way, to figure it out for myself. Just like I did at school. Just like I did when I started wearing eyeliner. Being out there cruising empowered other women to do the same. And now, there are so many women out there at the wheel. We made that change. And I'm proud of myself, of us."

Reflecting on her style, Perez is humble yet assured.

"I'm living my history right now in the best way possible, the best possible representation of my ancestors. When people see me, I hope they see perseverance, strength, pride, and courage," she says. "I'm not stereotypically beautiful. But I think people do pick up on my inner strength, on the inner lioness that comes out through my eyeliner."

Chapter Six

The Eye Dance

Kathakali and Kajal in Kerala

For wherever the hand moves, there the glances follow;
where the glances go, the mind follows;
where the mind goes, the mood follows;
where the mood goes, there is the flavor.

—NANDIKEŚVARA, *THE MIRROR OF GESTURE*

It's a muggy early afternoon in the coastal city of Kochi, Kerala, a full four hours until the classical Indian dance performance known as kathakali is set to begin. Three men—two older and one far younger—have started to prepare their makeup and clothing. Backstage, they've carefully laid out stripe-patterned reed mats. A single lamp in the center of the room illuminates a collection of clay makeup pots filled with reds, blues, and yellows, along with coconut tree leaves and coconut leaf sticks. The leaves serve as palettes for the men to mix their makeup, the sticks as applicators. Several contain a highly pigmented eyeliner substance known as kajal, a variation of the Arabic word *kuhl*, popularly known as anjana in Sanskrit-Hindu culture and sormeh in Urdu-Islamic culture.

Adityan, a young man, will play the role of Panchali, the female protagonist in *Kalyanasaugandhikam*, a Sanskrit drama. He sits cross-legged on the floor, taking a few deep breaths as he soaks in his surroundings as if preparing for a ritual—in many ways, he is. First, the man uses his fingers to lather onto his face a light yellow paste that's multiple shades fairer than his dark brown skin. He starts at the edges of his nose and spreads the paste toward his jawline. Once his entire face is covered in foundation, including his eyebrows, Adityan powders it to lock in the color and mattify any shine caused by the lingering humidity of a recent cyclone's showers. He returns to his foundation for touch-ups, ensuring no spots are missed, until he's formed a blank slate upon which to apply his eyeliner.

With his left hand, Adityan raises a mirror. Then, using a coconut leaf stick in his right, he steadily draws kajal onto his lower lash line. He begins a few millimeters beyond his eye socket, at his nose bridge, stenciling a wing that stretches to his hairline. Employing the grace and precision of a maestro, with each stroke, he thickens the bottom line until it's about half a centimeter in diameter, filling in the silhouette. In several dramatic swooshes, he lengthens the line; it ultimately runs parallel to the stretch of a drawn-on S-shaped eyebrow with a pronounced arch.

The sounds of birds and crickets chirping in the distance and the hums of four ceiling fans don't distract him. Neither does the Instagram influencer who's there with two friends and an assistant for a photo shoot. Her ring light hovers along with her, disturbing the lamp's soft yellow ambiance while illuminating her kajal-adorned eyes. Adityan's hand doesn't flinch: he's done this dozens of times, learning the art of extreme kajal application at school and later practicing privately. When he's finished, a second, thinner black line along his upper lash has met the lower one at the eye's corner. The result is a wing whose thickness is accentuated by the lower line rather than the upper (the latter of which is more common in Western winged liner looks).

"To enhance the eyes, their movements, and expressions, kajal is heavily used as makeup and is crucial in classical dance," says Sukhada Khandge, a kathak dancer and researcher who specializes in folk arts (like kathakali, kathak is one of eight major forms of Indian classical dance). "We often say many dancers dance with their eyes."

Adityan uses leftover kajal to draw swirls of baby hair around his forehead and temples and to outline a red bindi on his forehead. Following his makeup application, he's given a wig of long synthetic hair before carefully stepping into an elaborate, billowing frock coat, supported beneath by bunched-up, sturdy grain bags. (Kathakali costumes can weigh up to forty pounds and require multiple knots to hold them together.) Masses of gold bangles adorn Adityan's arms, his neck is decorated with pearl necklaces, and he wears chandelier earrings. Lastly, the performer dons a breastplate painstakingly constructed with tin and covered with red felt; below it are multicolored mini pom-poms.

Adityan has transformed himself into a woman, much in the same way drag queens do. While kathakali actors tend to be male, men and women are made up similarly, their makeup not considered a gendered accessory. The process takes about four hours, one of which is devoted entirely to the eyes. Nevertheless, Adityan appears far from exhausted: the real work begins onstage.

Nearby, Balasubramanian, sixty-eight, prepares to play Bhima,

Panchali's green-faced partner. His kajal is more extreme than Panchali's—in kathakali makeup, the less "pure" or more "evil" the character, the heavier the eyeliner. Balasubramanian, as a matter of habit, starts his makeup application with his eyes to devote as much time to them as possible. (He'll later be assisted by a makeup artist, who handles the trickier aspects of the facial makeup. That process, which requires Balasubramanian to lie down on the reed mat for easier application, involves paper and rice paste—rice flour combined with cotton and water—used to create a protruding beard.) Bhima's lines are similar to Panchali's, though thicker and more pointed, shooting up at an angle so steep that, at a distance, they resemble lightning bolts, ending not with a wing but a square-shaped tip. "This isn't a mask," Balasubramanian insists, pointing to his eyes. "We're transformed into extrahuman characters. The eyeliner is crucial to projecting the eyes onto the audience by enlarging them. Everything is precisely applied, with the intent that the eyes evoke the character's feelings."

The kajal has been preprepared by their makeup artist, using a technique that has existed in India for centuries. First, various herbs, gingelly oil (derived from sesame seeds), or other materials are burned, then covered with a clay pot; the smoke creates soot that is then scraped off and mixed with coconut oils. "The eyelids [are] blackened with antimony, so that the eyes appear enlarged, which is the Hindu ideal of beauty," writes the author Richard Tremblay in his book *The Kathakali Explorer*.

For kathakali performers, dance and eye makeup are a way of life—a passion that emerges in childhood, grows into young adulthood, flourishes in middle age, and matures to perfection in older age. Balasubramanian started learning kathakali and makeup application at the age of thirteen, at Kerala Kalamandalam, a university of arts and culture that teaches dance. He was a student of kathakali for ten years before joining the university as a lecturer for an additional thirty-two, and finally becoming a principal for two, before ultimately retiring in 2011.

An art form that developed in Kerala in the seventeenth century, *kathakali* translates to "story play," and synthesizes music, dance, and oral traditions. Its stories are adapted from Hindu epics and ancient Indian scriptures known as Puranas. Kerala plays a central role in the history of kathakali: some of the dance form's elaborate makeup patterns are inspired by murals found in the state's temples; many of its bodily movements have taken inspiration from the area's traditional martial arts practice; and the vocal music is thought to be an offshoot of a local style of singing.

The stories are told partly through performers' emotive facial expressions, with the eyes serving as windows into the surreal. Basic hand gestures known as mudras move in tandem with eye expressions—twenty-four mudras communicate up to six hundred words. In kathakali, musicality and mime are controlled and deliberately paced: performers are taught to isolate their eyes, eyebrows, cheeks, and eyelids as they act out specific emotions. The performers' eyes are lined extravagantly with black eyeliner to draw attention to them onstage; the kajal also helps the audience distinguish between characters from afar. "Kathakali has perfected the art of theater," Balasubramanian says. "Makeup is a crucial part of that; without the heavy eye makeup, the audience wouldn't be able to interpret the dance in the way they do now."

Adityan and Balasubramanian stick the seeds of a chunda flower under their lower lids to redden them and further accentuate their eye expressions. The eyes remain red for up to four hours after the seeds are inserted into the sockets, though it doesn't harm them, Balasubramanian insists. Along with the kajal, the seeds are said to act as reinforcements, protecting the eyes from other foreign substances. The kajal also offers a cooling effect that counters the burning triggered by the seed, he says.

Now that both characters are ready, they silently pray and bow before heading onto the stage. They conduct last-minute checks on hidden mirrors dangling from fabrics attached to their clothing; during the performance, they'll stealthily examine their reflections to ensure their makeup is intact.

In Indian tradition, the third eye—a mystical eye that cannot be seen—is considered the gateway to the upper levels of spiritual consciousness. Kathakali as an art form partly relies on the physical presentation and framing of the eyes and their ability to convey profound meaning. On the kathakali stage, the eyes communicate everything from the divine and desire to strength of character and wrath. The actors aren't merely actors, they're gods, and the sleek black lines around their eyes aren't simply drawn for aesthetic purposes—they guide the viewer to a portal into another world.

"Oh, Doe-Eyed Creature!"

We enter that world at twilight. Over one hundred spectators have taken their seats in an open-air auditorium in Changampuzha Park, a recreational facility built to honor the Malayalam poet Changampuzha Krishna Pillai. There isn't a single tourist here (save for me), and some of the audience members have traveled hundreds of miles from all over Kerala to marvel at the dance-drama's eccentric makeup and majestic costumes—to witness the past come alive in the present. For several moments, there's no sound; phones have fallen silent. Even the birds seem to hush. Finally, a curtain with a print of Bhima's piercing, lavishly lined eyes is raised to unveil the god and his partner, two drummers and two percussionists, one with a cymbal and another with a gong.

Panchali's and Bhima's eyes begin to move to the percussionists' beat, and as it crescendos, so does the speed of their eye movements. One of the percussionists starts to sing as he clashes his cymbals; he continues to do so throughout the performance, narrating some of the tale. Mere minutes have elapsed, but the audience is by now wholly engrossed. The eye motions are transfixing, borderline hypnotic. To watch kathakali is to exist in the world created by its characters, with their eyes as the centerpiece and their kajal as a frame.

Kalyanasaugandhikam's tale centers on three characters: Panchali; Panchali's husband, Bhima; and Bhima's brother Hanuman, the monkey god. Both male characters are sons of the god of wind. A breeze from the Himalayas carries a sougandhika flower, or water lily, to Panchali. She darts her eyes circularly, observing the bees swarming around it. Its scent appears to make her delirious; she's mesmerized, her eyes popping out of their sockets. When she gathers her wits about her, she demands her husband fetch her more of the flowers. She dances around him seductively, swaying her torso left to right, and right to left, while her hands mimic her eye movements, and vice versa.

Finally, she leans onto her husband, coyly tracing his body with her eyes, while raising and lowering her eyebrows in tandem. "Oh, lotus-eyed one," the singer narrates, "noble women express desires only to their husbands. Oh, doe-eyed creature, as you desire." Bhima, wanting to please his wife, edges closer to her, swinging both hands in the air, indicating he's decided to embark on the treacherous journey to locate the flowers, "even if on top of mountains, even if in heaven." He excitedly roams around the stage on tiptoe, his artificial metallic nails—which are more than two inches long—glinting in the light of an onstage lamp.

Bhima must now cross through a thick forest "full of rocks and thorns." As he stomps down his path, he interrupts the meditation of his older brother, Hanuman, who's unrecognizable to Bhima as he's assumed his form of a monkey. Hanuman, considered one of the more sinister characters in kathakali, has eyes so heavily lined that the kajal has run amok, metastasizing as it forms harsh patterns against his orange-colored forehead.

Frustrated, Bhima chastises the monkey and demands it make way for him. "Hey, monkey, move fast without obstructing my path!" Bhima says. His gestures are dramatic; he waves his hands in a disorderly fashion and squints his eyes repeatedly. The monkey, though, remains unmoved. Bhima attempts to lift its long tail with a cudgel, but realizes it's too heavy. The monkey then resumes his human form, and Bhima lowers his head in shame and deference, realizing Hanuman was his sibling all along. Having learned his lesson, Bhima is forgiven, and Hanuman points him toward the flowers he was seeking. Bhima retrieves the water lilies for Panchali, whose kajal-decorated eyelids flutter in delight once she receives them.

"A Talisman of Sorts"

The Indian subcontinent is saturated with rituals and customs that have been passed down for centuries—some remaining untouched, others evolving. Kajal for spiritual, superstitious, beautification, and medicinal purposes is a custom that's endured to the extent that the cosmetic is today the single most widely used makeup item in India. (While a decade ago local brands such as Jai Kajal, Lakmé, Ambar, and Shahnaz Husain's herbal kajal dominated the market, today, international names including Maybelline, L'Oréal, MAC, and Guerlain have released kajal pencils to cater to Indian women. To promote their offerings, some of these brands have enlisted big Bollywood names for advertisements, like Alia Bhatt and Aishwarya Rai.)

People of all religions and generations use kajal regularly, if not daily, both within and across India's borders, including in the neighboring countries of Pakistan, Bangladesh, and Sri Lanka. Dr. Vinu Kumar, a Kerala native, says his eight-year-old daughter wears kajal, applying it by herself every morning as she stands in front of a mirror with a makeup kit. "It's part of our culture," he says. "A part of growing up." Kajal wearers make the pigment at home, using soot from the burning of materials such as ghee, castor oil, coconut oil, camphor, aloe vera, or sandalwood paste.

Kajal is fundamental to Indian and South Asian culture; Anjana, Kajal, and Kajri are common Hindu names for girls. Kajal

Aggarwal and Kajol, for example, are famous figures in modern Indian cinema who often wear eyeliner. Kajal is used on newborns to ward off the evil eye and to help them sleep soundly; culturally, many Indians believe in the evil spirit. While some parents have stopped using store-bought kajal on newborns due to the lead content commonly found in various brands, others apply homemade kajal to their children's foreheads or cheeks, behind their ears, or on the soles of their feet as a mark of protection.

Some Hindus make the cosmetic during Diwali, the festival of lights celebrated in October and November—enough to last for months. Culture blogger Pooja Sodhi says she and her ancestors have followed this kajal-making tradition for three centuries. "My mother learned [the custom] from her mother, and she, in turn, would've learned it either from her maternal family or the family she was married into," says Sodhi, who is from the ancient city of Varanasi in Uttar Pradesh. (Hindu families in Uttar Pradesh and Bihar regularly make kajal at home during Diwali, she adds.) Diwali is a celebration of the triumph of good over evil, so the role kajal plays in warding off evil is apt. Kajal is also worn on special occasions, including weddings: In South Indian weddings, for example, brides and grooms sometimes dot their cheeks with it to ward off the evil eye; in the North, sisters-in-law apply the cosmetic to the eyes of grooms-to-be before they leave their homes to wed their brides.

In the South Asian diaspora, kajal has become a way to embrace one's identity. "As a Pakistani American teenager growing up in a Philadelphia suburb, traditional kohl was a talisman of sorts. . . . When I felt I didn't belong, lining my eyes with even the lightest touch of kohl instantly reminded me of Pakistan and made me feel confident in my beauty," writes journalist Iman Sultan for *Allure* in March 2022. "Wearing kajal was a way of comforting myself when I felt lonely or alienated among white people, because it was familiar," she tells me separately.

Farah Siddiqui, a forty-year-old art consultant and curator, says that whereas "Bollywood and the media have perpetuated unrealistic beauty standards set by our colonial past and inherent Hindu caste system, which included light skin and light-colored hair," in the last decade, South Asian women "have embraced their uniqueness and color," and have continued to turn to kajal as "an essential part of South Asian heritage, whether Islam or Hinduism." Kavitha Iyer, also in her forties, has been wearing kajal since she was eighteen. While her friends at college used eyeliner, she instead turned to kajal for its convenience. "It's an accessible and convenient makeup product that does the job without requiring time or aftercare," she says. "Lower rim only or also the lid, [it's] so versatile. It gives my face an instant lift."

Delhi-based researcher and teacher Sarah Khan wears both kajal *and* eyeliner, though she prefers kajal, as she says it's smoother, giving her a more "natural" look. "It's the only makeup routine I have," the twenty-five-year-old says, adding she was inspired by her mother growing up, as she often watched her apply surma to her eyes with just one stroke. (Surma is predominantly worn by Muslims in South Asian countries.) "It symbolizes effortless beauty to me."

For Amrita Thayyil, who started using the cosmetic after she got married, the application of kajal is also a daily ritual. "I don't step out of the house without wearing kajal," the thirty-eight-year-old says. "I personally feel I look tired or sick without it. I just wear it to look fresh. It adds depth to my eyes." Thayyil says she admires the kajal looks of actors Smita Patil, Chitrangada Singh, and Nandita Das, to name a few.

"Kajal makes me feel good," says forty-two-year-old Smita Nair. "I see this daily ritual of wearing kajal as a way of preparing myself for the long day ahead. It's a reminder of a routine, a sense of normalcy." Nair, a Mumbai-based journalist, closely associates the cosmetic with memories of her mother. Nair's mother would often use the bend of a safety pin to apply the pigment to her daughter's eyes; for easy access, she'd wear the pin on a necklace and take its coiled back to scoop up the black wax from its container. "It's a memory of days when I was dependent on her for everything," Nair says. "Today she buys me kajal sticks and keeps them in my drawer. In that sense [kajal represents] a relationship between my mother and me." When she feels nostalgic for those days, she buys Jai Kajal, a local brand from Maharashtra. Otherwise, like Thayyil, Iyer, and Khan, she prefers products including Maybelline's or Lakmé's.

"Kohl of Love"

Kajal is heavily referenced in Bollywood films and their whimsical songs and dances. Bollywood's stunning kajal-eyed actresses are at the center of the industry, where their distinctive looks are glorified and romanticized. In countless Bollywood songs, which often explore themes of unrequited love, heartbreak, and separation, kajal is mentioned in reference to a beloved's eyes. The 1981 indie film *Chashme baddoor* features the song "Kahan se aaye badra," about a forced separation of lovers due to "dark clouds" of misunderstanding; in its lyrics, the breakup makes the woman restless and causes a monsoon of tears to rain from her eyes, washing away her kajal. In the 1996 film *Sapoot*, the song "Kajal kajal teri aankhon ka ye kajal" tells the story of how the kajal of a woman's eyes drives her lover crazy—as the music is performed in the film, background dancers hold up scarves with large motifs of kajal-adorned eyes to illustrate the lyrics. And in the 1968 film *Kismat* (Destiny), the protagonist cross-dresses as a woman in heavy kajal, dancing to the hit song "Kajra mohabbat wala," to escape the movie's villain; the song refers to the "kohl of love" in a woman's eyes.

Shailesh Jukar, a Bollywood makeup designer, traces the use of kajal on the eyes of Indian actresses as far back as the earliest days of the country's cinema. "Makeup evolved prominently around the eyes, and thick, heavy eyeliner with mascara became a highlight for the actresses," Jukar says. The introduction of color on previously silver screens bolstered the golden era of Hindi film, which ran from the 1940s to the 1960s. Writers and directors boldly experimented with aesthetics, storylines, music, and characters. Costumes were made colorful and sensual, makeup was bold, and song and dance sexualized femininity. Women began to appear on screen as vamps, vixens, cabaret dancers, and femme fatales; celebrities such as Sadhana, Sharmila Tagore, Mumtaz, and Helen embraced dramatic looks that often included a big bouffant, elongated eyelashes, winged liner, and prominent eyebrows. During the 1960s, the Indian actresses Nargis, Saira Banu, and Madhubala wore abundant kajal with upturned wings.

Kajal served a purely practical purpose, too. Early film stocks, such as those by Kodak and Fuji, would diffuse light, so makeup had to be heavily applied in layered strokes to intensify actors' features, Jukar says, similar to makeup practices at the dawn of cinema in the Western world.

"In old black-and-white Hindi movies, the makeup for female characters used a lot of kohl, eyeliner, and mascara, as the only way to add drama or enhance the face was through the eyes," agrees Namrata Soni, a makeup artist who's worked on commercially successful Hindi films and is credited for the iconic makeup looks featured in the hit 2007 film *Om shanti om.* "The winged liner look became a statement for the women in Hindi cinema," she says. Historically, actresses were often draped in a sari or salwar kameez (loose-fitting trousers and a tunic); women on screen had yet to express their sexuality and femininity by way of revealing clothing. "It was all about the eyes then. So, the eye makeup expressed different forms from seduction and romance to drama."

Soni began working on the sets of Hindi films in Mumbai as a makeup artist in 2004, where she was an anomaly in the male-dominated industry. But she made a name for herself when she helped debut actor Deepika Padukone find her signature look: sweeping winged eyeliner. "Give me a kajal pencil, and I will change the way the person looks over any other aspect of makeup," she says, adding that, for inspiration, she observed prominent Hindi film actors such as Sharmila Tagore, Vyjayanthimala, Mumtaz, and Meena Kumari, all four of whom have sported the look. As many Indian women have almond-shaped eyes, agreeing with Iyer, Soni says that kajal can give the illusion of a face-lift, beyond enhancing the eyes themselves.

The cosmetic also features prominently in Soni's personal

style. "I'd never leave my house without a kajal pencil in my bag," she says. "A little hint of it can completely change the way the eyes look, especially Indian eyes, which have intense and varied shades of brown."

"The Full Experience of Real Feeling"

School is out at Kalamandalam's thirty-one-acre campus in the heart of Thrissur, the colorful Kerala city that's home to numerous sacred sites. The university, which hosts hundreds of students, was founded in 1930, with a second campus opening in 1971; it's surrounded by tall trees and rich foliage and comprises dormitories, a theater temple, a canteen, two libraries, and a visitor's center. Kathakali performers' ability to control their eye movements with such a high degree of precision is a skill acquired through up to a dozen years of practice at the specialized school—boys and girls begin their journey into the art from around age twelve, and students wake up as early as 3:30 a.m. to practice their dances. Alongside physical exercises, they sing and play music, while those specializing in kathakali costume design and makeup artistry refine their techniques. Given the importance of aesthetics, the makeup class is as rigorous as the dance and theory classes.

Aashiq, twenty-one, arrives at one of the campus libraries just after lunchtime to prepare for his final exams. He says kathakali, which he began studying at age thirteen, is his passion because he "loves classical art forms and makeup." While he's bare eyed when not in costume, he says kajal is essential because "it helps transform people into character, and it frames the eyes, the key to the soul." As he says this, he demonstrates several core eye movements expected of kathakali performers, moving them left to right, right to left, up and down, down and up, in a half-moon, diagonally, squarely, and then in a circular motion. Kathakali facial expressions can convey a wide spectrum of emotions, including humor, love, sorrow, fear, and calm. "The eye is most important when expressing feelings. The expression is more prominent when the eye is made up," he says. "An eye without makeup is naked. When I'm in kajal, I feel like a different person; I become the character." The eyes must become so free that they can move whichever way they'd like, unencumbered, he says, and though the liner frames the eyes, it does not confine them—rather, it liberates them.

Aashiq's thoughts on kajal acting as a beautifier *and* a protector are reinforced by historical, philosophical, cultural, and scientific texts, where it's sometimes referred to as anjana (the root of the word, *anj*, means "to smear") or collyrium, an antique term for a cleansing eyewash. The *Ashtanga hridayasamhita*, written in the seventh century, describes collyrium as a type of medicine to treat eye diseases. Likewise, in the third volume of the *Sushruta samhita*, a foundational book on medicine and surgery, anjana is defined as a substance used for healing purposes. The late nineteenth-century book *The Materia Medica of the Hindus*, compiled from Sanskrit medical works, asserts that anjana is therapeutic. The author also details four types of collyrium: sormeh; sulfide of antimony from the mountains of Sauvira, a kingdom along the Indus; pushpanjana, an alkaline substance; and rasanjana, an extract of the wood of Asian barberry.

"The two eyes are to be touched with collyrium," instructs the

Natya Shastra, which contains six thousand poetic verses published between the second century BCE and the second century CE. The ancient Hindu Sanskrit text and oldest manual of theater and dance, which is an authoritative guide to the performing arts, also refers twice to collyrium in Sanskrit verses describing a maiden's beauty. "Why are your eyes without collyrium and why are you resting the cheek on the palm of your hand?" reads one verse. A chapter on mudras illustrates the sandamsa or "pincers" movement, in which the forefinger and the thumb are crossed, and the palm hollowed, to represent the wick of a lamp, or the coloring of an eye with collyrium. According to Dr. Priyanka Basu, a lecturer in performing arts at King's College London and an odissi dancer—odissi is another classical style of Indian dance—kajal is universally accepted across India as it transcends class, caste, and religion. This is made evident in part by virtue of it being mentioned in the *Natya Shastra*, Basu says. The text also emphasizes the importance of sentiments (rasa) and states (bhava) as conveyed through thirty-six unique types of eye movements.

The *Subhashitavali*, a fifteenth-century collection of comic and erotic poetry, lists the solah shringar—the sixteen adornments commonly cited in Indian culture to celebrate feminine beauty and the art of grooming before meeting a beloved. These include a neck garland, tooth polish, clothing, a bindi, bangles, earrings, a nose pin, an anklet, an elaborate hairdo, a mirror—and kajal. With a focus on aesthetics, the *Sangitaratnakara* (Ocean of music and dance), published in the thirteenth century and considered the most definitive text on Hindustani and Carnatic music, advises the eyes be "decorated with collyrium."

Nayantara Parpia, a kathak dancer and teacher, says kajal

is one of the few cosmetics whose use hasn't changed much. Like kathakali, "eyes are the dominant component" in kathak, as performers "use mime to communicate stories from mythology through facial expressions and hand gestures," she says. The dancer has a popular online presence in which she bridges the past and the present. One of her YouTube makeup tutorials, viewed over three hundred thousand times, demonstrates how to achieve the "flawless" classical dancer look by using gel eyeliner.

According to Parpia, kajal is core to Indian aesthetics and is intertwined with femininity—even women in rural areas who are otherwise reluctant to use makeup embrace it. This is partly due to kajal's prevalence in popular culture, whether literature, dance, or music, the teacher says. Some of her performances have centered on couplets referencing kajal—she's danced to love songs about Krishna and his companion, Radha, who performed the ritual of solah shringar, and to songs revealing his unfaithfulness.

Even though classes are out, the Kalamandalam campus is filled with sounds of the chenda and maddalam, instruments taught at the school and used during kathakali performances. A din of voices draws us to Greeshma, fifteen, a dancer in training who's about to perform her final exams in front of a panel of two teachers, and friends and family who've come to support her. She's studying mohiniyattam, which translates to "dance of the enchantress" and has roots in the *Natya Shastra*. "The art of makeup and the history of dance, both of these things appeal to me," she says.

As a young girl, at just three, Greeshma was inspired by a

kathakali dancer; she'd dance for hours at a time as a toddler, to her parents' amusement. "Where life happens, dance happens," she says. "And dance reminds me of my pride in my culture." Greeshma's eyes are expertly lined with kajal to the extent that I feel embarrassed by my amateur lines; she says she applies it herself every morning within minutes. "Kajal makes me beautiful," she responds adorably, after I compliment her.

In addition to classical dancers, kajal is often found on the eyes of those in folk art forms, including gavlan, lavani, and kajari. In dance forms such as kathak, kajal is also used as an invisible prop by performers who demonstrate how the cosmetic is applied with their mudras. The performance is intended to portray a heroine getting ready to meet her lover, for example, or how one prepares for a festival. The makeup of mohiniyattam performers—who are predominantly female—is lower key than that of kathakali. Even so, their lips are usually painted red, and kajal is prominently applied to highlight their eye movements during the dance. (This style of makeup can also be found on the faces of middle-class women in Kerala, according to writer V. Kaladharan.)

Greeshma has been practicing for her test for months, from April to June, waking up at 4:30 a.m. daily and dancing until 12:30 p.m. to perfect her moves. She's visibly nervous, pacing around as she practices her mudras, and showing me her textbooks—but she's also excited. This is her third year at Kalamandalam; she wears a bright orange and green sari to indicate the level of her studies. When she finally performs for her jury, she's poised, roving around the classroom as she sways her torso from side to side like a slight wave in a vast ocean, her bare feet tiptoeing and delicately supporting her tiny body as it contorts.

The two teachers crack a few smiles as she dances before them, clearly taken by her performance. She emerges victorious and giggly, ready for her summer vacation before she resumes her studies next year.

A few doors down, Sivadas, fifty-two, is surrounded by makeup pots and applicators. Sivadas has taught makeup application at Kalamandalam for twenty years and has been a kathakali dancer for thirty-five. "Makeup is the most important part of kathakali," he says. With the use of kajal, "feelings are more easily transmitted to the audience. Enhancements like these provide the full experience of real feeling."

Kathakali was historically performed by the light of coconut oil lamps, in the absence of electricity or sound systems, so makeup played a crucial role in ensuring the performers' facial expressions were more visible to the audience, according to Sivadas. The colors would guarantee their faces glowed in the light, offering a technical benefit similar to how thick makeup helped make features more visible on early television and silver screens.

Sivadas turned to makeup as a discipline in kathakali because he had an artistic eye as a young boy. He teaches his makeup class from 4:00 a.m. to 6:00 a.m. daily; the dancers in training use the bottoms of clay pots to practice makeup techniques, drawing faces onto them and applying kajal to their features using the same materials and tools employed by professional performers. The kathakali characters students make up on the pots include gods, kings, and demons; on the bowls in front of Sivadas are various iterations of Hanuman's and Bhima's makeup, some eyes fully made up, others half-done.

"In Indian culture, everything comes back to art, and makeup is art," says thirty-seven-year-old Thulasikumar, who teaches dance, including scripts and the meaning of the mudras. "While all the costumes and colors are important, kajal is especially important because the eye is the organ where the expression should come first, and most communication happens through eye and eye movement." Thulasikumar says he was born into kathakali, surrounded by kathakali temples and dancers, and that he'll die with it. While he is just shy of forty, he has already performed at least five hundred times. "Kathakali is my life," he says. "I'm living with this art form. It gives me my livelihood, it gives me faith, and it's the greatest passion for me. When I'm ninety, I will still be performing kathakali. If I'm breathing, I'll be performing, and I'll still be wearing kajal."

"Tearful Black Eyes"

Indian and South Asian history is steeped in kajal. In 1935, British archaeologist Ernest John Henry Mackay discovered several bronze, clay, and cosmetic pottery jars in present-day Pakistan; they were found with other pots believed to have been used in vanity areas. While some of the jars were roughly hewn, others were intricately crafted (one jar features four fish carvings arranged around the opening of the pot). Applicators were made of copper or bronze, and also sometimes featured creative designs— for example, one handle is shaped in the form of a duck's head. Some of these pots still had traces of black pigment inside them at the time they were located, indicating that they may have been used for kajal.

There are also dated pictorial representations of kajal, some of which can be found on intricate murals inside India's caves. In the Ajanta rock complex in the country's Maharashtra state, murals of medieval Buddhist life suggest women and men—royals and peasants alike—applied kajal to their eyes. In one painting dating back to the fifth century, the Bodhisattva Padmapani, a young male deity, has kajal-rimmed eyes. Everyone from meditating Buddhas, dancers, and goddesses to queens, kings, maids, and commoners is brought to life in the paintings, their eyes exaggerated and elongated with wings.

As the Prophet Muhammad was said to have worn ithmid, early Muslim Arab traders who traveled to the Indian coast in the seventh century were thought to have helped spread the use of sormeh or kohl throughout the subcontinent. It may also have become more prevalent as Muslims of the Mughal dynasty from the sixteenth to the nineteenth centuries began to settle around parts of India. Separately, the *Nilamata Purana*, a religious text compiled between the sixth and seventh centuries BCE containing 1,453 verses on Kashmir's history, recommends anjana use as a form of decoration for worshippers, or as an offering to the benevolent goddess Uma, wife of the Hindu god Shiva, if one seeks prosperity.

Kajal and its production are also noted in folk songs eulogizing Lord Krishna or the goddess Lakshmi. Kajari, derived from the word for kohl in the North Indian language of Bhojpuri, is a popular form of folk dance and a genre of semiclassical singing in Uttar Pradesh and Bihar. The songs describe a woman's longing for her lover or husband as she spends her days at her family home, anticipating the meeting. "They call upon the clouds that hang low in the skies to break into showers and end the period of separation," Khandge says. "They express the pangs of separation that cause tears to wash away the kohl in the maiden's eyes, denoting the black monsoon clouds in the sky and the tearful black eyes."

"What Heaven Looks Like"

The journey of kajal and its intersection with Indian art forms is still being written today, by contemporary kathakali dancers and their peers. To an extent, it is being rewritten.

For centuries, kathakali was limited to male performers and the "high caste." It was considered socially inappropriate for girls and women given the physical effort required to train, the heaviness of costumes, and travel demands, and because most performances dragged into the late night and early morning. But as societal norms shifted, in 1975, a group of women in Kerala came together to form Tripunithura Vanitha Kathakali Sangam, an all-female kathakali troupe. The ensemble still performs today, inspiring many to become kathakali dancers; others have since followed suit. Instead of men prettifying themselves to look more feminine and become female characters—using the upturned wings of kajal as a tool—women began dressing up as female characters (and performing male characters, too). Roles weren't necessarily reversed; they became interchangeable.

In tandem, teachers at Kalamandalam have observed that kathakali has become even more popular over the years, and the school has seen an increase in the number of applicants. In 2021, the administration allowed girls to learn kathakali at the institution; today, of sixty kathakali students, only nine are female, but that number is expected to rise. Teachers see this as progress, given there's been no shortage of demand from girls to join Kalamandalam. Elsewhere, kathakali is more widely performed at various public arenas across India, providing opportunities for people of all religions to learn the art without having to attend a private school. Social media has also helped boost the popularity of kathakali and other classical Indian dances; there are even Instagram makeup tutorials inspired by kathakali.

Renjini, forty-nine, began learning kathakali when she was a little girl, in the decade the all-female troupe was formed. She was a child of the 1970s, continually energized by her father, who was a dedicated kathakali artist and teacher alongside his day job at a fertilizer and chemicals corporation. "I was born into this art form, and I fell in love with it," she says. "I was constantly watching kathakali, hearing kathakali, and living kathakali. I found the costumes and the makeup beautiful, so I decided it would be my career path, too." By the age of three, with kajal on her eyes, Renjini would perform in front of her two brothers and her father's students—a private audience, cheering her on.

As a little girl, Renjini was short and stout, but certainly not shy. She was talkative, fun loving, and mostly easygoing. That said, people teased her at school. Kathakali helped Renjini overcome her insecurities by allowing her to step into a character through makeup—especially kajal. "Once I put on the makeup, I felt like I was somebody else," she says, noting it takes her about forty minutes to apply the cosmetic for the stage, and far less time when she's off the stage. She wears it when she's in and out of costume, though the style and thickness vary depending on her audience.

It was virtually unheard of to see women learning kathakali in the early 1970s, "and those who did do it weren't taken seriously," Renjini says. Even so, by the time she was five, her Kalamandalam-educated father was convinced she was serious about kathakali, and so he began teaching it to her more formally. "He was a rigorous teacher and disciplined me if I didn't perform to his standard," she says. "But he was a very loving father, and even though women weren't expected to perform kathakali, at home, there were no gender differences between me and my brothers." Reversing traditional gender roles, sometimes, her mother would spend the day at her office job as an engineer, while her father looked after the children and prepared meals for the family. Renjini often found herself emulating her father: she watched him apply kajal to his eyes in awe before he started applying it to hers, and then she started doing it herself. Her favorite kathakali character was Hanuman, the Hindu monkey god, she reflects, partly because his kajal is so extreme.

As Renjini has a round face, speaks loudly, and has what she refers to as a "masculine temperament," her father felt she had the ideal appearance and personality to perform male characters instead of female ones. (Renjini says he was also short in stature, and so saw himself in her.) Today, the dancer has performed as a male so many times, her co-performers have come to view her as a man. "There is no gender in kathakali," she says. "The way we are taught, there is no difference. Everyone is treated the same. Men and women wear makeup and kajal, not just women."

As she came of age, Renjini joined the Tripunithura Vanitha

Kathakali Sangham troupe. Some of the women left the group as they attended college and started families. Others stayed. They continued to dance together, forming close bonds. Even as Renjini trained to become a lawyer, got married, and had two children, she remained committed. "I only stopped performing briefly, during the pregnancies and delivery periods, because the costumes were cumbersome," she says.

Renjini has small eyes that are enlarged with the help of kajal. "You'll never see me without kajal," she jokes before poking fun at my wings, which she says "aren't in fashion." Offstage, Renjini uses the brand Ramachandran's Ayurvedic kajal. She prefers it to alternatives because it doesn't smudge and is derived from camphor, which—like kohl in Petra—is extracted from a tree. She adds that she's been wearing some form of kajal to ward off the evil eye since her twenty-eighth day on earth, following the so-called twenty-eight-day "moon cycle," which the Hindu calendar is based on. (Amavasya, the first day of the moon cycle in Sanskrit, has been considered a powerful time period.) While both boys and girls are lathered with kajal as newborns, in Indian tradition, girls continue to wear it as they grow older, and most boys stop.

Renjini's mother used to make kajal at home, in a copper pot or on a plate held atop a flame burning ghee (clarified butter) or camphor. But Renjini says that today, she buys packaged kajal, as she's short on time. Onstage, she uses the real stuff, though. "Your eyes have to be big, and they have to be open during kathakali, and kajal helps with both," she says.

Renjini lost her father in 1998. Partly to combat her grief, she later decided to open a kathakali school—Karunakaran Smaraka Kathakali—to honor him. Today she teaches primarily girls and married women. Eventually, she stopped practicing law to commit herself fully to the school and her dancing career. "Kathakali is a passion turned profession," she says. The school also teaches makeup and, by extension, kajal application.

While recalling memories of her father, Renjini tears up, her kajal intact as she dries her eyes, not a dot of pigment on her tissue. He was a stern man as a teacher, rarely telling his daughter to her face that he appreciated her performances, but often boasting about her to strangers. It brings Renjini great joy that people remember her father when they see her perform—and though she sometimes feels burdened by the responsibility of living up to his greatness, it's a burden she has consistently been able to overcome, because becoming a kathakali artist has given her "a strong heart and even stronger eyes," she says, pointing at her kajal pot. More than once, she cites kajal's medicinal properties as the reason why she doesn't wear glasses.

Renjini insists she's sustaining not only her father's humility and his legacy as a performer, but also his beauty. Beauty, she explains, isn't superficial—it's not about a woman's face, her neck, her breasts, her stomach, or her legs. "I don't feel beauty when I'm Renjini, but I do bring beauty to my characters onstage. Kathakali performers are not normal beings, because we take our audience to beautiful places with our mudras, our body movements, and our eyes. The audience is taken somewhere else, to some other world. When you watch kathakali, it's not the person you see; it's not me, Renjini. It's the world the artist brings to you," she says.

"You've never seen what heaven looks like, but a kathakali

artist can transport heaven to your imagination. Beauty to us isn't physical; we give you the *feeling* of beauty. How do we do that? you may ask. Through the eyes. When you look at the eyes and the way they are moving, and when you look at the makeup and the kajal, you'll experience something truly beautiful, something profound."

Chapter Seven

Geisha Gaze

Mebari in Kyoto

Miehina, thirty-four, politely asks me not to film her while she's sans eyeliner. The soft-spoken woman's eyebrows are tinted auburn, her lips are painted crimson, and her face is slathered in oshiroi, a white foundation consisting of rice powder and water. The geisha, or geiko, as they're known in Kyoto, wears an elaborate wig that sits high atop her head, resembling a crown. Its sections, which fold and flow into one another, are held together by rhinestone-decorated pins. There's nothing low-key about this look, but somehow, Miehina herself is low-key—borderline chill. Although the geiko has had a good night's sleep, she says something's amiss absent eyeliner. "I don't look the same, I'm not yet presentable," she chuckles. "I look a bit stupid right now, like I'm lost! A woman's eyes without eyeliner look lazy."

After offering me tea, soup, and nibbles, including battered shrimp, daisy-shaped crackers lined with seaweed, and mizu yokan, a red bean jelly dessert, she disappears behind a curtain to fetch her makeup. The padded layers of her kimono, which is white with pinstripes and delicately decorated with flowers, trail behind her as she glides from room to room of the quaint teahouse in the Miyagawa-cho district of Kyoto.

When she reappears, she rests one floral cloth on the wooden floor table and another on her chest. From the makeup bag, she draws pots of blacks, reds, and pinks. With her left hand, she raises a mirror. And with her right, she starts dotting the corners of her eyelids with peach-colored eyeshadow. "I have no desire to get married, but I'm not against it," she says casually, almost cavalierly, as she dabs the pigment on with a bamboo brush. "If the right person comes along, great. If not, also great."

Marriage would mean Miehina would have to give up her career as a geiko, a centuries-old hospitality profession centered on hosting and entertaining by providing luxury experiences, including serving seasonal foods, flower arranging, dancing, singing, playing instruments, and making conversation (*geisha* translates to "person of the arts"). Miehina enjoys her job, but not so much that she can't fathom walking away—it's "just a job," after all.

The geiko dips an applicator into a pot of water and then into the red powder to catch the pigment before elegantly lining the edges of her eyes with it, a practice known as mebari or mehajiki. Mebari is like contemporary eyeliner use in that it stencils the eyes. But, when using red pigment, mebari differs in that it isn't intended solely to accentuate the eyes, but also to protect them. Miehina says she's so used to applying heavy makeup, it's become second nature to her: she's comfortable doing it in private and in company and adapts quickly to the lighting in new environments.

While it used to take her an hour to get ready earlier in her career, today it takes her half that time. Back then, makeup helped buoy her confidence as she struggled with acne. Though she hated touching her face, she appreciated how the products directed attention to her eyes and eyeliner.

The shades of geisha makeup—red, black, and white—are traditional Japanese colors, which tend to be used in local art and beyond. As is the case with India's kathakali performers and drag queens everywhere, thick layers of contrasting pigments allow audiences to see the faces of the geisha clearly, even from a distance. According to Sumi Asahara, a researcher and journalist, geisha makeup also contributes to a "sense of otherworldliness," which enhances the clients' feeling that they have been transported away from their daily lives and into another dimension.

The makeup application doesn't stop at the face—the nape of Miehina's neck is painted white, excluding a small portion of it, which is shaped like a W. While the whiteness elongates the neck and gives the illusion of a mask, this hint of bare skin gestures toward what lies beneath. The skin exposure, like Miehina's eyes—which peer out from under a heavy layer of makeup—reminds observers that there is a woman carrying a multitude of stories behind the aesthetic.

The World of Geisha

Geisha first emerged in areas including Yoshiwara, a red-light district in Tokyo, roughly during the middle of Japan's Edo period, which stretched between 1603 and 1867. The earliest geisha were male; their role was to assist sex workers by dancing and playing the shamisen, a three-stringed traditional instrument. These male geisha were called houkan and were focused less on appearance and beauty, and more on providing comical or otherwise entertaining performances.

Female geisha originated in Fukagawa, Tokyo, and were unlicensed; their purpose was to charm guests by singing and dancing. After an incident in which dozens of geisha were arrested for engaging in sex work, the government decided to provide licenses to geisha in Yoshiwara on the condition their roles and the roles of high-ranking courtesans known as oiran be formally divided and regulated. Geisha were permitted to sell 芸 (art or performance) and oiran were permitted to sell 色 (color; a metaphor for the body or sex). The distinction between the two was communicated through physical signals such as hairstyles and how kimono sashes were tied.

During the Second World War, geisha worked in factories to support the war effort; their number soon after started to dwindle. Throughout an era of postwar economic resurgence, the trade flourished, however, reaching a peak in popularity in the 1950s and 1960s, Asahara says. Eventually, with the import of Western forms of entertainment such as bars and nightclubs, geisha services became less popular. Fewer people were attracted to what now seemed like an outdated profession; these shiny new recreation options were far cheaper and, as a result, more accessible to the wider population (similar to today, the cost of a geisha's services varied depending on her popularity).

The early 1990s were among the most challenging years for geisha. Then prime minister Morihiro Hosokawa declared that ryotei, exclusive Japanese restaurants that geisha frequented, were "evil," as meetings between politicians there sometimes resulted in corrupt deals. In response, politicians stopped convening at geisha houses. "This had a significant impact on revenue and forced geisha to open doors to a wider group and target new consumers, including women and tourists," Asahara explains.

Over the course of the COVID-19 pandemic, the geisha industry faced another downturn due to social distancing rules and travel restrictions that kept tourists, who were a reliable source of income, out of the country. As of late 2022, however, it had once again gained its footing as a form of middle- and upper-class entertainment. Everyone from sumo wrestlers, Kabuki actors, tourists, businessmen, and young women interested in traditional Japanese arts and makeup patronized teahouses. And hiring a geisha is generally more affordable today than it was in the past. While the cost can run anywhere from hundreds to thousands of dollars, depending on the geisha, a visit aimed toward tourists can set them back around ¥5,000, or about US$38. That said, the broader industry is still in decline. In Japan, prior to the Second World War, there were some eighty thousand geisha across the country, many of them concentrated in Kyoto; today there are only about one thousand. (By 2020, there were just three hundred geiko and maiko in Kyoto combined, and that number had dropped further to about two hundred in late 2022.)

Geiko and their apprentices, maiko, are still beloved in this charming Japanese city. Images of maiko with subtly lined eyes can be found all over—on notepads, hand towels, key chains, and posters in train stations. Pre-pandemic, tourists and fans of maiko could engage in cosplay and get their makeup done at photo booths. In 2023, Netflix released a nine-part series titled *The Makanai: Cooking for the Maiko House*, adapted from the manga *Kiyo in Kyoto: From the Maiko House* by Aiko Koyama. The series tells the story of two young friends who move to Kyoto to become maiko, but ultimately go their separate ways. According to the academic Jan Bardsley, contemporary depictions of maiko have changed for the better, offering women more agency as performers of femininity in millennial Japan. Typically, maiko undertake a four- to five-year apprenticeship, often from the ages of fifteen to twenty, in which they're guided by their okiya, or lodging house; the okiya pays about half a million dollars for the all-inclusive training period. The cost runs high as it encompasses years of room and board, training, and clothing and kimonos, which are made of luxurious materials such as silk. Though the elaborately coiffed maiko is essentially the city's mascot—and, to some young girls, a cultural icon—it's the geiko who are the matriarchs.

Eyes have been central to the elaborate adornment process in karyukai, the world of geisha (translated as "the flower and willow world"), with the blackness and redness of the geisha's eyeliner contrasting with their skin's whiteness. Miehina relies on eyeliner the most to accentuate her beauty both in and out of costume. "I don't have beautiful eyes," she says. "But with eyeliner, they become beautiful." Teruha, a twenty-three-year-old maiko in Tokyo, says she loves using eyeliner because it makes her eyes look bigger. (She, too, doesn't like her naturally "small" eyes; she relies on the local Mitsuyoshi brand of liner to widen them.)

Teruha is also inspired by her favorite geisha, Kyoto-based Mame-fuji, who is known for her prolific use of eyeliner. A glance at #Mamefuji on Instagram reveals portraits of a devastatingly beautiful geisha, her red liner popping over the black.

These flashes of red are crucial to the geisha aura, and not just aesthetically. They're thought to keep evil spirits from entering the body: red eyeliner wards these spirits away from the eyes, and red lipstick prevents them from entering through the mouth. Some maiko also apply red pigment to their ears, believing it makes their faces appear more youthful. In ancient times, men and women wore red makeup for spiritual and religious purposes, mainly around the eyes and mouth. Author Azusa Tatebayashi notes in her academic paper, "The Cultural Theory of Makeup," that the combination of white and red also helps faces stand out in candlelight, creating harmony; against white and black, the red adds liveliness and vibrancy to the overall look.

Geiko and maiko use stage makeup for their faces, given its durability (in the past, they likely used charcoal to draw their black lines). Though their makeup and hair seem similar at a distance, a sharp eye will notice subtle differences. Maiko wear natural hair; geiko can wear wigs. Miehina's lips are painted red, signaling she's a geiko; maiko apply lipstick to only their lower lip. Maiko wear blush, whereas geiko tend not to; a geiko's kimono is also less colorful than a maiko's. The redness around the corners of a geiko's eyes is less prominent than that of a maiko, with the black eyeliner taking precedence—many maiko either don't wear black eyeliner at all or wear it so delicately, it has a barely there look. This application style changes as the maiko rises through the ranks of her apprenticeship, with each level allowing for a little more leniency and a little more liner. According to Asahara, geisha makeup practices also vary across regions, given the geisha community's diversity in beauty ideals, traditions, and fashions.

"A Woman, like Any Other"

Harutomi, Miehina's oka-san, or geisha "mother," hovers around as we speak. Oka-san act as mentors to maiko and young geiko, managing their engagements. "Geiko look like entirely different people without eyeliner on," Harutomi, fifty-seven, says. Her memories of wearing it for the first time remain vivid even after all these years. "I was so nervous, I couldn't draw a straight line," she recalls (and speaking of lines, there isn't a wrinkle to be seen on her pristine face). "I looked like a little raccoon dog. But I felt I could see more clearly as soon as it was on. Of all makeup, eyeliner is most important. You don't have to put anything else on; as long as you've got your eyeliner, you feel sharp." She says the shape of the eye matters—depending on whether you have double eyelids, the line may be thicker or thinner, for example. (Mid-conversation, Harutomi compliments me on how I'd applied my eyeliner, and I gush. Coming from her, this is high praise.)

Megumi, a Tokyo-based geisha, says many geisha strive to attain traditional Japanese looks, which eyeliner allows them to do. "The aesthetic we try to aim for is portraits in traditional Japanese paintings or wood-block prints, with the slit, elongated eyes. Eyeliner is very effective to achieve this look—not making the eyes look wide and round but making them look longer. We tend to draw eyeliner thicker around the outer corner of the eye. [With makeup] people can reconnect with their historical roots through geisha culture and enjoy a sense of nostalgia."

To Sayuki, née Fiona Graham, a white Western woman who says she is a geisha and anthropologist by training, eyeliner is so crucial to the geisha getup, she has it tattooed on her lids. "It just makes things easier," she says. "It is one of the most important elements of geisha makeup. You've got to get it perfect. On top of the white makeup, you really can't make any mistakes." Sayuki is naturally blond and blue-eyed but uses makeup to blend into the geisha community and appear "more Japanese." She says she wears brown contact lenses when in costume and has quite literally raised her eyebrows (apparently by concealing them and redrawing them higher on her face) as hers were too close to her eyelids to look Japanese. Her lips are lined to create the geisha's trademark small, heart-shaped pout. Though not Japanese by birth, Sayuki immigrated to the country at fifteen, and is now a permanent citizen. Of her decision to enter the geisha industry, she says, "I'm participating like anyone else in the activities of the country in which I live."

After completing the red lines at the corners of her eyes, Miehina turns to black liquid eyeliner—an essential step, she says. She uses Rubotan, a heavy-duty eyeliner, as she's in costume (when she's wearing "Western-style" clothes, she uses Kate eyeliner, another Japanese brand). Miehina seamlessly applies the pigment to her upper lids with the brush applicator, going over them twice to ensure the lines are smooth. Next, she extends them far beyond the eye's edges, to meet the ends of the red liner. Using a cotton swab, she makes some tweaks, then closes her eyes and fans her mirror to dry the liquid. Finally, she draws small triangles around her tear ducts, which help elongate her eyes further. She then opens her eyes, studies herself in the mirror, and smiles. "My look is complete," she says. "I feel like I'm alive again."

Miehina is the first woman in her family to become a geiko. She hails from Kyoto's Fushimi district and was born into a middle-class family. Her older sister is an aesthetician, and her father works with sports equipment; her mother passed away when she was young. Miehina entered karyukai around junior high, when she was still a teenager—her family had a preexisting relationship with her oka-san. So, when the oka-san made the suggestion, Miehina, who then went by her birth name, thought, *Sure, why not?*

Miehina was determined to find her own path; independence was more important to her than the means through which she received it. Her reasons for being open to the profession weren't profound—why do most people do the jobs they do, she asks, noting that not everyone feels called to a particular vocation. Miehina went in with no expectations and found that she appreciated her work as she became firmly embedded in its cultural practices, which afforded her certain luxuries and experiences she wouldn't otherwise be able to access. "I thought: *Wow, I'm wearing a kimono, which most can't afford to wear. I'm meeting interesting people. I eat at the best restaurants. I travel abroad. I make myself up. I'm experiencing things most girls my age don't.*"

Teruha, by contrast, says she was interested in becoming a geisha specifically because she admired kimonos and traditional

Japanese aesthetics. Historically, per Asahara, women became geisha because they were born into underprivileged families. This created a distorted power dynamic and at times facilitated exploitation, as girls would work to pay back the debts their parents owed for borrowing money from the geisha houses. Others entered the profession because they were born into or had a connection to a geisha house, making it an obvious choice.

If Miehina seems a bit casual about her position, it's because she is—though she concedes that life as a geisha isn't all smooth sailing. Initially, she found the transition to geiko in practice overwhelming. Even makeup application felt like a drag—becoming and being a geisha is physically and mentally taxing and involves evidently endless training. When Miehina made mistakes, she ruminated over them to the point that she considered quitting the profession altogether. Now, she feels satisfied and proud—being a geiko means having more freedom than a maiko, including the ability to engage in sophisticated conversation and the option to take liberties with her appearance, such as wearing heavier eyeliner. But she's also open to trying something different down the line. (In another lifetime, given she's an introvert who "values her private time," she would've avoided hospitality, and possibly pursued a career in design or "something that doesn't deal with people," she says.) While some of Miehina's peers describe her as strict and disciplined and not the type to party, others would say she has a "cheeky" side that is revealed through flashes of humor and her razor-sharp wit.

All things being equal, the role of a geiko is like "any other job," she says. Geiko have unions and pensions. They have good days and bad days; Miehina has some clients who are great and others who try her patience. "Maybe I'm lucky, but I haven't had any truly terrible experiences," she adds. "Just a couple of drunk idiots once." Geiko get paid at the end of every month via invoices that are referred to as "love letters." (Generally, geisha salaries are standardized and kept secret, though some may earn more than others by way of gifts and tips given to them by clients.)

In her free time, Miehina turns to lighter makeup, which usually includes eyeliner. She likes reading manga, her recent favorite being *Jujutsu kaisen*, about a schoolboy who fights cursed spirits. Besides Japanese dramas, she enjoys Western films, and especially loved *Sister Act* and *The Greatest Showman*. (She asks me if I've seen *Memoirs of a Geisha* and if I liked it—yes, I say, and no—and then raises an eyebrow and says, firmly, that she doesn't concern herself with, let alone engage in, lazy Western stereotypes of the geisha community.) The gym, which she frequently visits for Pilates lessons, is the only venue where she doesn't wear eyeliner. Among her preferred musical acts are the Bee Gees and Boy George, whose elaborate eyeliner she appreciates. She enjoys karaoke and watching horse races, which she bets on "in her head." And she adores traveling—Helsinki, the Finnish capital, is one of her favorite destinations, along with New York, which "feels like being on a TV set." Though social media has been a boon for geisha, helping them dispel misconceptions and highlight the artistic aspects of their profession, Miehina avoids it because she finds it a "waste of time."

The commitment of geiko and maiko to their beauty and overall presence is greatly appreciated by Miehina—the ideal is, to her mind, "someone who's lighthearted and fun" but still poised, someone who cares about their mannerisms, elocution, facial expressions, and demeanor. "It shows in their face. That's beautiful to me—what comes from the inside," she says. She appreciates when women go to lengths to look beautiful, the beauty being in the effort itself. "When you see women wearing lots of makeup, when you see them wearing eyeliner, you can know they're proud, and that's beautiful to me," she says. Miehina places more of an emphasis on charisma and charm than physical attributes. "I'd rather be known for that than my beauty. Sure, some women might be physically beautiful, but for how long? I also hated being called 'cute' as a maiko. I wasn't 'cute.' I was a woman, like any other."

Before Miehina dances for me, she kneels on the ground, the fan placed before her. Her oka-san plays the shamisen, singing somberly to a lover who's imploring her to come and meet him. Miehina's movements are controlled—she seems almost to converse with the fan, which she opens and closes as she twists and turns. Her arms are outstretched; her movements fill the entire tatami room, which is barely eighteen square feet and covered with straw mats. Miehina seems to retreat into herself as she dances; her gaze is steady, averting mine. But occasionally, she glances over at me, her lined eyes gleaming against the soft lighting. She ends by laying the fan on the ground and bowing. "When I'm dancing, I'm focused not on myself, but the lyrics and the moves, and making my client happy," she says. "It makes me happy to know you are."

Through the Ages

Traditionally, the eyes and their gaze have been linked to authority and power in Japan. The Japanese terms 目下 (eye-below) and 目上 (eye-above) respectively—refer to subordinates and superiors, and have deep historical roots. Rulers and commanders would sit in a higher physical position than their subjects, ensuring they could look down on them. The practice of お見合い, or look and match, was used during formal marriage arrangements; it also stems from the belief that eyes have inherent power. Throughout the Edo period, men would wait around the entrances of teahouses, and women would pretend to "accidentally" pass by to exchange glances. The term 目合う, meaning "eyes interact," was a euphemism for sexual intercourse. Eye contact carried significant implications, so people were cautious about how and when they exchanged it.

Scholars typically divide Japan's history of makeup, and by extension eye makeup, into four periods: primitive, continental, traditional, and contemporary.

Primitive

Gishi Wajinden, a Chinese textbook on Japanese culture written during the Kofun period (around 300 to 538 CE), refers to the use of tattoos and the practice of ohaguro, or teeth blackening—a look maiko once sported when they debuted—as well as red makeup. Haniwa figurines from the fifth to the sixth century, which served ceremonial purposes and were buried with the dead, were covered with red pigment, especially around the cheeks and eyes. The dye was made of cinnabar and iron oxide, and the red hue was believed to protect against evil. That belief may have stemmed from heliolatry, the worship of the sun, as red is associated with the sun, fire, and blood, and thereby symbolizes life. (Shinto, an ancient religion in Japan, involves the worship of nature—the sun goddess, Amaterasu, is an important Shinto deity.)

Continental

The Asuka and Nara periods (538 to 794 AD) were marked by prolific cultural exchange with China with the help of several official Japanese missions to Tang China starting in 630. Makeup practices and cosmetics such as oshiroi and beni (rouge made of safflower) were imported into Japan along with other elements of Chinese culture and society, including Buddhism. Makeup started to serve a more ornamental and aesthetic purpose, as opposed to a superstitious one; it was used by the ruling class and signified high social status. Items such as rouge were produced in Egypt or what came to be known as the Middle East and transported to Japan through the Silk Road. These periods formed the basis of the tricolor makeup tradition in Japan.

Traditional

During the traditional makeup period, which coincided with the Heian era (794 to 1185 AD), Chinese influence eased after the series of Japanese envoys to the country came to an end in 894. Interest grew among aristocrats in pursuing a unique Japanese aesthetic, known as the kokufu or "style of Japan." Consequently, fashion, hair, and makeup practices evolved to become more distinctly local.

The Edo period, from the seventeenth century through the late nineteenth century, enjoyed political stability, economic growth, urbanization, and the widespread appreciation of culture. As makeup became more widely accessible, a focus on individual style became increasingly important, and multiple new trends emerged. As in Persia, makeup even indicated whether a woman was married or unmarried. Teeth blackening, which had, since the Heian period, been linked to a woman's coming-of-age and marriage, developed into a common practice from the middle of the Edo period onward. Women would blacken their teeth just before or after their wedding and shave off their eyebrows after birthing their first child.

Women used rouge to paint their lips and fingernails and line the corners of their eyes; the substance was so commonly worn this way, it was sold in containers such as sake cups and shells. The practice of mebari was initially popularized by Kabuki and traditional Japanese theater actors and then copied by townspeople. Women would use their ring fingers to spread the rouge around their eyes (they called this finger beni-sashi-yubi, which translates to "rouge-applying finger"). Rouge was also applied around the edges of the eyes with a brush, similar to how winged liner is applied today. Red was believed to help counter epidemics including smallpox; because of this superstition, items such as hospital clothes were sometimes dyed red. Red was also treated as a form of protection during childbirth rituals that included wrapping a newborn baby in red cloth and applying red paint to their face. It also had a place in rites of passage: the inner linings of traditional bridal outfits were red; today, many geisha, including Miehina, wear red undergarments.

Miyako fuzoku kewaiden, a beauty handbook published in 1813, advised people whose "eyes are too thin and small that they almost look shut" to "wipe their eyelids, just around the lashes, with a damp cloth [to remove some of the white powder], and apply very thin rouge," to just the upper lashes, not the lower. It was important not to be heavy-handed: eyes that appeared to be *too* big were deemed unattractive, a notable contrast to contemporary Western beauty standards. *Miyako fuzoku kewaiden* also included tips on how to make the eyes look smaller or more "moderate," which included applying white powder to one's eyelids.

Modern

Toward the end of the nineteenth century and the beginning of the twentieth, during the Meiji period, makeup practices and beauty ideals shifted once again. Under the slogans "Fortifying the country, strengthening the military," "Civilization and enlightenment," and "Out of Asia and into Europe," the Japanese government promoted westernization across various sectors of society. Teeth blackening and eyebrow shaving were banned, as such customs were perceived as "barbaric" by Westerners who visited Japan. "Natural beauty," including natural eyebrows, white teeth, and skin free from white powder, became the norm. Although it's unlikely products titled or packaged as "eyeliner" were imported into Japan at the turn of the century, actors and entertainers such as Sadayakko Kawakami, who was also a geisha, applied greasepaint around their eyes onstage, according to a curator at the Beni Museum in Tokyo.

More women joined the labor force throughout the Taishō period of 1912 to 1926. Like Western women, Japanese women proactively began using makeup to express their individuality. The pressure to look "Western" intensified, with women aiming for bigger eyes and three-dimensional features, as opposed to smaller eyes and "flat" facial features, as was the tradition in previous depictions of beautiful women. This shift led to a growing interest in makeup that helped emphasize specific parts of the face by creating shadows. Among the most popular tools for this purpose was eyeliner.

The emergence of moga, or modan gaaru (modern girls), seemed to signify a new era for women's liberation. These young Japanese women enjoyed experimenting with fashion, wore their hair short, thinned out their eyebrows, and began to apply eyeshadow and eyeliner more heavily. Eyeliner could now be seen extending beyond the corners of the eyes out toward the temples, imitating the styles of Hollywood starlets. That said, from the Meiji to the late Taishō period, eyeliner was still primarily regarded as stage makeup or "evening" makeup, and wasn't yet sought after among the general population.

In the early 1910s, the Takarazuka Revue, an all-female musical theater troupe, was founded. The ensemble, whose performances include Western and Japanese plays and adaptations of films and love stories, enjoys an immense, almost cultlike popularity to this day. The concept of Takarazuka is associated with a "dream world" that transports viewers into another land, with actors performing both female and male roles. Older members of the troupe teach younger members how to do their makeup; eyeliner application depends on the performers' roles but tends to be bold. In Japanese plays, for example, performers would apply geisha-style makeup, lining the corners of their eyes with red, according to Ewa Barylińska, a researcher on Takarazuka culture. Gender also plays a part: male roles require eyeliner to create the illusion of a double eyelid, and the pigment is also applied to the lower waterline. Meanwhile, female roles require round eyes to achieve a "cute" effect, so eyeliner is applied only to the upper waterline or lid to make the performer's eyes appear more open.

In the early 1920s, Japanese women's magazines and beauty handbooks began to feature makeup practices that mimicked eyeliner use. Some instructed women to use rouge or eyebrow ink around the corners of their eyes to accentuate them, to practice mebari by applying ink at the roots of the eyelashes, and to use a smidgen of pencil at the edges of the eyes for evening events. One even instructed women to keep their eyes wide open "when creating mebari with eyebrow ink" to allow them to "draw a clear line towards the corner of the eyes." While packaged eyeliner products weren't yet widely available, people turned to traditional makeup tools such as ink or even artists' pencils to draw lines at the corners of their eyes. During this time, according to the Beni Museum, people still referred to eyeliner use as mebari.

By the end of the Shōwa period, in 1989, the makeup industry was thriving in Japan, and shops offered women a slew of new and modern products, which varied in type and quality. This was a welcome development. During the Second World War, makeup was prohibited as a luxury. In 1939, the Ministry of Education specifically barred female students from wearing lipstick, white powder, and blush. However, like Western women during the war, and like the ancient Egyptians before them, Japanese women were committed and resourceful, and used materials such as burnt matches to draw their eyebrows and darken their eyes.

Before the war, makeup use was still limited to those with a keen interest in trends and fashion; after the war, it became ubiquitous. The postwar US occupation and presence of US forces in Japan had a significant impact on makeup and style. Western cultural icons and celebrities became beauty idols—in the 1950s, many Japanese women imitated the hairstyle and makeup of Audrey Hepburn, including her trademark winged eyeliner and thick eyebrows. Though eyebrow ink was still likely being used as a substitute for eyeliner products, by the middle of the decade, the term *eyeliner* appeared for the first time in beauty magazines. Foreign and local products flooded the market, and cosmetics ads drew consumers' attention to the importance of the eye. In 1967, British model Twiggy visited Japan; her miniskirts and catchy eye makeup, which included double eyeliner and false eyelashes, shot to fame. To further emphasize the eyes, women thinned their eyebrows into near oblivion.

At the beginning of the 1990s, following the burst of Japan's so-called bubble economy, makeup wearing was relatively restrained and muted, with women turning only to foundation and lipstick as staple items, reflecting a deep sense of malaise triggered by economic stagnation, according to research conducted by the writer Kaori Ishida. But makeup practices began to rebound once more in the mid-1990s, with the emergence of the joshi kosei or "high school girl" aesthetic (previously, most Japanese women did not wear makeup until they graduated from high school). Researchers including Ishida have attributed these distinct makeup trends to the desire to foster a sense of individuality during tumultuous times. Media coverage of youth trends featured high school girls hanging out in the trendy Shibuya or Harajuku areas of Tokyo, decked out in the latest fashions and makeup styles. Their eyes were overly done, their lashes long and curled, their lips glossy, and their hair bleached. This "high school girl" aesthetic grew more daring as teens experimented with their looks, using fake (and sometimes colorful) eyelashes with black eyeliner to contour their eyes. High school girls also dabbled in what came to be known as the yamamba, or "mountain witch," trend, named after a Japanese folklore figure. The look entailed artificially and heavily tanned skin, white eyeshadow, and black eyeliner. Eyes emerged as the focal point for aesthetics among Japanese women of all ages by the turn of the century, with the slang term 目力, or "eye power," becoming prevalent.

The ageha, or "swallowtail butterfly," look of the noughties focused on デカ目メイク, a style that featured pronounced eye makeup to make the eyes look two to three times bigger than their natural size—with the help of copious amounts of eyeliner and mascara. The aesthetic was inspired by Japan's hostess club culture, and it emphasized exaggeration: in addition to applying heavy makeup, women added significant volume to their hair. According to Ishida, the growing focus on "eye power" was partly spurred by westernization and the proliferation of Western beauty ideals, as well as the idea that people would need to improve their appearances if they were to optimize their lives and be successful in their careers.

Some of these intense makeup styles can still be spotted, particularly in Tokyo's Harajuku district. But often, they're regarded as trends of the past. As of 2023, eye makeup in Japan, by comparison, seems to be more neutral and understated. Researchers at the Shiseido Japanese Beauty Institute have attributed these shifts in behavior to the Great East Japan Earthquake and tsunami of 2011, which left over fifteen thousand people dead.

Analysts have observed that during a national time of confusion, mourning, healing, and recovery following a large-scale disaster, lighter makeup has felt more appropriate. Makeup colors are more likely to include softer shades of pink, brown, and white over black and other stark colors; pencil eyeliner is preferred over liquid eyeliner to impart a delicate look. Making eyes look tareme, or "drooping" and "downturned," with the outer corner of the eye appearing lower than the inner corner, also became a popular practice.

Westernization and successive natural and economic disasters may suggest a dilution of distinct Japanese styles—at least on the surface. But many traditional techniques have persisted in creative communities, including among geisha. And with the help of social media, which has encouraged more cross-pollination than ever before when it comes to sourcing beauty inspiration, young Japanese women have created their own bold aesthetics, drawing from multiple trends, cultures, countries, and periods, responding to trying times in distinctive ways.

"Exploring Different Styles"

On a hot and humid late August afternoon, along the bustling Takeshita Street in Tokyo's Harajuku district, Japanese youth are decked out in the latest and edgiest visual kei / kawaii culture couture. Away from the main streets of Tokyo, where millennial and older women dress in more minimalist clothing and makeup, their platform shoes defy gravity. There's not a pair of skinny jeans or mom jeans in sight; low-rise baggy jeans and ultra-mini pleated skirts have taken over. Purses plastered with prints of Miffy, the popular cartoon of a rabbit, are carried without the slightest hint of irony. Phone cases have Pikachu ears. Face masks are striped, starred, and spotted. Gen Z hairstyles display dashes of purple and pink, often with matching eyeliner and eyeshadow combinations. The eyeliner is ubiquitous—there are red graphic lines extending to the temples, bat wings, neon-green fishtails stenciled with glitter, and amber floating creases. (I feel dreadfully outdated in my tapered denim and Amy Winehouse wings.) Striped shirts are tied diagonally across the chest, and fanny packs are nowhere near bums. The odd male goth with black smoky eyes makes the occasional appearance. Vintage tees with anime characters are matched with tartan skirts and Converse shoes. EarPods are out; wired headphones are in.

A subway ride away, at downtown Tokyo's Don Quijote, a multilevel department store selling everything from strawberry cheesecake–flavored Kit Kats to spatulas, an entire section is devoted to eyeliner. There are shelves of blues, greens, and oranges, featuring offerings from local brands, including D-Up Silky Liquid Eyeliner (my favorite shade is Pistachio Latte, a brownish green) and Flowfushi's Uzu Eye Opening Liner, whose brown-black shade lasted a full eighteen hours on me, smudge-free, even in 87 percent humidity. The product adopts the traditional Japanese brush known as the kumano, which is firm, yet flexible. MSH Love Liner Liquid and Heroine Make SP Smooth Liquid Eyeliner are also popular, the latter's sales pitch being "You must cry beautifully" (as the liner is long-lasting and waterproof).

In addition to lining their lids, Japanese women contour their under-eye areas with eyeliner or eyebrow pencils to make their eyes appear more three-dimensional. In Japanese, eye bags, or namida-bukuro, are referred to as tear bags—both men and women in the country use cosmetics to emphasize shadows and add highlights and glitter to the under-eye area, while making it look puffy. These products are called namida-bukuro liners; examples include Tear Eye Liner by Etude (a Korean brand popular in Japan), and the Saem Saemmul Under Eye Maker. Also in demand are double-sided products with dark-colored pencils to add shadows at one end, and highlighter or glitter to add sparkle at the other. "I draw the shades [onto my eye bags] with eyeliner to make them look more three-dimensional," twenty-seven-year-old Mika says. The product is "really subtle but adds the shades in a natural way."

Sayaka, twenty-six, says she wears eyeliner daily and turned to it during the pandemic for comfort. "I've been wearing less lipstick and blush because of mask wearing, but eye makeup is a must whenever leaving the house," she says. Sayaka, who works for a marketing firm in Tokyo, uses a combination of gel eyeliner and liquid eyeliner for her wings, but has yet to find her signature look: "I'm exploring different styles to figure out what works best," she says. Sayaka personally wants to make her eyes look bigger and more lifted—they're "slanted downward" and she's trying to "fix that with wings." She's so committed to getting her lines right and flattering her eyes to the best of her ability that she's started attending one-on-one classes to learn how best to make them up. "I feel much more confident after starting these lessons," she says. Sayaka also likes watching the show *Glow Up* on Netflix to compare makeup styles in Japan with those of the West, and has even made a habit of looking up YouTube videos of geisha to watch how they apply their makeup. "It's very otherworldly—the kind of makeup you'd never do in real life."

When people hear the term *Asian beauty*, local women say, they think of narrow and elongated eyes. But Japanese women tend to favor big eyes, according to a 2019 survey conducted by the Shiseido Japanese Beauty Institute. For the survey, Japanese women were asked what they thought the most "beautiful" eye shape was, with 46.6 percent saying "bright eyes with double eyelids," 24 percent responding "almond-shaped eyes," and 14.7 percent answering "round eyes." The preference for this wide, bright-eyed look relates to the kawaii, or culture of "cuteness," in Japan, which can be found in everything from anime characters to mascots such as Hello Kitty and Pikachu. To make eyes look bigger, women use techniques such as emphasizing or feigning the look of double eyelids, which sometimes involves the use of tools such as tape and glue.

Before starting her makeup lessons, Sayaka was paranoid about the "Japanese idea that wearing heavy makeup is bad," she says. "I used to associate it with kyabajo [hostesses] or gyaru [a countercultural group of young girls with excessive makeup, who are seen as vulgar or kitschy]. While in Western countries, wearing heavy makeup can be seen as 'gorgeous,' in Japan, we use negative terms like *kebai* [showy and loud] to describe it. Whenever I flick through Japanese magazines, all the makeup influencers talk about wearing 'natural/subtle makeup,' or wearing makeup in a way that nobody can tell. But I always liked heavier makeup."

The makeup of K-pop stars, especially the Blackpink girls' pop group, and K-beauty trends in general, have impacted Japanese makeup culture. With the rise of K-pop in Japan, Korean cosmetics and makeup styles, or the Japanese interpretation of Korean makeup, have gained traction. While its popularity decreased after initially peaking in 2011 and 2012, the K-beauty look started to gain momentum again circa 2015. The aesthetic involves liquid eyeliner to create a sharp wing or cat eye, as well as natural, straight eyebrows coupled with pale skin and tinted red lips.

"For every album or new single, Blackpink changes their looks entirely," Aki, who imitates their makeup, says. The twenty-seven-year-old watches YouTube channels offering makeup tips on their style and uses colored liner in the summer and darker colors in the winter. "When I was in school, the dominant trends in Japan were gyaru or Japanese girl groups like AKB48, which look innocent or childish," she says. "I wanted to look more mature—Korean beauty looked more adultlike." The life span of beauty trends is much shorter in Korea, she adds, with new styles constantly cropping up, making dabbling in the country's fashion more exciting. "Korean idol culture is my window into makeup and other beauty practices. I use liquid eyeliner from different Korean brands. Eyeliner gives me confidence. I also want to make my eyes look elongated—that's iconic of Korean beauty," she says. "In Japan, they like round, cute eyes. In Korea, they like the sharper, cooler, or more mature look."

Twenty-seven-year-old Kanako, from Tokyo, rejects both the Korean and Japanese eyeliner aesthetics. As she couldn't wear eyeliner at school due to strict rules banning makeup, she started in college. "My goal was to have 'big eyes'; I was trying to follow Japanese beauty standards, which put Westerners on a pedestal," she recalls. "I used lots of black liquid eyeliner and wore fake eyelashes. I used to love Western Caucasian or Middle Eastern faces, where they have very defined facial features—that's what most Japanese like."

That approach changed when Kanako lived abroad and decided to focus less on matters such as single or double eyelids and more on developing her personal style. As she watched YouTube videos that taught makeup application techniques designed for East Asian faces, she began exploring what worked best for her. Finally, she opted for a subtle look and wears brown lines instead of black. "I do my eyeliner at the end [of my routine], but that final touch makes my face look sharper," she says. "For instance, when I walk into the office, I feel like I need eyeliner. When I go out in the evenings, I draw thicker eyeliner." Kanako seems to be rebelling against what she perceives as "homogeneous" beauty standards in Japan, including large eyes and pale skin. Korean beauty trends heavily influence Japanese women, she says, and "are even more homogeneous. They have natural eyebrows but intense eyeliner."

Yoko, twenty-eight, from Tokyo, also keeps her eyeliner light after spending years drawing harsh lines. "I just draw on the waterline, a technique my sister taught me," she says. "That's enough to make your eyes look bigger. In Japan, people aspire to look like someone they're not—people wear lots of eye makeup to make their eyes look much bigger than they are. I don't want to look like someone I'm not; that would make me feel very insecure."

Across Genders

Eyeliner isn't limited to women in Japan—the use of cosmetics among men dates back to the end of the Heian period. Male nobles of the court imitated women's makeup, and the application of white pigment to their faces became popular due to the era's stately architecture. As tall eaves blocked out the sunlight, the interiors of these buildings were dark, and the white powder helped men's faces stand out. Men also drew their eyebrows high on their foreheads to help elongate their faces and convey a sense of authority. Throughout the late Heian to the Kamakura period (1185 to 1333), warriors wore makeup during combat so their faces would look beautiful—in the event that they were decapitated.

Over the Edo period, makeup use spread from the ruling class to those in the entertainment industry, including Kabuki actors, geisha, and sex workers, and then eventually to commoners. Men were less likely to wear makeup during the Meiji period, as gender roles were solidified to enhance the nation's productivity; men's bodies were for serving the labor force and the army, according to the culture site Wakaru Web, and makeup was a practice intended and designed for women, who were assigned more nurturing, domestic roles.

Kabuki, a traditional form of Japanese theater, was performed by men and women until women were banned from the art in 1629, as the industry was thought to have links to sex work, and the shogunate was worried it was corrupting public values. Today, male actors perform both male and female characters (female Kabuki performers exist, though they are a tiny minority). Kabuki performances are highly stylized, their costumes glamorous, and their makeup, known as kumadori, highly elaborate. Similar to kajal in kathakali, eyeliner features heavily in the Kabuki aesthetic as it has the power to determine the desired gender of the actor as well as the character's personality traits, such as common or noble, evil or good, and brave or cowardly. Various colors have different implications, too: red symbolizes courage, justice, and strength; blue signifies coldness, holding grudges, and jealousy; and brown symbolizes animals or spirits.

Hiroto Murasawa, a cosmetics researcher, says the more modern use of men's makeup gained traction in the 1980s. Still, it was limited almost exclusively to celebrities and men in the entertainment and creative industries. Researchers have attributed the mainstream use of makeup products among men who *aren't* creatives to the aftermath of the economic recession of the 1990s and the shifts in understanding of masculine identity that came with it.

The government predicted in its 2021 report on the future of the cosmetics industry that men's or unisex makeup and grooming products will grow to become the norm within a decade. In tandem, cosmetic giants such as Shiseido and DHC have launched separate lines of products for men. The growth potential is promising—the men's cosmetic market grew from ¥600 billion (US$4.6 billion) to an estimated ¥623 billion between 2018 to 2019, according to the research company Fuji Keizai Group.

Prevailing beautification practices among men align with popular "self-help" narratives, says Christopher Tso, a researcher at the University of Cambridge. Instead of simply working at a company and earning wages, in the early 2000s, men were now expected to foreground self-optimization in every area of their lives. To level up one's appeal, personal "brand," and social status, men have begun to invest extra effort into grooming and using makeup to hide perceived flaws and, consequently, "increase their likability." As these men are also concerned about transgressing traditional gender norms, they tend to be somewhat secretive about what they use, the end goal being to conceal imperfections rather than to stand out or express themselves, Tso says. And even if these men do choose to wear eyeliner to augment their eyes, Tso suspects they would feel reluctant to admit it at the risk of appearing overtly effeminate.

Despite these pressures, there is a demand for male influencers who offer makeup tutorials, and Instagrammers such as Kondo Yohdi and Hiroki Takahashi have garnered considerable followings instructing men on how to wear eyeliner in undetectable ways. Their tutorials suggest men apply eyeliner to the inner rims of their eyes, fill in gaps between their eyelashes, and wear a brown product that blends well with one's skin tone so these enhancements are less obvious. They also recommend applying a subtle amount of eyeliner to create the illusion of a crease on their eyelids or to accentuate their eye bags, in the same way scores of Japanese women do.

The "genderless" subculture has offered men interested in makeup and clothing a haven for self-exploration. For example, to enhance the eyes, Takahashi encourages men to use brown eyeliner and apply pearly eyeshadow. Like Aki, many of these young men are fascinated with K-pop stars, and closely follow Korean celebrities' makeup styles and K-beauty trends.

Kodo Nishimura, a Buddhist monk, makeup artist, and

LGBTQIA+ activist, says that while he was interested in embracing makeup—especially eyeliner—as a young man in Japan, whenever he went to a makeup store, he was asked if he was shopping for his "mother or girlfriend," and could never share that it was for himself. Nishimura grew up admiring Disney princesses and the Japanese manga *Sailor Moon*; he hated what he referred to as his "Japanese-looking" eyes. "In Japan, you grow up with rigid notions of beauty, such as the need to have big eyes and double eyelids," he says. So when Riyo Mori, a Japanese woman, became Miss Universe in 2007, Nishimura was shocked—he could never have imagined someone who was not blond and blue-eyed being considered beautiful on a global stage. He deeply appreciated that her makeup didn't hide her natural features; she wasn't trying to make her eyes look "bigger" or use double-eyelid tape, like many Japanese.

Nishimura couldn't always buy eyeliner comfortably. But with multiple shifts in his personal life—among them moving to the US and starting design school—and broader societal changes such as the rise of LGBTQIA+ awareness, he began to embrace the cosmetic. When he moved to the US, he noticed transgender people and drag queens wearing makeup and shopping at cosmetics stores like Sephora. The first eyeliner he ever bought was by CoverGirl; he chose the brand because he's a fan of Drew Barrymore, who modeled for them. He loved her performance in the 2000 film *Charlie's Angels*, and "admired her for being strong," whereas he felt he could never speak up for himself. At Parsons School of Design, where he studied, he began wearing heels and experimenting with fashion and makeup.

Today, as a makeup artist, Nishimura draws inspiration from

drag queens and their extravagant eyeliner, though he never wears makeup when performing rituals as a monk. He approaches makeup as one might approach cooking—by assessing tools and ingredients and creating something out of them based on one's mood (to build a solid eye look, he uses eyeliner pencil as a base, liquid liner to accentuate the eye shape, and waterproof liner on the waterline). Whereas previously, he just wanted to make his eyes look bigger, now he says it's all about "achieving balance": "Eyeliner is like salt," he says, in that it "accentuates what's already there," while colors are like "spices," adding flavor to the overall look.

Eitaro Matsunoya, thirty-five, isn't fazed when asked what it's like to be Japan's only male geisha who performs as a female. He was born into an okiya, and his late mother, Mariko Matsunoya, was a geisha, too. His life has been shaped by geisha culture—so much so that gender seems almost irrelevant to his ethos.

"Male and female distinctions don't matter to me; I don't see myself as special for being a male geisha," he says. "I'm purely pursuing this path because I like the culture and want it to survive in the future. What matters most is that geisha culture becomes widely appreciated and something that people are more familiar with."

Eitaro grew up watching his mother immerse herself in the geisha aesthetic and started practicing geisha performances and dabbling in makeup when he was just six years old. He first performed for clients when he was ten, hiding that he was a male (he's unable to conceal his gender these days, given he's become "bigger and more masculine" with age). "Sexism against women and male dominance is a widespread issue in Japanese society," he says. "But my mother and I usually joked that we deal with female dominance in geisha culture."

When Eitaro was twenty-three, his mother, who was dedicated to reviving the local geisha community amid years of decline, passed away after a long battle with cancer. "I'm not sure I would've pursued this path had my mother been healthy and still alive," he says. "I supported my family and mother economically and had to run the business." As a direct consequence, Eitaro took on his mother's role as the master of the Matsunoya geisha house in Tokyo's Omori port district. He inherited her ambition to promote and revitalize geisha culture, while also facing pushback due to his gender.

Omori, where Eitaro was born, was one of Tokyo's most prosperous geisha communities during the Meiji to early Shōwa periods. There used to be over three hundred geisha in the area at its peak, whereas today, there are only around four okiya and roughly fifteen geisha. But thanks to Eitaro, the area has received extensive media coverage.

Eitaro identifies as a cisgender male but feels when he's in costume, like drag queens, he transforms into a female. "The act of wearing geisha makeup is powerful; it has a magical power, in a sense. It affects your feelings and soul. You change dramatically," he says. "That's why it feels as if your soul is being 'drained' or [that makeup is] taking away your natural self. It's shocking and impactful. It pulls your soul into another dimension. It almost made me feel like I could no longer be a man, and I felt this strongly even as a child. Many of these makeup practices are based on tradition and have historical roots, but personally, I feel like it's becoming a form of self-expression."

One of Eitaro's most vivid childhood memories was when his mother would apply eyeliner to his lids. He often fell asleep when she did, so when his head jerked or twitched, the eyeliner would "go all over the place." "It's not like normal makeup where all you have to do is remove the eyeliner," he says. "You have white makeup on, so that's also ruined. Then you have to start all over again, so sometimes my mother would get mad at me."

Eyeliner is the key to geisha makeup, Eitaro says. When onstage, he wears "thick" eyeliner; sometimes, he uses modern applicators, but other times, he uses traditional makeup tools or paintbrushes. The transformation to female is so stark that when out of costume, Eitaro refrains from wearing makeup altogether, including eyeliner, to help him revert to his male sense of self, and his private life, as a husband and father. "The act of wearing makeup almost blurs your natural identity," he says. "I really had to make sure to separate my daily life from it. Otherwise, it was tormenting my heart."

The change is aesthetic *and* spiritual, he explains. "Japan is a polytheistic culture. Compared to Western dance, like ballet, where performers tend to look up, like standing on your toes to reach out to the heavens, Japanese dance usually looks down," he says. "We step on the ground firmly, and it also links to how we have harvest festivals: gods are on the ground. Japanese traditional performance has this kind of spiritual significance, and of course geisha—and the way they wear their makeup and their eyeliner—are a part of this."

While I was traveling in Japan to conduct research and reporting for this book in August 2022, the country seemed virtually free of Western tourists—and resultantly the Western gaze—due to COVID-19 travel restrictions. As I moved around, cognizant of my own gaze, it struck me that there were pockets of beauty and godliness in practically every corner of every city, from the tatami room and the temple to the most unexpected places.

This feeling overwhelmed me as I observed two hundred photographs at an exhibit titled *Family Portraits: Bonds Torn Apart* in the Hiroshima National Peace Memorial Hall. The images taken before the 1945 atomic bombings of Hiroshima and Nagasaki displayed smiling women with their families. Some of their eyes were made up, especially the geisha, their mebari visible from a distance, even with the graininess of the pictures. A young Japanese woman peered at one of these photos for some time, her eyes lined in red and purple, pops of color in an otherwise somber setting that served as a stark reminder of an immense tragedy.

Despite the time periods setting them apart, I considered the line connecting the two women, and the centuries-old cultural practices uniting them. And in that line, beyond the pigment on their faces, I saw an unshakable and profound beauty—one that had been untouched by time and tragedy alike.

Chapter Eight

"Naked without It"

*Drag and the Transformative
Power of Eyeliner*

My makeup bag. The passport that contains a bunch of crèmes, potions, polyfilla, and over-the-counter drugs that diminish the muscles of an overbearing gender binary, allowing me to wrestle it down, even just for a night. These tools are the hardware that allows me to finally live out my childhood fantasies, every one. They're also margin comments in a history book, connecting me to the radical queens, queers, butch dykes, and trans folk who fought for me to be able to paint my face the way I want to paint it and wear it out in the world.

—CRYSTAL RASMUSSEN, DRAG QUEEN

I think of eyeliner as building a house of bricks.
You start from the base and then you go up.

—MATHIAS ALAN, MAKEUP ARTIST

Lucia Fuchsia

As Lucia Fuchsia takes to the stage in her amber silk gown, lip-synching the opening lyrics to Queen's "Bohemian Rhapsody," she seems nervous. Her platinum-blond wig is blown out to the ceiling. Her winged eyeliner, exaggerated with gray strokes, is so extreme you might telescopically see it from space. Today is a big day for the drag queen—she's competing for the Entertainer of the Year title at the fifty-fifth Miss Fire Island contest.

Lucia's mother is in the crowd, beaming with pride as her child confesses, per Freddie Mercury, that she's just killed a man. At twenty-two, she's one of the youngest contestants—the eldest is ninety. The beauty and talent pageant, held on this tiny strip of land lined with protected beaches just off Long Island, brings together dozens of drag queens—and this year, drag kings—from New York and beyond. Here is an opportunity for these performers to parade their carefully prepared hair, makeup, outfits, and lip-synching skills. Here is a sanctuary for them to find community, to step away from adversity, homophobia, and transphobia and into an event whose sole goal is to celebrate them in all their glory. Here, Lucia feels she belongs.

The queens exude an energy that is so potent that the audience is briefly transported away from the harrowing realities of the previous pandemic year, and into a colorful universe of all things fabulous. Each look is strikingly inventive, but all of the competitors are wearing eyeliner. You might even call it an eyeliner extravaganza.

Lucia's makeup is immaculate. Her contour sharpens her already sharp nose and elevates her already pronounced cheekbones, its terra-cotta hue bringing out the peach-pink color of her plump lips. Her eyeliner is presented to us like a layer cake. At the top, just below her drawn-in eyebrow, is a line of light gray; below that, a luminous line of white; below that, a line of darker gray; and below that, a thick line of black that rests just above a set of even thicker upper lashes, magnified by falsies. The liner doesn't stop there: on the lower lash line is another dash of white that meets the upper line seamlessly. "Eyeliner is everything," Lucia says of her commitment to the product. "I just wouldn't be able to be Lucia without it. Eyeliner is the anchor, it's what makes everything make sense."

In drag aesthetics, eyeliner is the crown that completes a queen's attire, the star atop a Christmas tree, the diamond on an engagement ring, a chef's kiss. "Just think of a clown—a clown would look *crazy* without that red smile," Lucia says. "Drag makeup just doesn't make sense until you put on the eyeliner. It holds everything together." Lucia is so in love with her eyeliner, in fact, that she has a tattoo of a heavily lined eye with wispy eyelashes on her right bicep.

When she's out of drag, the tattoo serves as a reminder of the confidence her makeup brings her, the pride she takes in her profession, and her ability to transcend her insecurities and shift genders (she also has a tattoo of the singer-songwriter Frank Ocean—her queer idol—and another that reads "enjoy the journey").

Lucia's platinum-blond bouffant and decorated eyes are balanced out by the extravagance of the lengthy gold chandelier earrings that meet her shoulders, her bejeweled neck, and the sparkling cuffs and circular clasp of her cutout dress. Her bare chest is flecked with glitter that glimmers under the stage lights and outdoors under the September sun. The choice of the song "Bohemian Rhapsody" is, in and of itself, unique; the other drag queens lip-synch to classics by female divas such as Celine Dion and Whitney Houston. But somehow, despite all the statements Lucia is making, she comes across as subtle, shy, and humble—she may even underestimate her quiet power.

The contest has drawn spectators from Manhattan and around the country, coinciding with the twentieth anniversary of the 9/11 attacks. (Some of the contestants have marked the anniversary with ink on their clothing, including "never forget" and a silhouette of the Manhattan skyline, with the Twin Towers. The event opened with a solemn rendition of "The Star-Spangled Banner," followed by "The Ballad of Miss Fire Island," a classic anthem of the pageant.) Soon after the official opening, the beer and tequila begin to flow: "The more you drink, the more you're going to have fun today," says the MC. Within minutes, empty plastic cups are strewn on the ground. As the pageant's judges arrive, the venue swells with songs by eyeliner-wielding singers such as Ariana Grande, Lady Gaga, and Madonna.

Fire Island has historically been a haven for the LGBTQIA+ community; approaching it by ferry on this late summer's day, from a distance, one could see a large pride and trans flag, hoisted on its shores and fluttering alongside an American flag. The pageant was born in 1966 and is held at the Ice Palace Nightclub at the Grove Hotel on Cherry Grove, a picturesque beachfront filled with restaurants and bars that attracts queer crowds during the warmer months. It is the brainchild of bartender Johnny Savoy, who was inspired by the pomp and glamour of the Miss America pageant and wanted to create a version of the event for drag queens—an inclusive celebration for those who have faced discrimination as part of the queer community. "The Ballad of Miss Fire Island" is his creation, too: a variation of Bert Parks's infamous "Miss America" song.

As the music crescendos, and Lucia bellows out her second "Mama," she dramatically does away with the top of her wig, simultaneously releasing an explosion of hand-throw streamers, the twisted ribbon confetti floating around her before settling on the excited crowd. Beneath that top layer of long flaxen hair is a damp and disheveled mane, revealing an exultantly unhinged Lucia, one free from any nerves she may have had. The crowd cheers for her as she makes eyes at them and sashays, waving her arms around while she mimics Mercury. At one point, she even kneels on the ground and plays a riff on an invisible guitar. Lucia gathers her dress with her manicured hands by its ruffles as she courts the crowd, which is fully enraptured. For the five-minute, fifty-five-second duration of the song, Lucia, in her nude stilettos, goes from laughing to weeping, and from screaming to blowing kisses to the audience. "The song has so many levels, it's cathartic," Lucia tells me. "Nothing really matters," she says, quoting the song's lyrics—"I live by that."

It took Lucia three hours to get ready for today's six-minute performance (though, in a pinch, she can compose herself in forty-five minutes). To create her signature look, she turns to stage makeup brands used on Broadway, including Ben Nye and Kryolan. "I do pretty much the same kind of makeup every time, and I just tailor it to what I'm wearing and what the show is," she says. "But I always wear eyeliner."

> I first witnessed drag on the then-mean streets of New York as a courageous action, an attempt at a fuller expression of self and self-defined identity. Then I watched as drag became a performance of identity and politics and, finally, I have watched drag become an art form.
>
> —Penny Arcade, performance artist

It took some time—and several detours—for Lucia to arrive. When she's not in drag, she reverts to her birth name, Julian Blum (he/him). A native New Yorker, Julian grew up on the Upper East Side, before moving to the leafy, bougie Park Slope neighborhood of Brooklyn. Though he intermittently lived in other states, including Illinois and California, "everything brings me back to New York," he tells me. When we meet at a café in nearby Crown Heights, Julian wears a plaid shirt, khaki shorts, and no eyeliner. He presents as understated and warm. Living in the city allowed Julian to immerse himself in drag early, from the time he was a teenager—his father, "a Studio 54 guy" who left Chicago for New York in his twenties and became a fixture in the clubbing scene, encouraged him. As a teenager, Julian frequented the Kit Kat club, a queer hot spot in the 1990s.

Mixing with those vibrant circles led Julian to the infamous Susanne Bartsch, a Swiss events producer who describes herself as "New York City's patron saint of transformation and inclusion," having thrown parties in the city and other party capitals for over three decades. ("I can't thank Susanne enough for what she has done for the community here in NYC and around the world!" wrote one YouTube commenter on a video in which the famed drag queen RuPaul Andre Charles interviews Bartsch.) Bartsch is also known for her pronounced eyeliner looks, which at times appear more like architecture than makeup; she often uses sharp geometric designs that extend upward to occupy swaths of her forehead real estate.

At first, Julian merely observed the drag queens, immersing himself in this exciting new world, before finally deciding to try the art himself, at eighteen. He dabbled in the looks of the Club Kids, an underground party movement of the 1980s and 1990s that has influenced drag aesthetics. "I loved it so much," he says. "The rooms, the sets, the parties, the costumes, the eyeliner, everything." Julian also spent time with smoky-eyed drag queen Sherry Vine and the Jessica Rabbit–esque transgender model and performer Amanda Lepore, formerly a Club Kid herself, asking questions and learning from them. (Lepore and Vine are both, unsurprisingly, eyeliner enthusiasts.)

Julian quietly came out at age twelve. Though his parents supported him, he struggled with his gender identity. He liked skateboarding but was expected not to gravitate toward "masculine" or "boyish" things. At the same time, he was attracted to beauty, makeup, costume, and specifically to eyeliner. The push and pull between more rigid societal expectations and his own personal fluidity caused Julian to question where he belonged. Eventually, when he discovered drag, he found the balance—and drama—he was looking for. "I'd always felt like an outsider. Drag is a community that finally made sense to me. I never could find my niche or my specific group within the queer community before finding this one."

Julian is introverted (he says he "really dislikes people"); Lucia is extroverted. Julian sometimes struggles with his masculinity; Lucia revels in her femininity. "It's fluid for me, but Lucia has her own thing: her own time and place. Lucia forces me to be outgoing and to be a bigger personality than I am," he says. "She helps me build courage. Although it's really draining and really difficult [to be Lucia onstage], it feels rewarding."

Julian's love for makeup started when he was in the seventh grade, around the time he came out to his parents. He was going through an emo phase, identifying with music and fashion associated with sensitivity, social alienation, and angst. One day, when he received his weekly allowance, he decided to invest in eyeliner from a local store. Hoping to create the typical emo makeup look, which involves copious amounts of dark eyeliner, he attempted to apply it to his lower lash line but hit his eyeball instead, he recalls, letting out a small laugh. The budding performer continued taking an interest in makeup during high school, appreciating the product's potential for creativity and self-expression.

He also began experimenting with drugs, which precipitated an incident that deeply rattled him. Julian didn't wish to discuss it in detail, but it "put a spin on everything," he explains, and "made it much harder to genuinely connect with people." He was later diagnosed with post-traumatic stress disorder, finding that smaller traumas compounded existing ones as he resumed his journey of self-discovery.

This incident cast a long shadow over Julian's life. At the California Institute of the Arts, where he studied music production, he was lonely and "didn't have the energy to create new relationships." He became distracted from his studies and attended drag shows and parties. Though he enjoyed the shows, and found solace in them, he also fell into smoking and drinking addictions and lost his way (he has since quit smoking). "College was really scary and really not fun," he says.

Following that experience, Julian dropped out of school to take a year to focus on his mental health in Chicago, where he worked at Sephora and practiced the art of makeup and eyeliner application. Most days, he gave suburban housewives makeovers, patiently lining their eyes and blushing their cheeks. "They were like, 'Oh, there's no way you can have the same skills as a woman would,'" he says. "It was as if I needed to fit into some sort of expectation; makeup brought that to the fore."

But Julian wasn't dissuaded. In fact, his passion for makeup only grew. Following his stint in Chicago, he moved back to New York to formally train as a makeup artist. He found a job at the makeup store Riley Rose at the height of the pandemic. But he couldn't immerse himself in creative expression in the way he wanted to, which left him feeling unsatisfied: applying makeup to others wasn't quite the same as applying it to himself and bringing Lucia to life. So, when New York started to relax pandemic restrictions, Julian quit his day job and pursue drag full time. "As a drag queen, you pamper yourself so much," he says of his decision. "I use my darkness to make light. I make myself feel special; it just puts me in a good mood and gets me in a specific headspace."

Lucia's first New York show was at the Vault in Bushwick (now permanently closed). Julian says Lucia performed at 3:30 a.m. in a room that felt like a sex dungeon; there were few people there. In that surreal context, she felt she could let loose entirely—she even pulled her hamstring because she decided to do the splits despite never having done them before. Performing to "Make a Move," by the rock band Icon for Hire, she "got such a buzz from the experience that I was like, I need to do this over and over for the rest of my life."

Today, Lucia produces her own events, and is planning to compete in more pageants (Julian has taken on a side job again to support Lucia's endeavors). She hopes to perform in an off-Broadway production, perhaps even for people overseas. She's increasingly passionate about putting on shows with the help of over-the-top makeup looks. "It's a very special moment when people really enjoy what you do," Julian says. "It's hard to take in the moment, but when you look back at it, it's very heartwarming."

(In her favorite-ever drag show, Lucia tied a piece of yarn to each of her fingers. She passed out the yarn to people in the audience, and they pulled on the pieces of string to maneuver her as she performed, like a puppet. She then, with a pair of scissors, cut them all off, freeing herself to go back to moving around as she pleased. "I was just feeling tied down to one kind of expectation of what drag queens do. But there's so much more to it than that, and with the strings I wanted to show how easy it is to get away from [those expectations] and do whatever you want to do," he says.)

Despite loving what she does, Lucia also feels the pressure to look a certain way. Today, Julian says, "a lot of drag is about looking really pretty and looking like a female," whereas "it used to be very campy. It used to be more about the performance, less about the look. You had a wig on with shoes and maybe eyeliner, and people knew what you were doing."

Lucia in part blames influencers for this pressure. While Instagram has positively affected drag by introducing performers to a wider audience, it has its downsides, according to Julian. "The Kardashians are very much an inspiration for drag queens because they always look very pretty. They're always getting brand deals. And that laid grounding for what our jobs were to be," he says. "But that leads to some sort of body dysmorphia, after a while. I did experience body dysmorphia, and I still do."

Julian says the culture has also negatively affected *RuPaul's Drag Race*, the popular reality TV drag competition series, as fewer subversive looks are likely to be featured, because the show itself has become more mainstream. "They're all people who have had work done, who all look very pretty, who don't have any flaws. So, you can't help but be intimidated by what they show and feel like, 'Oh, maybe if I do what they're doing, I'll look better.'" That said, Julian insists Lucia won't resort to getting work done—with the potential exception of a teeny bit of Botox.

At the Fire Island show, the queens parade their gowns around the stage, competing in the daywear category. Many wear floral dresses. One wears a red, white, and blue jumpsuit with stars and stripes; another has on a ruffled white peplum blazer, clinched at the waist with a red star; and another channels British royal glam in a fitted red coatdress. There are purple nine-inch heeled platforms, fuchsia evening gloves, pearl chokers, padded shoulders, glitter belts, and jeweled fishnets. Corsets and padding help give the illusion of shapely or sharp silhouettes, depending on the desired outcome. There's a Minnie Mouse–shaped hatbox; there are hoop earrings so large they may as well be Hula-Hoops. The contestants' hair is, for the most part, beehived, though there are some bobs and tumbling curls, and styling in the way of 1920s Hollywood waves. One queen brings a martini glass onstage, sipping it as the audience cheers. On the contestants' eyes is every form of eyeliner imaginable: cat eye, wide flicks, double flicks, classic bars, open wings, and graphic liners in blues, greens, purples, and pinks, some embellished with rhinestones. The queens lip-synch to songs such as Celine Dion's "It's All Coming Back to Me Now" and ABBA's "The Winner Takes It All."

In the background, decorated with red and blue tinsel, is a collection of trophies. Following dozens of performances—including Lucia's lip sync—across several categories, the queens are called back onto the stage. Miss Fire Island Zola Powell, the reigning queen, prepares to hand over the batons.

Lucia is onstage once more, now in a new mermaid gown, with her hair back in a bouffant. The borrowed garment is hand beaded—sheer at the top, a solid amber yellow at the bottom, with a silver fringe drop. Her eyeliner is pristine, just as it was hours ago. As she's given the Entertainer of the Year award, which she so rightfully deserves, she remains demure; hints of Julian's nerves flicker behind Lucia's confidence. It's a powerful legacy to inherit, and Lucia seems momentarily overwhelmed by the thought of taking the baton—overwhelmed, but gratified. "I felt very proud of myself," she reflects. "It felt like I'd really entered this community, that I was carrying on a legacy, and participating in queer history."

It behooves us to study personal histories,
to fight against the erasure of history and
to honor lineage, because it belongs to us
all. If we do not—we too will be marginalized,
hidden, made obscure and devalued.

—PENNY ARCADE

⌒

In the past decade, drag has achieved unprecedented levels of mainstream popularity, boosted in no small part by *RuPaul's Drag Race*. But the art form originated on the margins of society, with its roots firmly in the underground. The modern history of drag is, as such, challenging to outline, due in part to discrimination against the LGBTQIA+ community and inadequate historical documentation. Consider accounts of the Stonewall riots, which are often conflicting. "Precisely because of this backdrop of social and cultural policing of non-normative gender and sexuality, we argue that there can be no single accepted version of drag history, rather there are many threaded lineages that connect drag to many kinds of performance," write Mark Edward and Stephen Farrier in their book *Drag Histories, Herstories and Hairstories.*

Drag makeup, though, can trace its origins as far back as the roots of cosmetics themselves. Makeup—and indeed eyeliner in all its iterations—has been central to the development of drag. Cosmetics tended to be heavily applied to ensure the radical transformation associated with cross-dressing, and the enhancement and exaggeration (or diminishment) of performers' features—especially their eyes. With its countless forms, textures, and applicators, eyeliner has helped queens experiment with their looks, enlarge their eyes, achieve facial symmetry, and adopt an overall more feminine appearance. "I wear eyeliner to transform myself into somebody new and to be seen in that new light," Virginia Thicc, a New York–based drag queen, tells me. "That gives me confidence, and I always try to be seen in a way that showcases my art."

Similar to how actors used eyeliner in black-and-white cinema, and how kathakali and Kabuki actors use eyeliner onstage, drag queens have relied on eyeliner so their facial expressions could be read better from a distance. (With the dawn of social media, queens also consider how their eyeliner looks on mobile phones.) Full-coverage makeup had to last for the entirety of hours-long performances during which drag queens would entertain under bright lights, so durability was a top priority in drag makeup technique; queens, as such, have often used stage makeup and face paint rather than what you might find on cosmetics stores' shelves.

"Threads of transvestism are woven throughout the ancient cults," writes Simon Doonan in *Drag: The Complete Story*. Indeed, when ancient Egyptian women adorned themselves with kohl—led, of course, by Queen Nefertiti—so, too, did men. "Buckets of black eyeliner, figure-hugging floor-length shift dresses, towering headdresses encrusted with gold . . . and that was just the men," Doonan says. Ancient Egyptians embraced this androgyny and were aesthetically gender-fluid. "In contemporary Western society, few figures are held in greater contempt, or considered more useless or perverse, than the drag queen," Mark Thompson argues in the multiauthor book *Out in Culture*. "But in many non-Christian and preindustrialized cultures, those who bridged the genders were placed in a position of honor and ritual purpose."

The influence of ancient Egyptians hasn't been lost on drag queens. The late Pepper LaBeija, the queen of Harlem drag balls who starred in the 1990 documentary *Paris Is Burning*, embodied what came to be known as the "Egyptian Effect" in her aesthetic. Her runway performances carried forward a different type of drag than what had previously been the norm, one that was less about showgirling and more a celebration of the culture of house music and people of color. It still prized high fashion, but was focused on grit, breaking ground, and paying homage to queens of the past, rather than solely on glitz and glamour.

At a Kansai John Moschino ball in 2000, the House of LaBeija dressed up as pharaohs, with kohl-rimmed eyes, tall headpieces, and lavish collars. Following the procession of pharaohs, five men carried Pepper into the ballroom on an open bed; one of them cooled her with a fan—she was bedridden for the final decade of her life as she dealt with diabetes and had both of her feet amputated. Pepper was dressed as Nefertiti, with a cream satin cap-crown embellished in gold and red jewels and a matching satin caftan. She "danced like an Egyptian" as she was brought onto the stage, and her large eyes were lined—the cat eye visible even in the grainy video of the event. As the mother of the House of LaBeija, by invoking ancient Egypt and, specifically, Nefertiti, Pepper was honoring not only drag performance, but also Blackness and Black history.

The roots of drag makeup sprawled across continents over the centuries, from the pharaohs of ancient Egypt to Japanese Kabuki performers and their heavily lined eyes to actors on William Shakespeare's stage in Elizabethan theater, who also darkened their eyes against faces plastered in white. The mythical King Theseus, founder of Athens, is said to have worn drag in ancient Greece. "Classic scholars describe hordes of shrieking eunuchs, in wigs, makeup, and garish female dress, roaming the towns of the ancient world, clinking cymbals and begging for alms," a tradition that persists today with the hijras (intersex, transgender, or "third gender" people) in India and "their kohl-rimmed eyes," writes Doonan. Romans are depicted in the 1888 portrait by Sir Lawrence Alma-Tadema, *The Roses of Heliogabalus,* which includes the emperor Elagabalus, believed by some historians to be transgender. In the painting, the emperor is clearly in drag, with darkened eyes; modern renderings of him often dress his eyes in eyeliner. Across empires, boys were forced to dress as girls for initiation rituals or chose to do so to evade punishment, according to Doonan. During the baroque period, men in the court of

Versailles cross-dressed, with blushed cheeks and thin lines of eyeliner on their upper and lower waterlines. Likewise, operatic performances featured men in makeup and women's clothing, as well as women in men's clothing.

In Japan's Kabuki performances, which were made off-limits to women in the 1600s following audience riots, males are made up as females. Like drag queens, they use a waxlike substance to tame their eyebrows, paint and powder their entire faces white, and frame their eyes with eyeliner. Chinese opera, known as Peking opera, combines ballet, acrobatics, dance, dialogue, monologue, martial arts, and mime. In the 1700s, women were also banned from performing in these operas, so men wore drag. The various facial makeup patterns, including the whole, quarter, three-tile, six-division, tiny-flowered, and lopsided face, required different types of eyeliner application to help enhance or diminish different aspects of the face. Eye designs were drawn to depict specific character traits. For example, figures with large eyes were considered brash and bold, writes Hsueh-Fang Liu in "The Art of Facial Makeup in Chinese Opera." Conversely, performers with wide eyes were deemed "gentle and reserved." Curved-up corners indicated cunningness, and slitted eyes signaled wickedness. The expressions fell under eight eye types, among them villain eyes (in which liner was used to draw a gently tapering triangle), straight eyes (depending on the shape of the eye, the lines would be square or circular), elderly eyes (in which the liner was downturned at the eyes' edges to give a droopy effect), and ring eyes (in which circles were drawn around the eyes, often to indicate aggression).

Back in the West, drag was partly a reaction to the conservativeness of the Victorian and Edwardian eras. Julian Eltinge (1881–1941) mimicked the bourgeois women of the time and loved the pageantry of corsetry and makeup. Considered a glamour girl by Doonan, Eltinge published magazines including *Julian Eltinge's Magazine of Beauty Hints and Tips*. During the 1950s, some drag queens dressed as sex workers with darkened eyelids, perhaps to live vicariously through the women, as they may have been thought to represent a kind of hyperfeminine ideal.

With the 1960s came a loosening of sexual norms, and the emergence of a counterculture of queer and Black power. Drag activist groups, like the Cockettes, the Sisters of Perpetual Indulgence, and the Radical Faeries, arrived on the scene. Balls and pageants allowed the queens to take to some stages with confidence. *The Queen*, released in 1968, documented the Miss All-America Camp Beauty Pageant, held in New York. In the film's promotional poster, four images are shown. The first is a bare-faced man, the second and third show the same man applying eyeliner, and in the fourth, the man wears full glam, with chandelier earrings, a wig, and extravagantly made-up eyes. The queens in the pageant all wore flicks. The documentary was groundbreaking, not only in its portrayal of drag as an art form that has given sexual minorities and people living on the margins of society visibility, but also in the way that it addressed the discrimination people of color faced in the industry despite the key contributions they'd made to it.

Impersonations of starlets such as Bette Davis and Marilyn Monroe gained popularity as drag melded with cabaret and burlesque performances. Wigstock, a festival for the queer community first held in Manhattan's East Village neighborhood in 1984, raised the profile of drag culture. New York's drag queens found a home for their performances at the East Village's iconic Pyramid Club and, toward the 1990s, in the venues where Susanne Bartsch threw parties. The works of Andy Warhol and Jean-Michel Basquiat also inspired riskier, more colorful eyeliner looks among queens that straddled the line between fine art and fashion. Jackie Curtis, a drag icon and one of Warhol's Superstars, starred in Warhol-produced films, including *Women in Revolt*, a satirical movie that tells the story of the women's liberation movement through three female experiences (the actors are actually drag queens). In the film, Curtis, along with her co-stars, wears prominent eyeliner.

Comedy drag as an art form and a reaction to years of oppression also featured more pronounced, cartoonish looks, with eyes lined imperfectly to mock rather than embrace standard makeup conventions. Drag queen Bianca Del Rio, for example, has been described as a "clown in a gown," and refers to herself as an "erotic clown." On Facebook, she once posted a photo of herself alongside a clown, with the caption "B*tch stole my look!" Drag comedians, when impersonating, sometimes also use makeup to mimic and mock the glamorous and out of touch.

Toward the end of the twentieth century, singers across the genres of synth pop, glam rock, punk rock, and disco began to cross-dress or wear drag. (In the 1984 video for "I Want to Break Free," Freddie Mercury presents as a vacuuming housewife, wearing a leather miniskirt, a sleeveless baby-pink top, a bob, and smudged eyeliner.) Boy George, the androgynous vocalist of the pop band Culture Club, wore bold and colorful guyliner; David Bowie wore high heels and smoky eyes; and the New York Dolls wore dresses, feathers, and platforms with cat eyes and bouffants.

Most of these performers were straight or believed to be straight in their offstage lives, and could remove their eyeliner and return to presenting as men without facing discrimination. ("We can't run around London with our eyes rimmed with kohl, trailing silk foulards and fringed man bags and driving a vintage Rolls painted with psychedelia, because we are gay and gay is verboten, but you can, because you are a young straight popstar!" writes Doonan of the trend.) That said, not all male pop stars who wore guyliner necessarily wore drag—many opted to darken their eyes without wearing feminine clothing.

In the modern era, numerous makeup styles that have gone viral are assumed to be the ideas of mega beauty influencers, including Kim Kardashian. But these "trends" often have roots in drag techniques and aesthetics. "A uniform, airbrushed makeup look has become the new normal: Thick, ombré block eyebrows, heavily contoured cheeks, blinding highlighter, fluttering false eyelashes," wrote Kristina Rodulfo for *Elle* in 2018. "Some call it 'Instagram makeup.' Some call it a 'beat' face. What it really is is decades of quiet, but powerful, influence from the drag community." In the piece, drag performer Vivacious laments the beauty industry's failure to formally credit drag culture for its innovations.

The use of hairspray to set makeup, the cut-crease eyeshadow technique, highlighting and contouring, wearing graphic liner, and "baking"—a practice that involves setting one's concealer or foundation with loose powder for a poreless matte look—are just a few styles and techniques borrowed from drag performers. Some superstar queens, such as Trixie Mattel and Kim Chi, now have their own makeup lines (Trixie Cosmetics and KimChi Chic Beauty, respectively). Both are known for their extreme, larger-than-life eyeliner looks; Trixie's "Beauty Secrets" makeup tutorial on *Vogue*'s YouTube channel has been viewed over five million times since it was posted in October 2019. "I wanted to show you guys an easy look," she says. "Well, easy for me, difficult for you."

On YouTube, TikTok, and Instagram, there are thousands more tutorials on how to achieve the perfect drag eye look. "Everyone is kind of obsessed" with eyeliner, drag influencer Tamara Mascara says in an episode of her YouTube *Drag Essentials* series, using a three-dollar Essence liquid eyeliner to demonstrate how best to apply it. (She prefers the cheap stuff, because "Mama has to work for her dollars!") As she expertly lines her eyes for her followers, creating a feline look, she demands they take the art very seriously: "When you do your eyeliner, be sure to have a moment of silence."

Anya Kneez

Identity, for me, became something that could be fractured into separate
fragments; all the decaying aspects of myself—my relationship with my parents,
my fear of being disowned for my sexuality, my heritage, the Arabic language, my
faith—I stuffed in a closet at home, in a fashion not dissimilar to Dorian Gray's
rotting portrait. The qualities that I wanted to be seen, I tried to excavate from my
depths, and to project them onto my artificial identity.

—Amrou al-Kadhi, British Iraqi drag performer and author

In the YouTube video by *Cold Cuts*, a zine focusing on queer Arab
culture, Charlie holds his liner as if it were a lightsaber. With its
magical properties, it may as well be. First, the thirty-two-year-
old draws a line of neon pink that starts at the inner corner of his
left eye. His thick eyebrows are already prepped and covered in
concealer. He flicks his hand upward, drawing over the inner
arch of the eye and past the hidden hairs of his eyebrow, before
steadily extending the line out toward his hairline. Next, he dips
his brush into the palette's blackest shade and draws a highly pigmented line from the outer corner of his left eye to the pink line at
his temple, creating an empty space. After gently softening the
pink by blending it into his dewy skin, he fills the space with
golden glitter eyeshadow. To make the liner look pop, below the
black, he adds highlighter. The demarcation creates a precise
boundary between the eye and the rest of the face, the eyes being
the focal point. Around both eyes, Charlie sprinkles on more glitter. Now, Charlie is ready for the falsies, which he plops onto his
natural lashes with the help of lash glue.

Finally, with both of his eyes made up, Charlie is no longer
Charlie. He's become Brooklyn's very own Lebanese drag queen,

Anya Kneez (which is, yes, meant to sound like "on your knees"). "The eyeliner and lashes is the moment that I feel like Anya's come to life," Charlie tells me. "That is the moment I'm like, 'Okay, she's done.'"

Charlie was raised by "very Lebanese," culturally conservative parents who immigrated to the US in the early 1980s during the fifteen-year-long civil war in the Levantine country. Makeup, fashion, and the worlds swirling around them were his gateway into another lifestyle, his breath of fresh air. "As a child of an immigrant, you have a life outside of the house, and you have a life inside the house, where it's very strict," Charlie says in an interview on the patio of his Bushwick apartment. "I was born here, but I always felt different." Though he appreciated many elements of Lebanese culture that his parents instilled in him—the food, music, and layers of history—the more conservative norms stifled him. Outside of the bounds of that strictness, Charlie experimented with his looks, sexuality, and gender, albeit in secret. He viewed eyeliner as a portal into an alternative way of life, in which women—and queer men—could adorn and transform themselves.

Charlie has adored eyeliner since he was a young boy. In a 2022 Instagram post marking his birthday, he shared a photo of his younger self cutting his birthday cake in which he'd failed miserably at applying the cosmetic, missing his lower lash line completely. "From the shitty eyeliner that I probably drew on with a marker, to the 'I'm a girl' t-shirt (that I secretly wish I still had)," he wrote, "I didn't even know what drag was at the time, but I was subconsciously doing it. . . . It's funny how our childhood memories will come back to remind us that the lives we lead today make total sense."

Charlie's desire to break free and immerse himself in an alternative lifestyle drew him to New York from California to study fashion in 2010. "It wasn't until I moved to New York that I blossomed into the flaming queer that I am today," he says. "New York is really what brought me to life. It opened my eyes to the world. So, when I moved here, it was like, 'Holy shit,' all the queers are here. So many of them are in Brooklyn!" While living in New York, Charlie shared an apartment with three drag queens who frequented shows around the city. In that safe space, he started putting together looks for the queens until he decided to start crafting looks for himself, as well. Besides, as a designer, Charlie had always been drawn to women's clothing, specifically the vintage romantic and chic looks of the 1920s, '30s, and '40s. He appreciated the softness of the overall aesthetic, combined with the statement eye makeup.

At first, Charlie's roommates painted his face and did his eyeliner—he had no idea how to apply makeup himself. After observing them do their makeup for months and watching dozens of YouTube tutorials, Charlie learned the ropes, sometimes copying other queens' faces and eye makeup. (He recalls being inspired by the American drag queen Raven, who opts for neutrals and browns on her eyes.) Realizing that his features were different and that he had "big Arab eyes," Charlie began studying the "beautifully lined, smoky eyes" of Haifa Wehbe, the salacious Lebanese Egyptian singer known for her curves and the not-so-subtle sexual innuendo in her songs. "Haifa has influenced the entire Arab gay community," Charlie says of the inspiration. "She's our Brit-ney, our Cher." Shifting gears, Charlie decided that mastering how to prettify his eyes would be highest on the list of his makeup-learning priorities.

After settling in NYC, it took Charlie two years to birth Anya Kneez. The idea came to him when he was invited by an Arab arts collective to perform at a Manhattan gay bar. He thought of the invite as an opportunity to come out to the world—or his cor-ner of it—in drag. The designer had previously separated his "queer life" from his "Arab life." His queer life was with his non-Arab friends, whom he was out to as gay; his Arab life was with his family, and he wasn't out to them. When deliberating which Arab diva he'd most like to emulate, he settled on Haifa. Anya would don a Haifa wig: long, thick, and jet black. Charlie de-signed a backless dress for the occasion and sewed four bras into its front to replicate Haifa's ample bosom. As soon as he stepped into the dress, and put on his eyeliner, he became Anya. "I love the idea that you can transform yourself," he says of his ability to jump from persona to persona and gender to gender.

On a bar that night, Anya performed an eight-minute Haifa medley. "I got off that bar, and it was like an epiphany where I knew I could be queer and Arab at the same time," Charlie remi-nisces. "It was such a moment for me." The crowd devoured the performance—they, too, seemed thrilled to see a drag queen who was also proudly Arab. (At most NYC drag shows, Charlie notes, Arab divas weren't represented.) "I got so much love and support that night," he says. "That was the night when I said, 'I want this to be a big part of my life. I want to be an advocate for Arab queer-ness.' Being Haifa—being Anya—brought me a sense of comfort.

"The day I birthed Anya was the day that I found myself as a person. All these things that were bottled up inside of me manifested. I've always loved fashion. I've always loved art. I've always loved performing and being onstage. I've always loved my culture. I've always loved queerness. I've always loved makeup and eyeliner. Being Anya was all these things that I love, combined into one. Everything that I'd been looking for happened that night. Before Anya, I was a very lost Lebanese gay boy."

Putting on makeup, [drag queens] mimic
the expressions that a woman
makes when she is alone with her reflection,
playing to no one but herself:
the haughtiness with which she tilts her
head back and looks down her nose
as she applies her eyeliner; the way she
watches, sidelong, as she brushes color
on her cheekbones; the slackjawed
concentration with which she puts on
lipstick and then, in a businesslike grimace,
presses her lips together to blot it.
Like drag queens, women rely on illusion. In
the interest of illusion,
they exaggerate certain features and
downplay others.

—HOLLY BRUBACH, AUTHOR, *GIRLFRIEND:*
MEN, WOMEN, AND DRAG

In a world where power is usually
taken from us, makeup lets us draw
our battle lines.

—Crystal Rasmussen

Like Lucia Fuchsia, it usually takes Anya about three hours to apply her makeup. For eyeliner, the penultimate step, Anya uses Haus Labs by Lady Gaga. She loves the brand not only because Gaga is beloved by the queer community and is practically an honorary queen herself, but also because the lines can be drawn seamlessly on top of eyeshadow or whatever other eye makeup she has on, including glitter, concealer, and lash glue—it doesn't streak or slip. Anya doesn't do much of a wing; she keeps her lines thin and sharp. (She says she's done thicker lines on occasion, just "for fun.") She also uses liner to draw two beauty spots above her upper lip and below one eye. "It depends on the levels of drama that I want to go with," Charlie says of Anya's eyeliner use. "I'd never leave the house without eyeliner. It's like you're naked without it. I mean, imagine putting a lash on without the eyeliner. Absolutely not."

Anya's drag is an amalgamation. She brings together the physical characteristics and performative skills of Haifa; Nawal al-Zoghbi, another Lebanese pop diva; Cher; and Charlie's mother—even though she doesn't know about her son's queerness and drag life, or even his makeup skills. (Once, when Charlie's mother was getting ready for a wedding, she was clumsily trying to apply her eyeliner while wearing her reading glasses. Charlie wanted to help her, but she flatly said no, being a perfectionist and not realizing her son was a pro.)

Charlie likes to think that Anya looks like and embodies the glamour of his mother. He had, in fact, already imitated her by becoming a designer—she was a seamstress in earlier years, and she taught Charlie how to sew. He once even styled Anya as his mother had been at a wedding when she was younger, sewing a similar dress and wearing her hair, eyeliner, and makeup in the same way. When he looked into the mirror that night, it was like coming face-to-face with her. "I'd love to show my mom Anya, because a part of me feels like she'd be so proud to know that I did everything from her makeup to the dress to her hair," Charlie says. "And my mom, she's a diva. She loves fashion and makeup like me."

In 2010, Charlie's parents moved back to Beirut, and Charlie decided to follow them in 2012. After relocating to Lebanon, Charlie became the head designer for Elie Saab, the Lebanese fashion mogul who's created stunning couture for the likes of Halle Berry and Jennifer Lopez. In Beirut, a city then known for its bustling nightlife and exquisite cuisine, things were going well for Charlie: he'd taken what he learned in NYC and applied it to a major fashion house. Women and men appeared to appreciate dressing up: there wasn't an unlined eye for miles.

But something was missing, and Charlie's journey into queerness seemed to have been put on pause—he felt he'd gained a queer community in New York and lost it in Beirut. "I was like,

'Where are the queers? Where are the gender nonconforming? Where are the nonbinary?'" he recalls. "The environment felt very toxic-masculine, and very femmephobic." Charlie worked with his friends and allies to help effect change—but had to do so within a strict set of boundaries (same-sex relationships are technically criminalized in Lebanon and most of the broader Middle East). And while Lebanon is home to Bassem Feghali—a female impersonator, cross-dresser, and comedian—drag was not a widely known and accepted practice.

At private queer parties, Charlie became Anya once again, and started to perform drag in bars including the now-shuttered Bardo on Clemenceau, a leafy residential street in West Beirut. At one venue, reminiscent of Pepper LaBeija's performance, Anya was carried over the threshold on an open bed by a group of men, as if she were Queen Nefertiti joining her subjects. Initially, some didn't understand the performances, he says, while others loved them. When people expressed confusion over Charlie deciding to keep his beard, despite being made up, he explained that he was a "hairy queen." "I'd tell them, 'Well, I'm not trying to be a woman. I'm not a woman. I don't identify as a woman. I'm paying homage to femininity. I'm paying homage to all these female icons of my life that have inspired me, including my mother.'"

As Anya gained popularity, more underground clubs booked her for appearances. By the summer of 2015, Anya and her friends seemed to have successfully launched a drag scene in Beirut, which attracted a younger generation of queer people who came to shows in nine-inch heels with glitter and cat eye on their faces. By now, Anya had become a khalto, or an "auntie" (she prefers the term over *mother*), to many young queer people in the capital, helping them feel safe while also nurturing and teaching them the art of drag. "We started seeing young queens come out on the scene, doing their shows, and being a part of our shows," Charlie says, manifesting the pride of a khalto. "Some venues in Beirut started hosting balls. I started judging some. We'd essentially created a safe space for these people to come out and be themselves." At the same time, Anya had to keep in mind that the queens needed to quietly navigate Beirut's streets; safety measures involved bribing government officials and police to avoid raids and arrests at venues where Anya performed.

News of the expanding drag scene spread by word of mouth and social media. All the while, Charlie was doing drag in secret while living with his parents. Pretending he had photo shoots, he'd leave the house as a boy, transform into Anya at the desired venue, and go home as a boy (though he'd sometimes still have traces of eyeliner on his face). At around the same time, *RuPaul's Drag Race* was going mainstream. The timing was fortuitous. While Anya played a part in popularizing drag in Lebanon, "drag itself was becoming such a global art form in mainstream media," he says.

The mini balls Anya and her peers helped organize grew to become the Beirut Grand Ball. The organizers flew in former *Drag Race* contestant Vivacious from New York to perform in 2018. ("The world is not ready for you here in Lebanon," Vivacious said during the performance. Incidentally, shortly after the grand ball, a general prosecutor banned Beirut Pride and threatened to detain its organizer for "incitement to immorality.") The balls paid homage to New York's ball culture of the 1970s and 1980s, as depicted in *Paris Is Burning*. The country of around

6.8 million now has over thirty drag queens—partly a result of Anya and her friends' work. The queens care for each other as if they're one family: they apply each other's liner; they lend each other money; they look out for one another. In a sense, Anya had become a khalto of the drag scene in Beirut in the same way drag mothers such as LaBeija had once nurtured and fostered it for the Black and Hispanic communities of New York.

Anya lived in Beirut for seven years until the crippling economic situation in the country, spurred by government corruption and mismanagement, forced her to return to New York in 2019. In August of the following year, the Beirut blast destroyed large swaths of the city, killing at least 215 people, wounding over 7,000, and leaving tens of thousands homeless. Mar Mikhael and Gemmayze, Beirut neighborhoods that were once safe havens for the LGBTQIA+ community, were heavily damaged by the explosion. Many members of the queer community frequented or worked at businesses in these areas to avoid discrimination. The blast, combined with the economic downturn, forced scores of the businesses to shutter.

After Anya returned to NYC, she experienced the guilt often carried by people in the diaspora, as if she had deserted her nieces in her homeland. But on a late night in Bushwick in October 2021, Anya seemed once more to be reveling in and reconnecting with her culture. What started as a low-key gathering of a seemingly majority-Arab audience had, by 1:00 a.m., become something of a rave.

Anya was the guest performer of the evening, hosted by Laylit, an organization that celebrates Middle Eastern and North African music and artists. The queen served the inebriated audience several looks modeled on Lebanese diva Nawal al-Zoghbi's performances circa the 1990s. Anya's first dress, which she had sewn herself, was a black velvet gown, beaded in gold paisley patterns at the bust (Charlie had replicated a photo of Nawal that he has on his dresser at home.) Anya lip-synched and belly danced to Nawal's big hits, including "'Ala bali" (On my mind) and "Elli tmaneito" (What I desired). Her outfits referenced some of the singer's iconic looks, among them a shirt and printed tank top with boot-cut jeans, a flowy kaftan, and a peplum skirt suit set with sharp edges that accentuated Anya's waist. Her eyes were, of course, lined—it'd be safe to say that Nawal, now in her fifties, has never been seen in public without at least some eyeliner.

Along with Anya, Arab drag queens have gained visibility in NYC. At around the same time that she returned to the city, Ana Masreya—whose name translates to "I'm an Egyptian woman"—established Nefertitties, a Brooklyn cabaret act that uses drag "to build bridges and create community spaces for Egyptian, Arab, SWANA folks and beyond." (SWANA is a decolonial acronym that refers to Southwest Asia and North Africa.) Besides her aesthetic, Ana Masreya thinks deeply about what her being a queen means for the Arab queer community, and how best to be an ally to others. Two moments in 2020 forced her to ponder this question, she told BuzzFeed Video: the Black Lives Matter protests, and the suicide of the queer Egyptian activist Sarah Hegazi.

"I want to see the Arab women with the big curly hair and the eyebrows. . . . I need to see the women that I saw on TV growing up. . . . If I can't see it, I need to make it exist here," the queen told the publication. "I'm so proud to be an Egyptian Muslim. Ana Masreya puts together all the struggles that I faced as a queer person living in Egypt and the beauty of everything that I love about Egypt and Egyptian culture and Egyptian women and Egyptian tante [aunties]. . . . Seeing Ana Masreya in the mirror, I felt like I was seeing a drag that speaks to me. That I was giving myself permission to do all the things that society taught me I couldn't do. And I felt free and empowered and f*cking beautiful."

Some of Nefertitties' earliest posters featured colorful illustrations of the bust of Nefertiti with Ana Masreya's features. In May 2022, the drag queen dressed as the royal wife at one of her shows, in head-to-toe rhinestones, with a tall, gold bejeweled crown, a lavish matching dress, and an intricate collar. Her eyes were lined, adorned with highlighter and glitter. In wearing her cat eye, Ana Masreya, like Anya, is paying homage to the queen's aesthetic.

With the help of eyeliner, Charlie, too, is empowered to embody every aspect of his identity, rather than creating an entirely new persona or hiding behind a false one. He can be everything—Arab, man, woman, artist, queer—at once. "I never feel like I'm masking anything," he says. "Anya's my gateway. Drag and drag culture are my gateway. Through drag, through makeup, through eyeliner, I'm able to represent Lebanon and the Arab world for a global audience and show them that 'Hey, we're not just this. We can also be this, this, and this.' Look at the beauty of our culture."

Chapter Nine

Back to Black

*Amy Winehouse and Liner
in the Public Eye*

Had Dame Edith Sitwell, who chronicled the lives of eccentrics of the 1930s, been confronted with the contemporary spectacles of some of her countrymen, one has to wonder if she would revise her remark that "eccentricity is not, as dull people would have us believe, a form of madness." For who, puzzling over how Amy Winehouse, in her state, gets her crazy eyeliner just right, or noting Pete Doherty's newfound propensity for wearing two hats at once, would not consider the possibility that these people are out to lunch?

—Eric Wilson, fashion journalist and editor, 2007

On June 18, 2011, Amy Winehouse sat restlessly in a room at a hotel near Kalemegdan, the largest park in Belgrade, Serbia, which regularly hosts music festivals. The British jazz icon was preparing to sing for some twenty thousand adoring fans. Winehouse, twenty-seven, usually applied her own makeup with skill: blush by Illamasqua; a bright pink lipstick by Chanel; foundation, also by Chanel; and her trademark eyeliner wings by Rimmel. The dramatic flicks were often so thick and long that they stretched out to the edges of her eyebrows.

But that evening, she appeared confused, overwhelmed, and intoxicated. Tyler James, a close friend who was with her, wrote in his book, *My Amy*, that Winehouse was so drunk that her eyes were barely open, and her head periodically flopped down and jerked back up as she mumbled. When she attempted to draw the signature lines that typically accentuated her deep brown eyes, she missed the mark, scribbling a messy black tick on her forehead instead. Her personal stylist and friend, Naomi Parry, helped her wipe the smeared makeup off her face.

Lacking the hand-eye coordination required to master her makeup, she took to the stage without her wings, looking barefaced. Winehouse's signature beehive was also nowhere to be seen, and her blond-streaked hair appeared disheveled; she fiddled with it as she reluctantly slurred the lyrics to her songs. (Parry had attempted to style the singer, but she resisted; to get dressed, she needed help from an assistant, and ultimately wore a tight, bamboo-print minidress.) At one point, as she hobbled aimlessly around the stage, she took off one of her ballerina flats and threw it into the crowd. This was the vision of a woman who wanted nothing more than to be alone, and certainly not before an audience of thousands of scrutinizing spectators.

As the concert dragged on, Winehouse became increasingly distressed and was apparently close to tears, perhaps at the realization that she was in no state to appease her agitated fans. She folded her arms—tattooed with pinup girls. She darted her eyes around, first at her band as if for reassurance, and then toward the crowd and onto the floor. Winehouse looked frail and vulnerable, much like a terrified child craving protection. If it seemed to the audience that the singer was aloof, it was only because they couldn't possibly fathom the demons that shadowed her. And yet, Winehouse tried to the best of her ability to push through the excruciating concert.

Photographers zoomed in on her appearance, giving audiences what they wanted: blown-up images of a woman clearly in distress.

"The paparazzi loved Amy. They couldn't get enough of her. They loved her beauty. They loved its blemishing even more," writes author Leslie Jamison in an essay for *Tin House* magazine. "They didn't just want her beehive hair; they wanted it ratty. They didn't just want her eyeliner cat's-eyes; they wanted them smeared." The UK press and even a Serbian minister later mocked Winehouse for her performance, blaming her lifestyle. "They Know That She's No Good," read one UK headline, a variation of "You Know I'm No Good," one of Winehouse's songs; "Amy Winehouse Embarrasses Herself in Belgrade," read another. To many, the singer appeared overconfident and reckless; people rarely assumed she was a nervous performer. Her father, Mitch Winehouse, wrote in his book, *Amy, My Daughter,* that part of the reason she sang so poorly that evening was her extreme stage fright. Winehouse had always taken pleasure in singing, he wrote, but he wasn't convinced that she felt the same way about performing.

"That was when I knew she wasn't well," Alex Foden, Winehouse's hairdresser for almost four years, who helped cultivate her beehive, tells me. "Amy's eyeliner and beehive didn't only give her confidence. They *were* her confidence. She never left the house without the hair and the eyeliner." (Foden was battling an addiction himself and no longer working for Winehouse at the time of her passing.)

Winehouse's team had an inkling the tour would go south: en route to the UK airport and following her arrival at Belgrade, the singer was also sans wings, and it was clear she was unwell. According to James, she had to be picked up off the sofa and put into the car, as she was barely conscious.

The forty-five-minute gig was Winehouse's last official performance. Just over one month later, she was found dead at her home in Camden, North London. Her untimely and tragic death shook the entertainment world, and indeed the world at large. The official UK inquest into the cause of death recorded a verdict of "misadventure"; Winehouse had five times the legal alcohol limit for driving in her blood when she passed.

I want to go somewhere where I am
stretched right to my limits and perhaps
even beyond.

—AMY WINEHOUSE, 1997

Amy Jade Winehouse was born on September 14, 1983, in Southgate, London. She came into the world like a hurricane, her mother, Janis, recalls in her book, *Loving Amy*, doing things her own way from the start. As a baby, Winehouse was bright and curious, and as a toddler, she was accident prone; her older brother, Alex, would refer to her as "a pain in the bum." When she was five, she sang to herself in mirrors, using a hairbrush as a mic. As a child, Winehouse was so naughty and precocious that she told her mother she felt she could get away with murder.

Winehouse was a chronically restless teen who had an overactive imagination, too. By both of her parents' accounts, it seemed difficult to calm her down; she was filled with frenetic energy. She poured that energy into music. In notebooks decorated with hearts and doodles, she wrote intense autobiographical lyrics; she regularly listened to all sorts of genres, compiling multiple play-lists, often at the expense of her schoolwork (she even formed a girl group with her friend and named it Sweet 'n' Sour, a play on the name of the US hip-hop group Salt-N-Pepa).

As part of her rebellious persona, perhaps even a culmination of it, Winehouse took an early interest in makeup. The defiant teenager had been contending with the aftermath of her parents' separation when she was nine. "When my parents separated, I was like, I can wear whatever I want, I can swear, I can wear makeup, this is really cool," Janis said of her preteen years. "I had a tattoo; I had everything pierced, I used to bunk off school, get my boyfriend round." According to her mother, while "Amy appeared to carry on as normal," Janis learned over time that she had "buried her feelings. Even though she was a loud and forth-right child, rightly or wrongly, and typically of children, she felt Mitch had left her and Alex too, and her behaviour was often about chasing Mitch's affection."

Winehouse especially took to eyeliner and lipstick—both of which would soon become staple items in her aesthetic. Her makeup bag as a teen contained numerous liners as she experi-mented with her looks, drawing thin, subtle strokes at first before graduating to more daring swooshes. Winehouse loved makeup so much that once, at age ten, she was caught shoplifting cosmet-ics from Asda, a supermarket chain.

As Winehouse came of age, she nurtured her explosive talent

in secret, spending hours on end in her bedroom, her sanctuary. But, as would quickly become evident, it's impossible to contain such greatness behind closed doors. When Winehouse was discovered by music executives at just sixteen, with the help of James, who was also a singer, her raspy, contralto voice was so stunning, it was thought to be that of someone far older. "I could not believe my ears, or my eyes—this tiny girl was singing like a 40-year-old jazz veteran who drinks three bottles of whiskey and smokes 50 Marlboro Reds a day—her voice was something else," wrote James.

Winehouse was propelled into the spotlight about four years later, in 2003, with her debut album, *Frank*, based on her experiences dating a man who, per the album's songs, was found wanting. Her music was described as Motown meets retro British pop, and her lyrics were raw and mature, wavering between nostalgic and crude. Winehouse made such an impact on UK culture with her persona that the press didn't know what to make of her. "There are so many reasons why Amy Winehouse could—should— be a huge star. Talent. Charisma. Songs. Voice. Attitude," wrote Garry Mulholland for *The Guardian* in 2004. "But there's one big reason why she may not be. That box she implores you to take? She just won't fit inside it. Sounds Afro-American: is British-Jewish. Looks sexy: won't play up to it. Is young: sounds old. Sings sophisticated: talks rough. Musically mellow: lyrically nasty." Mulholland was, of course, only partly right; Winehouse would soon shoot to global fame, beating superstars including Beyoncé, Rihanna, and Justin Timberlake at the 2008 Grammy Awards and performing alongside greats she admired as a child, such as Tony Bennett and Prince.

The lush mane was ratted and back-
combed into a frowsy beehive, the kind in
which hoodlums of legend used to conceal
their razor blades. Her basic eyeliner
became an ornate volute, a swath of clown
makeup, a cat mask. Her demure and
kittenish dresses gave way to tart frocks
that accentuated a cleavage impressive on a
woman of any size, let alone one barely
larger than a doll.

—GUY TREBAY, CULTURE AND STYLE REPORTER

As is the case with any young female celebrity, Winehouse was expected to project a particular look. After all, this was the early aughts—the decade of pop princesses including Britney Spears and Christina Aguilera—when soft yet sultry and suggestive appearances were demanded of women and girls. Hair was pin straight or beach wavy, jeans were uncomfortably low rise, butterfly clips and glitter were a thing, and desirable figures were athletic, rarely curvy (with Kate Moss's so-called heroin-chic look of the 1990s still very much in vogue). There were, of course, exceptions to these rules, primarily written by men, in which women could be considered "alt" yet still palatable. The grungy looks of Avril Lavigne, with her smudged lined eyes and part-loose, part-fitted clothing, and Pink, with her, well, *pink* hair, were just about acceptable to mainstream audiences. And both women were still desirable, albeit less conventional. But even then, Lavigne's fame wasn't as enduring as those who emulated the early tantalizing styles of Britney and Xtina.

Winehouse firmly resisted cookie-cutter looks, saying in an interview with the BBC's Jonathan Ross of that resistance that "if someone has so much of something, there's very little you can add." (To the delight of the audience, she jokingly said one of her managers had attempted to change her into a "big triangle shape" when asked if they had tried to "mold" her look or how she speaks.) Winehouse also had strong views on what constituted "girl power," as the Spice Girls rose to fame in the UK, popularizing the term. She resisted British pop and disliked being compared with her contemporaries, including the briefly famous Dido, instead embracing American jazz heroines Dinah Washington and Nina Simone.

At first, Winehouse's style was subtle—at least by contrast with her later years. During rehearsals and in the studio, she wore thin, barely there lines and her natural hair. In her debut music video, "Stronger than Me," her flicks were minimal, and her brick-red wrap dress was rather demure, at least by the pop standards of the time. But as her career progressed, and she brought on stylists and hairdressers to help her craft a look that she already had in mind, Winehouse came into her own.

That's not to say that she wasn't inspired by other artists, including women of color. The singer was heavily influenced by the retro looks of the swinging sixties, popularized by the likes of the Chiffons, the Crystals, the Shangri-Las, and the Ronettes. In addition to their unique sound, the Ronettes were known for their soaring bouffants, sharp fringes, winged eyes, and thigh-skimming skirts. Winehouse's look was so reminiscent of the pop trio that the late front woman Ronnie Spector once said in an interview that when she saw a photo of the British star, she thought it was her—until she put her glasses on. Winehouse was also a fan of the French actor Brigitte Bardot, whose half-up, half-down teased and tousled hair was sought after during the 1960s.

The diva had even taken a liking to the looks of Latina women she'd seen after a trip to Miami, wanting to blend their aesthetic—full eyebrows, heavy eyeliner, bright red lipstick, and large hoop earrings—with her passion for the 1960s bouffant look. She adored iconic divas such as Marilyn Monroe and had a drawing of Betty Boop inked onto her lower back, along with thirteen additional tattoos scattered all over her body, including three other pinup girls. (When asked about her interest in pinups during an interview, she said she "just like[s] pretty girls.")

Ultimately, Winehouse required little guidance and "dressed how she wanted to dress," Parry said in an interview about her style with uDiscover Music. "She was incredibly creative. . . . I never really felt like I was telling her what to wear, she had a really strong sense of self, so really, I was just enhancing her own personal style." The stylist described Winehouse's look as "modern rockabilly, not too heavy on the vintage, with a little bit of *True Romance* in there and definitely some 1980s influences."

Foden says Winehouse's beehive was also a collaborative effort. "I used to finish it, and it'd be perfect," he says. "And then she'd get the Denman brush out and start back-combing it, and it would be like a bird's nest. And I just used to sit there shaking my head." She once went behind his back to dye her hair blond, he adds, using Jolen Creme Bleach, as she was going through a "Marilyn phase."

Winehouse, who designed a collection of bowling shirts and miniskirts for Fred Perry (several items from which I own), was so invested in fashion and clothing that she aspired to create her own label. The singer liked her dresses short and tight, which wasn't trendy at the time, Parry said in an interview at the opening of the 2020 Amy Winehouse exhibit at the Grammy Museum. But she also loved dressing down, often wearing athleisure and low-key, casual outfits from the high street. Winehouse certainly had a knack for design. According to Foden, when the late fashion designer Karl Lagerfeld dressed her for one of her performances, she cut the dress's straps off and tied one around her neck, creating an entirely different look. Instead of being horrified, Lagerfeld, who stood backstage, per Foden, exclaimed that he "just loved it" (in 2007, the designer told *The Sun* that Winehouse was his muse). The singer also experimented with prints, including leopard and gingham, and accessorized with objects ranging from roses in her hair to flowy headscarves and large leather belts that accentuated her tiny waist.

Winehouse recognized and embraced the transformative power of eyeliner. She was friends with British drag queen Jodie Harsh and would watch in awe as she removed her dramatic eye makeup and reverted to being male. Winehouse was also inspired by her beloved grandmother Cynthia, who was similarly petite with enormous hair and wore eyeliner. The two were particularly close; one of Winehouse's tattoos was modeled after her. Like her granddaughter's, Cynthia's aesthetic and persona were eccentric and striking. She read tarot cards, dressed in bright red prints with blue and green eyeshadows, and regularly had her nails painted. Winehouse sometimes dressed up in her scarves and tops, and put on eyeliner and lipstick, telling her father to hide her makeup wearing from her mother. (Cynthia's death from lung cancer in 2006 shook Winehouse, with friends and family saying her downturn worsened substantially as a result.)

The singer's daring sensibility was perhaps cemented in her 2007 music video "Back to Black," from the album of the same name released the year prior. In the video, her hair and eyeliner were amplified to new heights. Foden, who styled her mane for the shoot, says the bold look was partly conceived due to Winehouse's boredom and restlessness on set. To keep her engaged, Foden had suggested that they "take the piss" with her hair, adding two and a half packs of extensions to it, versus one and a half—essentially giving her two full heads of hair. "I said, 'Let's just do a caricature of you.' And she was like, 'What do you mean?' And I said, 'Well, let's just go as big as we possibly can.' And we combed it right up. And her eyeliner was big, too. So then, when she walked out of the trailer, that was when all of the crew were like, 'That's it; that's the signature look.'"

All that said, according to Foden, eyeliner coupled with the beehive was more than just a "look" for the singer. "She used to tell me that 'the Old Amy is dead,'" he says. "She wasn't wearing a mask when she wore her eyeliner and beehive; she wasn't channeling a 'look.' It was her creating a new Amy. She was re-creating herself."

In the era of total exposure Winehouse
would serve herself and her listeners best
by working behind closed doors.

—Jon Pareles, music critic, *The New York Times*

When Winehouse's makeup artist, Talia Shobrook, relocated to the US, the singer began applying her makeup herself—consequently, "the winged eyeliner got bolder," writes Emma Garland of *Vice*. Winehouse was so committed to her eyeliner that she reapplied it throughout the day, drawing over the original lines repeatedly to ensure they remained crisp at the corners. If a beautician happened to apply the eyeliner themself, she'd later go over it, disappointed by their conservative hands, says Foden. (Per Parry, Winehouse mostly didn't have a makeup artist with her while on tour, either, and she would quickly make up her own eyes. "It wouldn't be perfect, but it was there, it was her look," the stylist once said. Despite the extent of her fame, Winehouse had a refreshing and endearing DIY quality about her; her "imperfect" look seemed to underscore how raw and genuine she was. In the era of ultra-manicured, media-trained, filtered celebrities we're living in today, it's hard to imagine a singer of her caliber adopting a similar approach to aesthetics.)

While Winehouse's life was often chaotic and fast paced, her liner was near constant. It may as well have been tattooed onto her face, Foden jokes. She wore her wings when she walked the dog, when she wrote songs, when she nervously performed those songs, and when she went to the grocery store, the pub, the beach, and Camden Town—even when she went to court. Ironically, she didn't wear it on Halloween in 2007, her bare face ostensibly being her costume. By wearing eyeliner the way that she did, according to Foden, Winehouse was also rebelling against her record label and rigid expectations of female pop stars.

As the singer's career progressed and her fame intensified—along with the many responsibilities and the vicious public scrutiny that accompanied her stardom—she battled substance abuse issues, anxiety, and other mental health difficulties, both privately and publicly. Winehouse wrote songs, she had explained, not because she craved recognition, but because she needed to make sense of herself, and she poured her emotions into her music to powerful effect. According to James, she "was never happy-go-lucky, she was complicated, solitary, and reclusive." As her life became increasingly complex, her eyeliner also became more pronounced, her wings inching their way from the corners of her eyes out toward her hairline.

"The more insecure I feel, the bigger my hair has to be," Winehouse said of her looks. "I'm very insecure about the way I look. I mean I'm a musician, not a model," she said, noting that she also turned to alcohol to self-medicate her anxiety. The artist developed bulimia in her late teens, a disorder she would battle for the rest of her life. Her tenuous relationship with self-esteem was undeniably worsened by her fame; as she was constantly inundated with recordings and photographs of herself and public commentary on her appearance, her self-perception became distorted and critical. Toward the end of her life, her father remembers her watching YouTube videos of herself and asking him if he thought she was talented and beautiful—she didn't trust herself enough to know.

The media often portrayed Winehouse as a "train wreck," its default for women celebrities who fall short of "perfection." In his book of the same name, Jude Ellison S. Doyle explains that "by zeroing in on the messiest and most badly behaved women, and rejecting them, we make a statement about what makes a woman good," and define how unconventional women are "allowed" to be. In that vein, commentary about Winehouse was often blatantly misogynistic, even when framed as a joke: "Singer Amy Winehouse was photographed in the street barefoot, wearing nothing but jeans and a red bra. Or as Britney Spears calls it, 'Chic Formal,'" Alan Cross, a *New York Times* reader, wrote to the newspaper, shortly after Spears, head freshly shaved and eyeliner heavy, was filmed attacking paparazzi with her umbrella.

For years, the press itself continued to harp on this narrative, even as Winehouse put a concerted effort into her treatment and recovery: "Angry Amy Winehouse Loses Her Cool as Fan Tries to Photograph Her at the Supermarket," "Bleary-Eyed Amy Winehouse Falls Back into Her Old Ways at Her Favourite Camden Haunt," and "Amy Winehouse Stumbles Out of Restaurant Exposing Her Potbelly," they wrote. One publication once even cited Winehouse in a piece about how unhealthy lifestyles can result in women looking four years older than their age; she was regularly described as "falling apart," her makeup "smudged" or "smeared" following long nights out.

According to Foden, Winehouse was never the shallow diva

she was portrayed as being in the media. "She was the little Jewish granny who looked after everyone and who had the softest heart ever," he said. "She was the perfect solution to all of your problems. It's just a shame that she wasn't able to put into practice her own theories. People thought she was unapproachable, but she used to make the paparazzi cups of tea. She used to give the fans that waited for her just outside her flat Haribo."

Winehouse was attracted to underdogs, Foden being one himself after having been bullied for years at school, he says. She was also maternal and wanted children, saying once that "when you're around kids, you can be a little kid yourself, and pretend that life is magic." And while the press would have readers believe that her ideal night out was a crack- and alcohol-fueled bender at the pub, what she really craved was a sense of normalcy. "I know I look like a train wreck," she said in an interview. "But I'm actually a really domesticated person," adding that her idea of a perfect night would be having fifteen of her friends over for dinner. "It's not very rock 'n' roll."

The relentless public scrutiny was practically inescapable. Once, in a restroom at a London pub, a woman touching up her makeup in the mirror spotted the singer and told her she looked just like Amy Winehouse, only "prettier." Understandably, the incident upset Winehouse, and was representative of the kind of commentary that troubled her and alienated her from her own reflection. Her larger-than-life aesthetic uniform, once a playful expression of the convergence of her influences and her individuality, became a suit of armor: "Amy was happy to let the beehive and the eyeliner and the car crash lifestyle become the only side of her the public saw," her mother, Janis, wrote in her book, "even though we knew she was a much more complex person than that." James described her beehive as "both a retro style statement and her comfort blanket," a distraction from the face she so often criticized.

Winehouse's relationship to her eyeliner arguably went even deeper: when she traveled to Saint Lucia in late 2008, where she remained for months as she attempted a detox, she dropped the beehive and sexy dresses for her fresh-faced, pre-fame self, but she still wore winged eyeliner. The look was simultaneously an affirmation and a bold assertion of her vision.

It was especially distressing, then, when her eyeliner sometimes appeared to have been imperfectly applied, smudged and asymmetrical. As her health declined, her loved ones were alarmed and concerned. "This is someone who is trying to disappear," her friend, the rapper Yasiin Bey, said of her downfall.

In one scene in *Amy*, the 2015 documentary about her life directed by Asif Kapadia, Winehouse is seen with no eyeliner and a blemished face. The budding superstar had fallen asleep in the back seat of a car and was awoken by a friend who was filming her with his mobile phone. She looked reluctant and shy, seemingly not wanting to be seen without makeup, covering her face with her blanket and speaking softly.

It's a striking physical manifestation of her vulnerability, a correlation between physical appearance and emotional volatility made so brutally apparent as to feel borderline exploitative to watch.

Winehouse wasn't alone in making eyeliner an essential part of her stage presence. From Prince and Madonna to David Bowie and Lady Gaga, eyeliner has played a critical role across musical subcultures and eras—including, to name just a few, goth, glam, grunge, and, of course, the swinging sixties.

The cosmetic is often used or understood to make a statement—personal, political, or both—much like it did for Winehouse. Nirvana's Kurt Cobain and his wife, Courtney Love, muddied or overexaggerated their eyeliner, which, along with their signature bedhead, signaled the antiestablishment nature of their music and personae. Cobain also toyed with gender norms, sometimes pairing floral, flowy dresses with his lined eyes.

Freddie Mercury, the Queen front man, elevated his style with guyliner (curious readers could scroll through @Freddies_ Eyeliner, an Instagram account devoted to his many looks). As the queer son of Parsi parents in an industry and a society rife with racism and homophobia, he crafted a carefully curated image that was intimately linked to his expression of his gender, sexuality, and cultural heritage. Mercury's daring looks asserted his defiant rejection of societal norms, and his eyes, generously framed with black liner, could be admired by fans everywhere in the crowds that amassed to revel in his memorable performances.

Male punk rockers, glam rockers, and rock stars including Iggy Pop, Gary Glitter, Rod Stewart, Alice Cooper, Marc Bolan of T. Rex, Steven Tyler of Aerosmith, David Johansen of the New York Dolls, and the members of Roxy Music and Kiss, also turned to guyliner during the 1960s and 1970s. Slade, a British rock band that rose to popularity in the seventies, was famously referred to as "brickies in eyeliner" by English singer Siouxsie

Sioux; the logo of her rock band, Siouxsie and the Banshees, featured an image of Sioux's eyes dressed heavily in eyeliner in a style reminiscent of the Eye of Horus.

In the 1970s and 1980s, Mick Jagger, the lead singer of the Rolling Stones and one of the most influential rock singers of his day and beyond, regularly wore guyliner, as did his fellow band members Keith Richards and Ronnie Wood and the members of British band the Cure. So, too, did heavy metal band members of the era, including Nikki Sixx of Mötley Crüe, Ozzy Osbourne of Black Sabbath, and Dee Snider of Twisted Sister, along with Dave Navarro of Jane's Addiction. Both Prince and David Bowie, legendary, enduring singers who spanned genres, wore eyeliner that inched well beyond the corners of their eyes, sometimes adopting cat eye and experimenting with shapes and color; their eye looks furthered their ability to bend genders and mutate personas. Elvis and Michael Jackson, by comparison, wore lower-key eyeliner looks to enhance their eyes. Later, Pete Wentz of Fall Out Boy, one of Winehouse's contemporaries, became perhaps the most iconic proponent of guyliner in the early 2000s.

During the swinging sixties, girl bands, particularly Black girl bands including the Ronettes and the Supremes, led the winged eyeliner look, inspiring Winehouse. "The louder they applauded, the more eyeliner we'd put on the next time," Ronnie Spector wrote in her memoir. The style would endure for years to follow, with soul, gospel, country, jazz, and R & B singers such as Shirley Bassey, Barbra Streisand, Whitney Houston, Tina Turner, Nina Simone, Aretha Franklin, Patti LaBelle, and Etta James also embracing cat eye and often the big hair to match.

Female rock and pop stars also donned eyeliner in the 1970s

and 1980s, perhaps the most widely known among them being Madonna, Patti Smith, Joan Jett, Dusty Springfield, Stevie Nicks of Fleetwood Mac, Chrissie Hynde of the Pretenders, Kim Gordon of Sonic Youth, and Debbie Harry of Blondie, all of whom embraced counterculture to varying degrees. While 1980s eye makeup featured jewel tones and bold blues and pinks, approaching the 1990s, a grunge aesthetic with more muted tones and browns emerged, led by the likes of Shirley Manson of the band Garbage. Similar to Wentz of Fall Out Boy, Hayley Williams of Paramore helped foment the pop-punk "scene" aesthetic of the 2000s, which involved flat-ironed hair that swooped over the eyes, piercings, chunky belts, skateboards, and (super) skinny jeans. The look was capitalized upon by the likes of retailer Hot Topic and traveling rock tour Warped Tour.

Many superstars, including Winehouse, have recognized the "queenly element" of eyeliner, says Sharon Dowsett, a renowned makeup artist and the former UK director of Maybelline. The cosmetic also allows the wearer to broadcast facets of their identity without saying a word: "The fact that it goes straight across the eyelid means it's quite serious, and you mean business. Generally, the more flicked it is, the more retro it is." Dowsett styled Swedish singer Neneh Cherry for the cover of her 2018 album, *Broken Politics*—in the images, Cherry's eyes are distinctly lined, lending her a majestic air. "Like Nefertiti, like Neneh, Amy was such a queen herself, though they are each regal in different ways. I like eyeliner to be fucked up. I like it if it's a bit destroyed in that it tells a story, it makes it far more engaging and interesting," she says (complimenting me on my imperfect, asymmetrical eyeliner in the process).

She didn't look like Halloween, but you
could go as her on Halloween, and there's
the difference.

—FILMMAKER JOHN WATERS, QUOTED BY GUY TREBAY

Winehouse's style has had a lasting impact on fashion and iconography, touching everything from Paris runways to Halloween block parties. "All makeup artists now know the 'Amy Liner'— that incredibly thick black flick," Pablo Rodriguez, Illamasqua's director of artistry, said in *Beyond Black*, a book about Winehouse beautifully curated by Parry. "Like a 'Linda Eyebrow' or 'Bardot hair,' it became a trademark. I remember her style was completely new at the time—no one looked like her. She's the one who brought back liquid liner, and for good." The soul singer defied convention with both her music *and* her looks. "You couldn't have such a big voice and leave everything else so small—you needed a big voice and a big character and a big signature look," Foden says of her eyeliner. In 2012, the French designer Jean Paul Gaultier held a show where his models were styled in homage to Winehouse, with cat eyes and beehives. "To me, the scandal is that no fashion magazine did an Amy Winehouse cover," Gaultier said. "She was so exceptional in her style, how she held her body, the way she dressed, mixing pieces from different decades."

There are numerous images and murals of Winehouse scattered around Camden, where she lived and died. A bronze statue of her was erected in the area in 2014, her signature wings etched onto its face; when I visited it in 2020, there were white carnations at the statue's heels. In 2021, Winehouse's winged eyeliner was voted one of the most iconic British beauty trends of all time. And a biopic about Winehouse, titled *Back to Black* and starring Marisa Abela, was in the works in early 2023; some have criticized it for exploiting the singer's death.

Foden hopes to eventually launch a hair and makeup collection making a paean to the singer. The collection will contain black eyeliner, black mascara, red lip liner, and red lipstick, in addition to hairspray that will be packaged in a large gold tube, with a big black beehive cap sitting on top of it. "She changed my career, she changed my life forever," Foden says of his vision. "She touched my heart, and she deserves to be immortalized."

> Regardless of what happened to her in terms of fame, addiction, she always stayed herself; she was very, very real—if that isn't strength, then I don't know what is."
>
> —Chantelle Dusette, *Reclaiming Amy* documentary

In the final stretch of her life, Winehouse appeared to have wanted to start anew. Following her divorce in 2009 from Blake Fielder-Civil, her health seemed to have improved—there were periods during which she was alcohol-free. She had numerous future projects in mind; she spoke of wanting to start a publishing company for songwriters. She was spotted looking happy, hand in hand with a new man, and she enjoyed spending quality time with her goddaughter. She started going to the gym again, tidied up her wardrobe, and organized her books and CDs. At times, she looked physically well, her eyeliner sharp and purposeful. It seemed she was indeed on the path to recovery.

But as *Reclaiming Amy*, a 2021 BBC documentary marking the tenth anniversary of Winehouse's death, makes clear, she continued to struggle in private. According to her friends, Winehouse's stints of sobriety were interspersed with stints of binge drinking, such that her body never really had the opportunity to recover. "She went from drugs to alcohol; that was the problem," Parry says in the documentary. But "the alcoholism, the addiction, that was a by-product of something else much deeper that needed addressing . . . [her] mental health. She didn't want to admit that she had mental health issues because it was at a time . . . [when] people didn't understand it. . . . She was trying to hide it; she felt guilty about putting her issues on other people."

After her death from alcohol poisoning in 2011, Winehouse's family established the Amy Winehouse Foundation to assist young people with building resilience and self-esteem in the face of adversity, offering music therapy and other recovery pathways to those who would not typically be able to afford or access them. Toward the end of *Reclaiming Amy*, one of the foundation's clients spoke about how Winehouse's legacy had not only changed her life—it had saved it. "I was really, really ill, and I didn't want to accept that I was an alcoholic," she said. "I was always really good at putting on a show, so I could fool the world into thinking I had confidence."

In the background, on the walls of the foundation's small office in London, sits a large black-and-white photograph of Winehouse. Immortalized in the print, her heavily lined eyes project a hypnotic, disarming gaze as the woman bravely shares her story—a reminder that Winehouse's life, legacy, and look haven't been lost on the world she left behind.

Chapter Ten

#GraphicLiner

Eyeliner in the Age of Influencers

For the beauty mogul's millions of followers today, her name is synonymous with glamour—but as a young Muslim Iraqi woman growing up in the suburbs of Tennessee and Massachusetts during the 1990s, Huda Kattan rarely felt beautiful. Her olive-brown skin and textured hair made her conspicuously different from her mostly white classmates, who often derided and bullied her. "I remember definitely not feeling pretty because I didn't look like everyone else," thirty-nine-year-old Kattan said on *Huda Boss*, a reality TV show that ran for two seasons on Facebook Watch. "I was one of the only brown people in my whole entire school. . . . When you're a child looking for that comfort and need to belong, and you're not getting that . . . it's the worst feeling ever. It still affects me to this day."

Kattan became "obsessed" with beauty around age nine, both as an outlet for her creativity and as a coping mechanism that eased her insecurities. Although her parents didn't have much money to offer their daughter to spend on herself, she still bought makeup products when she could, to experiment. By manipulating her appearance with powders, palettes, and creams, she found she could water down or enhance her ethnic differences. "The makeup made you prettier, made you feel more beautiful," she explained on *Huda Boss*. Cat eye would come to define her dolled-up style.

After earning a degree in finance at the University of Michigan–Dearborn in 2008, the budding entrepreneur ditched the US and moved to the UAE, where she took on a recruiting job but lost it a year later during an economic recession. At a crossroads in her professional life, Kattan finally decided to take her enduring passion for makeup more seriously and moved to Los Angeles in 2009 to train as a makeup artist. During that time, her name gained traction in the industry, and she started to build an impressive list of clients that would eventually include members of the UAE royal family and celebrities such as Eva Longoria.

Well before Kylie Jenner set up her own makeup brand, Kattan—whose first name means "guidance"—was already schooling the beauty conscious. When she launched her blog in 2010, the year Instagram was founded, she didn't have Middle Eastern role models to look up to; she said on *Huda Boss* that through her work, she wanted to lean into her insecurities and be an example for others. "When I started out, there weren't many bloggers with brown skin," she told *Metro* in 2019. "My goal was to represent for brown skin girls."

At a time when beauty influencing and tutorial videos weren't as common as they are today, on her site, Kattan offered tips on how to contour cheekbones, thicken and shape eyebrows, manage curly hair, plump lips—and create the perfect smoky eye. "I am obsessed with eyeliner," she wrote in a 2011 post. "The blacker, the better!" Distinguishing herself from the beauty establishment, the tone of these posts was conversational and informal, almost as if Kattan were talking to a friend about how best to make oneself up.

The influencer's content was so popular and relatable that the blog soon elevated her to celebrity status, first among Arab women, and then among beauty enthusiasts the world over. Kattan went to great efforts to connect with her Arab audience by addressing them in broken Arabic in her videos. Her fans appreciated her approachability and warmth; the intimacy with which Kattan addresses her followers has undoubtedly contributed to the cultlike quality of her fan base. (Which isn't to say the mogul is above reproach—as her platform and influence have grown, she has been criticized for her cosmetically enhanced appearance, sometimes-controversial makeup techniques, and tensions with fellow influencers.)

Brands took notice of her influence, sending her thousands of products in the hopes that she would recommend them to her following. But Kattan was always aware of gaps in the market, both as a brown-skinned woman and as a longtime makeup enthusiast, so—with the help of her siblings, Alya and Mona, and her husband, Chris—she decided to found her own brand, Huda Beauty, which launched in 2013. Her first product was a line of false lashes that proved to be a hit: Kim Kardashian herself was a fan.

Today, Huda Beauty is a multimillion-dollar brand stocked everywhere from Sephora in the US and Selfridges in the UK to vending machines in Dubai, where the company is headquartered. It is, by far, the most popular name in beauty across the Middle East and North Africa, and boasts over seventy-four million Instagram, YouTube, Facebook, and TikTok followers worldwide. Kattan's beauty and personal feeds, in which she regularly posts informative videos with lined eyes and dewy skin—as well as videos of other influencers using her products—are packed with giddy comments such as "my beautiful Habibti" (darling).

Although Kattan's personal eyeliner style was iconic, her brand wouldn't release its own version of the cosmetic until 2019. In her telling, Kattan refused to create an eyeliner until she felt she could do it better than everyone else. "There is so much power in eyeliner," she said of her desire to perfect the product. "If it's not going to smash every other eyeliner that's out there, it's not going to happen." When she finally released Life Liner, there was so much anticipation around the launch—a dual liner, with a mechanical pencil at one end and a liquid liner at the other—that the seven hundred thousand presales far exceeded the two hundred thousand units that were manufactured. Life Liner, Kattan said, was a "Middle Eastern woman's dream" in a shade of black that was "deeper than your soul." (The brand has since also released another iteration—Quick 'N Easy Precision Liquid.) "I cannot go a day without [eyeliner]," Kattan told *Dazed* after the launch. "It can honestly change the eye shape, lift the eyes, make you look more awake, and draw necessary attention to the eyes. Liner just makes me feel feminine, beautiful, and sexy."

While Kattan is committed to beautifying faces everywhere,

she seems also to be interested in shifting global beauty standards. "If I do something I'm not passionate about, how am I going to impact the world?" she once said. "And if I am not changing the world in some way then what the hell am I doing?"

From Instagram Face to Snatched Face

The dawn of influencing and the popularization of bold eyeliner looks in the aughts and 2010s in the West intersected with—and was arguably led by—the rise of the Kardashian-Jenner family. In the now-infamous reality TV show *Keeping Up with the Kardashians*, Kim Kardashian regularly wore smoky eyes, with thick lines framing her long "spider" lashes. Kardashian, who is of Western European and Armenian descent, would quickly become known for her "exotic" makeup, hairstyles, and curves, all of which contributed to her notorious "racial ambiguity"; the star has been accused of capitalizing on the aesthetics of brown and Black women.

But it was Kim's younger half sister Kylie Jenner who would become one of the biggest names in the industry with the launch of Kylie Lip Kits in the fall of 2015, when she was just eighteen. Earlier that same year, Jenner admitted to using lip filler to plump her naturally thin lips—a fact that did not hinder the success of her lip products, which often sold out upon release. It wasn't just Jenner's lips that her followers were after, but her overall appearance: sensual and sultry. To help her achieve that ethnically ambiguous look, Jenner, who is Caucasian, frequently wears a cat eye, drawing thin black lines on her top lids, with pronounced upticks for wings. The lines impart the classic feline, Nefertiti-esque aesthetic; some plastic surgeons speculate cosmetic proce-dures such as a brow lift have further enhanced it. The year after the launch of her lip kits, Jenner released a Kyliner Kit, which included an angled brush, a pencil liner, and a rich gel liner pot in black or brown. While the original product enjoyed some success, it's since been discontinued. (Currently on offer on her website are gel eyeliner pencils in shimmery and matte shades and a Kyliner Brush Tip Liquid Eyeliner Pen.)

At the time of writing, depending on Instagram's algorithm, over 376 million followers scrolling through their Instagram feeds will be presented with Jenner's carefully curated images and lined eyes. She is at the vanguard of the uncanny "Instagram Face," a term popularized by Jia Tolentino in a 2019 *New Yorker* article—a "single, cyborgian" face that is "distinctly white but ambiguously ethnic." Commenting on the "greatest hits" aspect of Instagram Face, celebrity makeup artist Colby Smith says in Tolentino's piece, "We're talking an overly tan skin tone, a South Asian influ-ence with the brows and eye shape, an African-American influence with the lips, a Caucasian influence with the nose, a cheek struc-ture that is predominantly Native American and Middle East-ern." In October 2020, Arab Twitter erupted in memes after Jenner posted a video of herself on Instagram and elsewhere mod-eling a new makeup drop with heavily lined eyes, lower waterline included—looking very much like a prototypical Middle Eastern pop star (the kind of pop star I watched in awe when I was grow-ing up).

The ripple effects of Jenner's aesthetic have been wide reach-ing, affecting countless girls' senses of self. "The Instagram Face can certainly influence a user's thinking of how they 'should look,' which can lead to a tendency to self-rate against these beauty influencers," says Dr. Lisa Orban, a London-based clinical psychologist. "This self-rating against a perceived standard of beauty can often lead to feelings of intense self-dislike and, in some cases, attempts to 'fix' themselves, such as through elective plastic surgery to achieve the same idealized features." In more extreme cases, Orban says, body image issues can manifest as body dysmorphic disorder, or BDD, an anxiety disorder in which a person has a disabling preoccupation with perceived defects or flaws in their appearance, which can result in depression and even suicidal thoughts.

In a 2016 *Nature* study, academic Isabelle Coy-Dibley coined the term *digitized dysmorphia*, which she argues is on the spectrum of BDD, but as "a socially conditioned dysmorphia, shaped collectively by societal pressures, constructs of beauty and the technology presently available to attain these standards in image form." People can now go beyond observing and critiquing their reflections; they can download apps that allow them to virtually tweak themselves to supposed perfection. Facetune and Makeup-Plus, for example, allow users to apply all sorts of makeup, including eyeliner of various shapes and types, to their otherwise bare eyes, simultaneously beautifying and distorting the face. "The unfortunate reality of this phenomenon is that in years to come, many of us will be unable to recognize ourselves within the images created through digital modification," Coy-Dibley writes.

Dr. Tijion Esho, a London-based practitioner of aesthetic medicine, says the dissonance between one's digitized image and real-life reflection leads some to seek more permanent alterations through surgery, with many of his younger patients requesting looks like those of the Kardashians. Esho says he performed "an ever-increasing amount" of facial procedures, including nonsurgical nose enhancements and lip treatments, during the COVID-19 pandemic due to higher demand. Most patients have been seeking upper or lower blepharoplasties, he says; the procedure removes loose skin to give a tighter and smoother appearance, allowing one's eye shape to appear more drastically different from the looks eyeliner alone can achieve.

Interest in beautifying the eyes via cosmetic tweakments and eye products including eyeliner soared during the COVID-19 pandemic, due to mandatory mask wearing concealing the rest of the face. According to Kantar, a data analytics group, in the months after the World Health Organization declared the pandemic in March 2020, sales of eye makeup surged by 204 percent globally. "Obviously, when you can't see the lips, eyes are super important," former L'Oréal CEO Jean-Paul Agon said on an earnings call in August 2020. Shortly after the outbreak of COVID-19, *The Washington Post* reported that employees at a Sephora warehouse in Las Vegas were working additional shifts partly to keep up with the demand for eyeliner.

The so-called Instagram Face had, by early 2023, receded somewhat into the digital background, with the more chiseled and less pillowy "snatched" Bella Hadid look coming to the fore. Hadid's face is distinctly angular and less rounded, her jawline sharp, her eyebrows steeply arched, and her cheeks so sculpted as to appear hollowed out. That said, this look can *also* require the help of surgery and cosmetic tweakments such as removing buccal—or cheek—fat. (The model has admitted to having had surgery on her nose at just fourteen, telling *Vogue* in 2022 that she wishes she'd have "kept the nose of her ancestors." Hadid denied, however, that she'd had any work done to her eyes or brow area.) "Instead of luscious lips and small noses, we're seeing defined jawlines and cheekbones," plastic surgeon Sagar Patel told *The Cut* in February 2023. "In 2017, it was about looking young and cute, but now people are like, *I don't want to look like I'm 15. I want to look like I'm 28 and sexy.*" Incidentally, some elements of this "new" look—especially the sharp angles—can be found on the bust of Nefertiti.

To help get the snatched face, models and celebrities such as Kendall Jenner and Ariana Grande have evolved the classic cat eye into a look called the "fox eye," an upswept eye makeup style. In the style, the wearer's brows are brushed up and drawn relatively straight (sometimes attained by shaving and redrawing the tails of the brows), and eyeshadow and eyeliner are used to help extend the outer corners of the eyes toward the temples and from the inner corners of the eyes toward the bridge of the nose. A procedure known as a thread lift, in which the upper eyelid is pulled and stretched with the help of dissolvable or non-dissolvable sutures inserted under the skin, can help achieve the aesthetic. (Hadid, in her *Vogue* interview, said she pulls off her fox-eye look with the help of face tape.) Influencers modeling the fox-eye trend often have their hair tied into taut, high ponytails or buns to further stretch and lift the edges of their eyes. In various images, content creators showing off this look can be seen pulling the edges of their eyes up with their fingers to make them appear more slanted. The result is an elongated "almond" eye shape that some Asian Americans have critiqued as appropriative when worn by non-Asians.

"The eye-pulls trigger flashbacks to my experiences in elementary school when my peers would make so-called 'exotic Ching Chong eyes,' pulling the outside corners of their eyes to mimic the size and shape of Asian eyes," Sophie Wang wrote in *The Stanford Daily*. "On [white women], this 'manufactured' eye shape is beautiful. On Asians, however, this inborn eye shape is a feature to make fun of. Whether the look is achieved with makeup, eye-pulls or plastic surgery, the effect is the same: It's still an age-old taunt." In an op-ed for *Teen Vogue*, writer Sara Li concurs: "It is not accidental that mainstream [US] beauty standards would, yet again, steal select features from another culture, when that very same feature has been weaponized against its origin community in the past."

The Rise of Graphic Liner

At the time of this writing, #Eyeliner had close to 18.7 million posts on Instagram, compared with 11.8 million for #Mascara. The hashtag reveals an explosion of color, craft, and creativity. #GraphicLiner, which often accompanies #Eyeliner and has over 700,000 posts, collects especially innovative looks. (Graphic liner first emerged in the 1960s—think Twiggy's iconic mod eye makeup—though the internet enables a wider variety of trends to be shared and emulated today.)

On Instagram, there are floating fluorescent lines, with sharp rises and falls, along with ovals, circles, triangles, and intersecting flicks. "Split eyeliner," in which one line grows into two or more, "parentheses eyeliner," in which the eyes are an afterthought, and "big-little-dotted eyeliner," in which dots are both large and small, are also popular. At the edges of the eyes, there are no limits: Lines can grow into leaves, Christmas trees, flowers, feathers, and fruit. Sometimes, they create negative space. There are lemons and limes, swirls and squiggles, candy canes and unicorn horns. More daring styles include flame, cloud, swan, and star stenciling, even hearts, lightning bolts, spiderwebs, and butterflies.

The variations are apparently endless. One influencer, @MakeupByRabe, even flexed her eyeliner skills to announce that she had reached one hundred thousand followers on Instagram. She used the product to draw "100K" on her lids, embellishing the writing with confetti. Her account presents several creative liner looks, some modeled on film and TV iconography—a *Criminal Minds* post, for example, has yellow lines with the text CRIME SCENE DO NOT CROSS written into them, a smattering of blood under the eyebrows, and the letters FBI drawn onto the lids, above the lash lines. Another creator posted graphic lines styled around the colors and designs of book covers; under the hashtag #BookLook, many authors and influencers have done the same.

Even celebrities have turned to avant-garde liner looks, especially over the awards season. Iranian American actor Yara Shahidi has experimented with blue negative space, American TikTok star Dixie D'Amelio has worn a punk cat eye, and English actor Cynthia Erivo showed off a purple liner look on the 2021 virtual Golden Globes red carpet, color-blocking her neon-green mesh dress and white leather gloves. Singer Dua Lipa, model Bella Hadid, and actors Hunter Schafer and Alexa Demie are frequently seen in graphic liner, the latter two while on their wildly popular HBO show, *Euphoria*—which is known for its futuristic, often glittery looks styled by makeup artist Donni Davy—and off. (Schafer, who's also an LGBTQIA+ activist and posts her liner styles on Instagram, told *Vogue* in 2021 that she thinks about her eye makeup "in the context of an oil painting, which is all about doing a lot of thin layers of colors to create something more dimensional. Or, it might be something super graphic, like a line drawing.") Meanwhile, US gymnast Simone Biles wore floating liner while competing in the 2021 US Gymnastics Championships. The singer Solange has been wearing the uniliner look for years, which travels uninterrupted from one eye to another; at Coachella in 2023, the Colombian American performer Kali Uchis paired an all-denim Dolce & Gabbana outfit with her cat eye. And pop star Doja Cat deserves special mention for the variety of her liner looks, from asymmetrical negative space to intersecting wings. Both Kattan and Kylie Jenner have been spotted in graphic liner, too—Huda Beauty offered neon eyeshadow palettes specifically marketed as ideal for creating graphic liner styles.

Trending alongside graphic liner is "puppy eyes," a Korean beauty trend in which flicks are turned downward instead of upward; "sleepy liner," which accentuates the eye's lower rim as well as the upper to give a "sultry" effect; "kitten eyeliner," a subtler variation of cat eye; "fishtail liner," whose wings swoop up and down; "batwing liner," with an upturned wing in the shape of a bat's wing; "transparent liner," achieved with concealer; "siren liner," with elongated flicks on the inner and outer corners of the eyes; and my favorite, by far—"the four dots trick," drawn with four dots of white liquid eyeliner around the eyes, which promises to "hypnotize" men or make them "fall in love with you." (PSA:

This has not worked for me.) Actor Julia Fox had a curious go at her own trend of extreme eyeliner; the look harked back to her days as a dominatrix and underscored her IDGAF persona.

Instagram also offers myriad eyeliner filters via its effects feature, as does TikTok. But none of these have taken off in the same way that graphic liner has. Not everyone is getting these looks right, though—according to the more than fifteen thousand members of the That's It, I'm Eyeliner Shaming group on Facebook. The community provides a space for "eyeliner elitists to complain about everyone else," as well as to showcase their own botched looks.

The New Guard of Influencers

For a new crop of influencers, the goal is to divert attention from the "perfect" Instagram or snatched face and to spark interest in these eyeliner patterns for their own sake. Rather than integrating the lines into a "full beat" or a full face of makeup, they take on a life of their own. "Beauty," in the conventional sense, isn't the point. It is, instead, about artistry and self-expression, and perhaps also an attempt to stand out in saturated feeds. These influencers may be onto something—research has shown that pops of color in the grid perform better than black-and-white or more muted content.

Some who struggle with skin conditions, such as acne, frame their eyes dramatically to deflect from perceived flaws—while also owning and normalizing them. The eyes become the most important facial feature, and what *can* be controlled is controlled with flair, while the rest of the visage is left bare. This minimalist/maximalist approach is favored by influencers such as Sofia Grahn, who runs an "acne-positivity" Instagram account. On @ISofiaGrahn, she forgoes full-coverage foundation and contouring altogether, preferring to focus her efforts on her eyes. "Starry-eyed with acne constellations," reads one of her posts, her lids lined with glittery stars. "I have made it my mission to merge my passion for makeup with my aim to portray my so-called flawed skin in its raw unfiltered state paired with eye-catching makeup looks," reads another—her scars uncovered, her eyeliner turquoise.

Rhianna Angell, a twenty-four-year-old emerging British creator, also strives to present unfiltered, authentic, and minimalist looks for the overall face, with maximalist, colorful looks reserved only for the eyes. Her goal is not to appear "attractive," per se, but approachable. When I interviewed her in early 2021, she was certainly that—soft-spoken and softly made up with rose blush, matching eyeshadow, and barely there eyeliner (she'd taken a well-deserved day off from her day job and Instagram). Speaking by video from her bedroom, surrounded by makeup products, she explained how she uses eyeliner as a tool for individuality and confidence. "How you can manipulate your look just from this one product is incredible," she says, noting that she can go from unadorned to Adele-esque with the swoop of a brush.

Angell's journey into influencing started with her grandmother, who regularly applied her makeup in front of her, from when she was about six. "I have very vivid, fond memories of how I'd watch her get ready. It was a sort of ritual," she says. Angell's grandmother made a habit of gifting her almost-empty makeup products, including several from high-end brands; she then taught her how to use them, allowing Angell to experiment with looks before she was even a teenager. She'd stash the items in a small drawer, which Angell would run up to in excitement every time she'd visit her. While her grandma didn't wear black eyeliner—she'd say it was too aging—she did wear brown or blue. Angell watched closely as she enhanced her looks with those lines.

When Angell landed a job as an assistant makeup artist before being laid off during the pandemic, her grandmother often visited her to observe her in her craft. "We went from me observing her, to her observing me," she says fondly. As a teenager, Angell was also influenced by alternative rock bands, such as Fall Out Boy and My Chemical Romance. "They rocked the eyeliner really well. I was like, 'I need to look like that.' I felt so confident when I put the liner on. How can eyeliner not help with confidence? Eyeliner has been a saving grace for a lot of people, especially during the pandemic. In a time when you can't control much, if you can control how you look or what you do, that's got to be positive. It's a form of self-care. It's a form of looking after yourself."

Though she started with more traditional or emo eyeliner looks, in keeping with trends, Angell's feed (@Rhianna_Angell) now features graphic liner styles, including purple cat eye with floating amber lines; vivid red, black, and yellow patterns; squiggly pink lines; and feathery multicolored dashes. The rest of her face isn't heavily contoured and sometimes has just a hint of blush or bronzer. Notably, her posts are sans filter, showing the texture of her skin as natural light shines brightly on it. She uses the hashtag #NormalizeSkinTexture, coined by Katie Jane Hughes, one of Instagram's leading influencers redrawing our perception of makeup's role in beautification.

Rather than portraying a beauty ideal, Angell seeks out what makes her feel good, eyeliner included, and focuses on sharing those tips and tricks. "My makeup videos have never been about, 'Oh, well, look at me. Look how great I can do these different looks,'" she says. "It's 'Let me show you how to do this. Let me show you how you can feel better about yourself, too.'" (Angell says she's aware of her privileges as a white woman with a conventionally attractive Eurocentric face—but candidly notes that she does have her own insecurities.)

Shalini Kutti, a twenty-four-year-old influencer from Chennai, India, takes a similar approach. "With my account, what I'm trying to make people understand is that makeup can be powerful if you use it in the right way," she says. "Makeup is a very personal experience that can empower one to be creative and express themselves."

Kutti works full time at an early stage cosmetics start-up in India called FAE Beauty, which specializes in inclusivity and innovation in the Indian beauty landscape. The influencer's niche is minimalistic makeup, with a focus on eyeliner and the eyes. So far, she has amassed almost ninety thousand followers on Instagram and YouTube.

Like Angell, Kutti inherited her love of makeup from the women in her family. "My first introduction to makeup was my mother's makeup collection," she says. And her culture played a significant role in her journey. "Something that was a gold standard for Indian makeup at the time when I was being indoctrinated in makeup was kajal for the eyes, which I never failed to wear. So, I guess you could say that that was really my gateway drug into eye makeup." Kutti's feed also features unfiltered looks with barely there foundation, glossy lips, and eyeliner, including golden and glittery floating lines, ample negative space, and coral and white stripes. "Minimal Makeup 101 + Unfiltered Makeup Therapy," her Instagram bio reads.

Kevin Ninh, known as Flawless Kevin across social platforms, creates content that explores LGBTQIA+ issues. The ethnically Vietnamese influencer is queer and nonbinary. Graphic liner enriches Kevin's look; he also experiments with colorful or pixelated liner patterns drawn from a love for anime, K-pop, and Pokémon. In one post, Ninh's eyes are silhouetted with Pride Liner—the colors of a rainbow—the caption reading, "Being able to inspire, empower and impact people to be more confident and take positive action on their lives is one of the greatest feelings. I'm so glad you can come to me as a safe space and express yourselves for the way you truly are. Know that whatever you're going through, I believe in your strength and resilience."

Other creators cater specifically to women in midlife and beyond. Samantha of @StungBySamantha is, per her bio, "shutting down stereotypes for women OVER 50" by providing eyeliner and makeup hacks for those with older skin. Makeup artist and author Lisa Eldridge, who has over 1.7 million followers on Instagram, shares cosmetics tips that are inclusive of older viewers (the creator is herself over fifty). Her feed, @LisaEldridgeMakeup, includes images of actors aged forty and up, such as Kate Winslet and Claudia Schiffer, whom Eldridge has made up for major events and shoots. With this proliferation of influencers catering to ever-more-specific niches, there's something for every face and every eye.

Social Media's "Double Potential"

Social media has also become a means for people living in the diaspora, or under authoritarian or repressive regimes, to exchange ideas and connect with each other. For example, Instagram has played a role in offering Iranian women an avenue to share their individualism and, in some cases, even foster economic independence (although social media apps including Facebook, YouTube, and Twitter are formally blocked in the country, they can still be accessed via VPNs).

Internet platforms have "the double potential to serve as ways of strengthening existing power relations and to serve as means of giving voice to the unheard and power to those outside the social and political elite," according to Ladan Rahbari, an academic. In these instances, creators have used makeup, especially eyeliner, as a tool to express themselves. Sadaf Beauty, one of the biggest Iranian accounts on Instagram, has around four million followers (in 2019, Forbes ranked Sadaf the second-most influential beauty influencer in the world), and Shakiba Azemati, who has over six hundred thousand followers, posts eyeliner how-tos on the platform. Model Elnaz Golrokh, who ranks among the top Persian influencers, with around seven million followers, had to flee Iran after posting photos of herself online without wearing the hijab. Today, the eyeliner-adorned content creator performs her tutorials out of LA.

Separately, an image of Marzieh Ebrahimi, a young Iranian woman, was shared widely online after she became the victim of an acid attack in 2014; it's understood that she was targeted because of how she wore her hijab. In the photo of her that went viral, the half of her face that remained untouched by the acid is made up—one of her eyes is lined with eyeliner. By sharing these posts of Ebrahimi, people have been able to show solidarity with women policed by the Iranian regime because of how they dress, while also raising awareness of their plight. (Iran's cybercrime unit allegedly investigated Kim Kardashian for possible espionage in 2016 due to the influence of her decidedly un-Islamic values on young Iranian women. Following the death of Mahsa Amini, activists have flooded Kardashian's posts with #MahsaAmini, in the hopes that she might post something about the tragedy to spread the word about the struggle for women's rights in Iran.)

In addition, Iranian members of the LGBTQIA+ community use various platforms to experiment with their looks, finding the internet allows them to transcend the public-private divide and share a wide range of nonconformist expression. Some of these influencers use eyeliner to blur gender lines, despite often being trolled or attacked for their posts. Cyrus Veyssi, a first-generation Iranian American, uses their Instagram account to "carve out a niche for queer Persian people in the beauty community," according to a *Boston Globe* profile. The influencer posts images of themself wearing bright-colored flowy shirts, oversize coats, and crop tops. Their large eyes are lined, and their long, abundant lashes are curled and lifted. In one post, Veyssi transforms themself from barefaced to smoky eyed, with wings stretching across the screen, in a gold-sequin bralette.

They also use their account to raise awareness of the restrictions on women in their home country and to reflect on their personal growth and relationship with their identity and appearance.

"For the thousands of times I used to look in the mirror and say evil things to myself about how I looked," they shared in one post, "I now create thousands of looks, using makeup as a tool to begin healing the scars of old wounds."

Eye makeup holds a special, comforting place in their evolution, which has been informed by their identity as a brown child of immigrants. "I always fall back to finding beauty in my eyes because I never linked them to my gender or body dysmorphia. My eyes have always grounded me, so I feel like they naturally became my most prominent and confident feature," Veyssi tells me. "This gave me the power to explore different ways to accentuate them, and for me, eyeliner has always emphasized my femininity in a way that's validated my gender identity, rather than causing me any friction or urgency to mold [myself] differently. I find safety and beauty in my eyes for that reason."

"Black Is Beautiful"

In January 2020, a viral TikTok video showed a Black makeup artist using black eyeliner to contour her face. "I wouldn't use eyeliner for contour if I didn't have to," she later said about the video's virality. The TikTok exposed the beauty industry's ongoing failure to cater sufficiently to people of color, despite some strides forward. Meanwhile, white or white-passing influencers continue to appropriate or capitalize on Black and brown beauty practices.

"Black women reshaped the beauty industry; the problem is almost exclusively white women were paid for it," British actor

and body-positivity activist Jameela Jamil wrote in an Instagram post in May 2021. "Wash, rinse, and repeat all of these statements of mine for all beauty influencers at the top. Not just the Kardashians." Jamil also cited the impact entrepreneurial Black women such as Flex Mami and Pat McGrath have had on the industry, demanding that they be credited, along with the South Asians and Middle Easterners responsible for "heavily influencing" the rise of kohl eyeliner and the smoky-eyed look. "Just a thought for the beauty industry that takes ethnic styles to emulate ethnic features on white/white-passing faces," she said.

While she was a high school student in Spain, between classes, Fatima Camara often peered at her face in bathroom mirrors, not liking what she saw. "Why am I Black?" she'd ask herself. "Why are my lips so big?"

Camara, who's originally from Gambia and Senegal, says she would sometimes suck her lips in, trying to imagine what she'd look like had she been born white and Spanish. The twenty-six-year-old eyeliner influencer's parents immigrated to Europe before she was born, and she grew up surrounded by Caucasian students and teachers, many of whom made fun of her appearance. Camara finds it ironic that countless Instagram personalities appropriate Black culture today. "When you open Instagram, it's like everybody wants to be Black!" she says. "So now everybody wants to have my lips? It's weird. Like, okay! You guys were making fun of me, and now, you want to look like me. Look at how the tables have turned. It irritates me that people cherry-pick some aspects of Black beauty while remaining racist in other ways."

To Camara, how people respond to women wearing makeup, and specifically eyeliner, often depends on their race and ethnicity. "Eyeliner on a white woman and a woman of color are not read the same way because they have a different history and face different prejudices," concurs Rae Nudson in *All Made Up*. While a white woman may look trendy or "exotic" in eyeliner, a woman of color may be viewed as "transgressive," subversive, or—like cholas—even dangerous. But Camara pays no mind to these stereotypes; in a way, she plays into and mocks them.

The creator says it took her years to realize she'd experienced racism in the form of blatant aggressions and microaggressions at school, even from her teachers. "I love my facial features now. But when I was young, I was insecure about them because they were different from the rest of my classmates," she says. After leaving Spain and moving to the UK at nineteen, she turned to makeup not only to build her confidence but also to embody and amplify the message that "Black is beautiful." "Being Black is the best thing that I have in my life. That's the message that I want to give."

When Camara isn't filming eyeliner tutorials from her bedroom, she's stocking shelves at a warehouse, four days a week. It isn't just the makeup industry that discriminates against Black women, she says, it's the influencing industry, too. During the pandemic, she believes most ad deals have gone to white women. "When white people do makeup that's not even close to as good as how we Black people do it, they'll have a million, or two million followers, and they get all the deals with makeup brands. As a Black woman content creator, I have to work one hundred times more than a white creator. As a Black person in general . . . I have to work ten times harder than a white person. That's just how it is. That's the reality." (The communications company MSL and the Influencer League found in a study that Black influencers are substantially underpaid when compared with their white counterparts.) "It's harder for a Black girl to get partnerships," Camara says. "When you do, you'll always get paid less than a white woman—always."

When BPerfect Cosmetics, a UK brand, asked Camara to take part in a photo shoot, she was shocked and delighted by the request. "Normally makeup brands go for mixed-race girls to tick the box of Black representation," she says. "For them to include someone whose skin tone is as deep as mine was great, and I hope that is a sign of things to come." Camara, who has a level three diploma in makeup artistry, hopes to eventually start her own makeup academy—and perhaps, down the road, to launch her own cosmetics brand, one that focuses on Black women and African culture.

Eyeliner is personal to Camara. She refers to the product as a "gift that continues to give," because she can create whatever shape she wants, in whatever color or combination of colors she pleases. Camara's feed is mostly bold and bright. Some of her Paul Klee–like styles and strokes of color are so vivid, they seem like they must have been digitally enhanced (they have not). From hearts and tiger prints to jewels and butterfly wings, Camara has mastered the art of graphic liner. In one post, she decorates her eyes with the colors of the Senegalese flag to mark the country's Independence Day. "Have you ever seen a Black fairy?" she asks in another, in which her lines are adorned with flowers. In her video tutorials, her hands are so steady, she may as well be performing surgery. During the holy month of Ramadan, Camara wears the hijab and has featured special Eid eyeliner looks on her feed. "I feel prettier when I wear hijab," she declares in one of her posts.

One of Camara's favorite brands is Juvia's Place, the Black-owned business that has an eye makeup palette honoring Nefertiti. (Huda Beauty has also paid homage to Nefertiti in one of its eye palettes.) To Camara, Juvia's Place does what most brands do not: it amplifies the historical contributions of people of color. At school in Spain, she learned about slavery and the Arab conquest of the country. But she was never taught about African queens and kings, or about Black kingdoms. She took it upon herself to learn about ancient Egypt and was thrilled to discover Nefertiti, her kohl-rimmed eyes, and the civilization's obsession with makeup.

Eyeliner, she gleaned, speaks a universal language of lineage and transformation, of beauty and power. This enduring cosmetic tool has traveled across centuries and continents, from culture to culture and community to community—from Nefertiti to Camara.

"When I wear my eyeliner, I feel like I'm connecting with my African queen," Camara says. "Channeling that representation is everything. Like my queen, I'm not a follower: I am a leader. Follow me. Or don't—your loss."

Acknowledgments

On my birthday in October 2020, at the height of the COVID-19 pandemic, I was stuck between continents, having packed up my flat in London to relocate to NYC. The move was stalled by the US's decision to temporarily halt immigration and the partial closure of consulates worldwide. While in limbo, I stayed with my parents in Lebanon. Though I'd toyed with the idea of this book, I felt, in particular in the aftermath of the Beirut blast in August that year, that a "trivial" subject would be a futile endeavor. How could I possibly write about eyeliner with so much tragedy unfolding in the world? I also felt weighed down by subjects covered in my first book, *Our Women on the Ground*. The many traumas the themes carried—relating to conflict and socioeconomic turmoil in the Arab world, the region of my ancestors, a region I'm no longer living in—circled violently in my mind. My mother, understanding but critical of these anxieties, told me that *Eyeliner* would offer a layered study of cultures of color and reveal untold stories about these communities, amplifying their contributions, while also bringing delight to readers. On that day, she walked me into the depths of Sidon's souks, and took me to a kohl seller to buy a traditional kohl pot. Surrounded by the copper and clay containers, as we surveyed the options, she said, with a terrifyingly straight face that Eastern sons and daughters will be familiar with: "You must write this book, ya mama." And so I did. Mama is always right.

Endless thank-yous to Shweta Desai, Moeka Iida, Roghieh Aghabalazadeh, and Salileh Aghabalazadeh, the incredible women who assisted me with research and logistics in local languages—this book would've been half of what it is without them. Thank you also to Lina Ejeilat for the most enriching birthday week in Petra, during which we interviewed over eighty Bedouin men and women, young and old, about their thoughts on kohl, while bonding over tea and live oud music. Shokran to her parents, Hayel and Nabila, for always welcoming me into their beautiful home. And especially for the ajweh cookies.

Many thanks to Laila Shadid, Nancy Correa, Desire Thompson, Peter MacIntosh, Steve Fine, Alexandra F. Morris, Nada Elrhalami, Farah Shoucair, Raphael Cormack, Katherine Zoepf, and Vinu Kumar for additional research or translation suggestions and photography assistance. Every fact in this book was diligently checked by Rachel Stone—my gratitude to you for your phenomenal work, Rachel. Thank you also to Habu and Sleiman, my deeply knowledgeable fixers in Jordan, and to Kana Van Sandt and Richard Farmer of InsideJapan.

When I traveled to Kerala, India, to conduct research for this book, in the third year of the pandemic, I fell ill with COVID-19 and was confined to my hotel room for twelve days. I couldn't be more thankful to the staff at the hotel, who sent me fruit plates and a goldfish to lift my spirits and keep me company.

To Jessica Papin, who far more than an agent has become a mentor, and to Gretchen Schmid, who's no longer my editor but continues to cheer me on from afar—I'm grateful to you both for believing in this idea (and me). I'm grateful also to Ellie Steel and Allie Merola for their sharp eyes and continued support, as well as to the editorial, sales, and marketing teams at Penguin Books and Vintage Books. I'll never get over *Eyeliner*'s book cover and illustrations—thank you, thank you, Lynn Buckley and Mercedes deBellard.

To the friends and family who offered unwavering encouragement, I am forever indebted to you: Hind Hassan, Yumna Mohamed, Joseph Willits, Nada Bakri, Nour Malas, Gabriella Schwarz, Tara Fowler, Justin Tasolides, Laura Hurst, Sahar Tabaja, Dalila Mahdawi, Kassia St. Clair, Simon Akam, Samantha Fields, Zeina Hashem Beck, Joumanna Nasr Bercetche, Aida Alami, Yara Romariz Maasri, Kareem Chehayeb, Tamara Walid, Ruth David, Anna Louie Sussman, Jessica Lehmann, Daniele Pinto, Ami Cholia, Dan O'Donnell, Rhea Rakshit, Adi Narayan, and Lenny Toussaint. Dalia Shukri, a shout-out to you, as the eyeliner skills you flaunted at AUB have stayed with me. Heba Ayoubi, I'm sorry I missed your wedding.

This book idea was born out of a discussion over dinner at a French bistro in London with my book sister Azadeh Moaveni. I'm endlessly thankful to you for our most fascinating chats, and our ability to share our cultures, ideas, and jokes.

Finally, Lina, Amal Rammah, and Ahmad Ghaddar—truly, you're my anchors.

Notes

INTRODUCTION

XXV **While they didn't use kohl:** Lisa Eldridge, *Face Paint: The Story of Makeup* (New York: Abrams Image, 2015).

XXVI **the global eye makeup market:** "Eye Makeup Market: Global Industry Trends, Share, Size, Growth, Opportunity and Forecast 2023–2028," International Market Analysis Research and Consulting Group, https://www.imarcgroup.com/eye-makeup-market.

GLOSSARY

XXXVI **Western eyeliner tends:** Mandy Zee, "So What Is Eyeliner Made of Exactly?," *Byrdie*, April 25, 2019, https://www.byrdie.com/what-is-eyeliner-made-of.

XXXVII **The Japanese practice of outlining:** Samuel L. Leiter, *Historical Dictionary of Japanese Traditional Theatre* (Lanham, Maryland: Rowman & Littlefield Publishers, 2014), 337.

CHAPTER ONE

5 **In 2010, scientists discovered:** Sindya N. Bhanoo, "Ancient Egypt's Toxic Makeup Fought Infection, Researchers Say," *The New York Times*, January 18, 2010, https://www.nytimes.com/2010/01/19/science/19egypt.html.

5 **That same year, ancient Egyptian:** "Ancient Egyptian Cosmetics: 'Magical' Makeup May Have Been Medicine for Eye Disease," American Chemical Society, January 11, 2010, https://www.acs.org/pressroom/newsreleases/2010/january/ancient-egyptian-cosmetics.html.

9 **Nevertheless, scattered clues:** This and other details on the queen's life in this section are from Joyce Tyldesley's *Nefertiti's Face: The Creation of an Icon* (Cambridge, MA: Harvard University Press, 2018).

15 **in such high demand:** Charly Wilder, "Swiping a Priceless Antiquity . . . With a Scanner and a 3-D Printer," *The New York Times*, March 1, 2016, https://www.nytimes.com/2016/03/02/arts/design/other-nefertiti-3d-printer.html.

25 **Some journalists even mocked:** William Ritt, You're Telling Me!, column, *The Vidette-Messenger*, March 25, 1946.

34 **end of the Second World:** Geoffrey Jones, "Globalizing the Beauty Business before 1980" (working paper, Harvard Business School, Boston, 2006), https://www.hbs.edu/ris/Publication%20Files/06-056.pdf.

35 **"It's a lasting style":** Ludelle Brannon, "Permanent Eyeliner: Eye Surgeon Tattoos Eyelids," *News Herald* (Panama City), October 13, 1985.

44 **Eyeliner's cultural significance:** Raphael Cormack, *Midnight in Cairo: The Divas of Egypt's Roaring '20s* (New York: W. W. Norton & Company, 2021).

CHAPTER TWO

58 **color of the face makeup:** Mette Bovin, *Nomads Who Cultivate Beauty: Wodaabe Dances and Visual Arts in Niger* (Uppsala, Sweden: Nordic Africa Institute, 2001), 18, 33–38.

61 **The origins of the Wodaabe:** David J. Phillips, *Peoples on the Move: Introducing the Nomads of the World* (Carlisle, UK: Piquant Editions, 2001).

CHAPTER THREE

69 **sources close to her:** Parisa Hafezi, "Iranian Woman Whose Death Led to Mass Protests Was Shy and Avoided Politics," Reuters, September 28, 2022, https://www.reuters.com/world/middle-east/iranian-woman-whose-death-led-mass-protests-was-shy-avoided-politics-2022-09-28/.

74 **Some would go as far:** Haleh Esfandiari, *Reconstructed Lives: Women and Iran's Islamic Revolution* (Baltimore: Johns Hopkins University Press, 1997), 6.

76 **Veils became looser:** Azadeh Moaveni, "'It's Like a War Out There.' Iran's Women Haven't Been This Angry in a Generation," *The New York Times*, October 7, 2022, https://www.nytimes.com/2022/10/07/opinion/iran-women-protests.html.

77 **The hard-line president demanded:** Vivian Yee and Farnaz Fassihi, "Women Take Center Stage in Antigovernment Protests Shaking Iran," *The New York Times*, September 26, 2022, https://www.nytimes.com/2022/09/26/world/middleeast/women-iran-protests-hijab.html.

77 **The literacy rate among women:** Garrett Nada, "Statistics on Women in Iran," United States Institute of Peace, December 9, 2020, https://iranprimer.usip.org/blog/2020/dec/09/part-5-statistics-women-iran.

84 **likely because per hadith:** Book 29: Hadith 24 (Sunan Abi Dawud 3878), https://sunnah.com/abudawud:3878.

84 **Abu Hurairah narration:** Book 38: Hadith 17 (Jami at-Tirmidhi 2539), https://sunnah.com/tirmidhi:2539.

92 **Inspired by new makeup trends:** Morteza Ravandi, *The Social History of Iran*, vol. 1 (Tehran: Amir Kabir Publishers, 1978).

94 **Cyrus the Great:** Hassan Pirniya, *History of Ancient Iran*, vol. 1 (Tehran: Negah Publishing, 2018).

99 **In pharmacies and retailers:** Author interview with Holly Dagres of the Atlantic Council in 2022.

103 **women couldn't even buy:** Ali Anizadeh et al., "Introducing the Items of the Museum of People's Culture Unit," *Journal of Iranian People's Culture*, no. 13, (Summer 2008): 211, 216–207.

CHAPTER FOUR

117 **In centuries past, Emirati women:** Shayma Bakht, "The Legacy of Kohl," *Azeema* (September 2021): 155.

118 **multicolored, double-barreled kohl pouch:** Artist Unknown, "Kohl-Container," 1920s–'40s, ornamented silk satin and bamboo, 47 cm × 26 cm, British Museum, London, https://www.britishmuseum.org/collection/object/W_As1968-05-7.

118 **Zarqaa al-Yamama (Blue Dove):** Jad Mhaidly, "Learn about the History of Kohl from the Pharaohs until Today," *An-Nahar*, March 2019, https://www.annahar.com/arabic/article/944420-اليوم-حتى-الفراعنة-من-الكحل-تاريخ-إلى-تعرفوا.

127 **The lives of the Bedouin:** Christopher C. Angel, "Umm Sayhun: Geography and History of a Permanent Bedouin Settlement Above Petra, Jordan," *Annual of the Department of Antiquities of Jordan* 55 (2011): 9–24.

NOTES

128 **Western tourists had been visiting:** Andrew Lawler, "Reconstructing Petra," *Smithsonian Magazine,* June 2007, https://www.smithsonianmag.com/history /reconstructing-petra-155444564/.

128 **The former capital:** Abby Sewell, "Meet the Man Living in a Lost City Carved in Stone," *National Geographic,* November 20, 2017, https://www.national geographic.com/travel/article/petra-unesco-world-heritage-bedouin.

CHAPTER FIVE

137 **Cholas have always presented:** Wendy Hackshaw, "Chola: That's Who I Am," *Latino Rebels,* December 1, 2016, https://www.latinorebels.com/2016/12/01/chola -thats-who-i-am/.

141 **The group was characterized:** This and other details on the Chicano movement are from F. Arturo Rosales's *Chicano! The History of the Mexican American Civil Rights Movement* (Houston: Arte Público Press, 1997).

141 **as patriotism surged:** *American Experience,* season 14, episode 8, "Zoot Suit Riots," written and directed by Joseph Tovares, aired April 15, 2023, on PBS, https://www.pbs.org/wgbh/americanexperience/films/zoot/.

142 **though largely Mexican:** Kathy Peiss, *Zoot Suit: The Enigmatic Career of an Extreme Style* (Philadelphia: University of Pennsylvania Press, 2011).

142 **The chola aesthetic evolved:** This and other details about the aesthetic are from Amaia Ibarraran-Bigalondo's *Mexican American Women, Dress, and Gender: Pachucas, Chicanas, Cholas* (New York: Routledge, 2019).

142 **The distinct style originated:** Barbara Calderón-Douglass, "The Folk Feminist Struggle Behind the Chola Fashion Trend," *Vice,* April 13, 2015, https://www.vice .com/en/article/wd4w99/the-history-of-the-chola-456.

143 **And this appropriation didn't occur:** Julie Bettie, *Women without Class: Girls, Race, and Identity* (Oakland: University of California Press, 2002).

145 **There were few films:** Amanda Martinez Morrison, "Cholas and Chicas, Spitfires and Saints: Chicana Youth in Contemporary U.S. Film," *Text, Practice, Performance* 7 (2007): 4, 5.

148 **The Indigenous group:** Anna Rebrii and Ariella Patchen, "Celebrating Zapatista and Kurdish Women's Struggles, on International Women's Day," *The Nation,* March 8, 2022, https://www.thenation.com/article/world/zapatista-rojava -womens-movement/.

155 **her community was targeted:** "San Jose Repeals 'Blatantly Racist' Policy of Barring Lowrider Cruising," CBS News, July 3, 2022, https://www.cbsnews.com /sanfrancisco/news/san-jose-repeals-blatantly-racist-policy-of-barring-lowrider -cruising/.

CHAPTER SIX

181 **In 1935, British archaeologist:** Ernest John Henry Mackay, *Chanhu-Daro Excavations 1935–36* (New Haven: American Oriental Society, 1943).

181 **Applicators were made of copper:** Madho Sarup Vats, *Excavations at Harappa,* vol. 1 of 2 (Calcutta: Government of India Press, 1940), 460.

182 **As the Prophet Muhammad was said:** Supriya Unni Nair, "Arab Flavours from 7th Century Still Sparkle in Kerala Cuisine," *Scroll.in,* July 10, 2015, https:// scroll.in/article/738373/arab-flavours-from-7th-century-still-sparkle -in-kerala-cuisine; Habeeb Salloum, "Kohl—the Cosmetic of Seductiveness," Arab America, December 28, 2016, https://www.arabamerica.com/kohl-cosmetic -seductiveness/.

NOTES

CHAPTER SEVEN

192 **The geiko dips an applicator:** "Red Makeup in the Edo Period," Beni Museum, accessed October 2022, https://www.isehanhonten.co.jp/beni/makeup/.

193 **Geisha first emerged:** Reuters Staff, "FACTBOX—What It Takes to Be a Japanese Geisha," Reuters, December 2, 2007, https://www.reuters.com/article/us-japan-geisha-factbox/factbox-what-it-takes-to-be-a-japanese-geisha-idUST27307020071203.

196 **the academic Jan Bardsley:** Jan Bardsley, *Maiko Masquerade: Crafting Geisha Girlhood in Japan* (Oakland: University of California Press, 2021).

197 **thought to keep evil spirits:** "Japanese Makeup Culture History," Pola Research Institute of Beauty and Culture, May 26, 2020, https://www.cosmetic-culture.po-holdings.co.jp/culture/cosmehistory/4.html.

203 **the eyes and their gaze:** Kaori Ishida, "Cultural Understanding of the Eye," *Aromatopia* no. 149 (July 2018): 32–35, https://www.fragrance-j.co.jp/book/b372610.html.

204 **Haniwa figurines from the fifth:** "Japanese Makeup," Pola Research Institute of Beauty and Culture.

205 **The Asuka and Nara periods:** Masayuki Suzumori, "Why Do People Wear Makeup?," *Journal of Japanese Cosmetic Science Society* 42, no. 1 (2018): 27–35.

205 **During the traditional makeup period:** "The Culture of Heian Period in Japan," Masterpieces of Japanese Culture, accessed October 2022, https://www.masterpiece-of-japanese-culture.com/period-of-japanese-history/culture-heian-period.

206 **makeup became more widely accessible:** "Red Makeup," Beni Museum.

206 **Women used rouge to paint:** Mitsuko Takahashi, "Isehan-Honten Museum of Beni—Explore Japan's Traditional Makeup Culture," Matcha, January 24, 2017, https://matcha-jp.com/en/3854.

207 **Under the slogans:** Editors of Encyclopaedia Britannica, "Meiji Restoration," Encyclopaedia Britannica, last updated March 29, 2023, https://www.britannica.com/event/Meiji-Restoration.

207 **More women joined:** Editors of Encyclopaedia Britannica, "Taishō Period," Encyclopaedia Britannica, last updated September 14, 2012, https://www.britannica.com/event/Taisho-period.

208 **The emergence of moga:** Michael Dunn, "Modern Girls and Outrage," *The Japan Times*, May 10, 2007, https://www.japantimes.co.jp/culture/2007/05/10/arts/modern-girls-and-outrage/.

208 **whose performances include:** "Performances," Takarazuka Revue, accessed October 2022, https://kageki.hankyu.co.jp/english/revue/index.html.

209 **In the early 1920s:** This and other details are drawn from an author interview with a Beni Museum curator.

209 **end of the Shōwa period:** This and other details on modern makeup in Japan come from Yasuko Tamaki and Kimiko Yokogawa, "A Study of the Change in Makeup Practices through History and the Acceptance of Makeup Fashion among Young Women," *Cosmetology* 11, no. 17 (September 2003): 83–94.

209 **Before the war, makeup use:** Tamaki and Yokogawa, "Change in Makeup Practices," 83–94.

210 **beginning of the 1990s:** This and other details on modern makeup in Japan are drawn from Ishida, "Cultural Understanding," 32–35.

213 **The product adopts the traditional:** "Flowfushi Japan UZU Eye Opening Liner 熊野の筆職人 Liquid Eyeliner with Kumano Brush," Alpha Beauty, accessed

NOTES

October 2022 https://www.alphabeauty.net/flowfushi-japan-uzu-mote-liner-liquid
-eyeliner-with-kumano-brush.

218 **Eyeliner isn't limited:** Author interview with Ryuen Hiramatsu, a researcher
on the history of cosmetics in Japan.

218 **makeup use spread:** "What Did Samurai and Nobles Do? A Great Dissection
of the History of Men's Makeup Where Men's Aesthetics Dwell," Waraku Web,
April 5, 2021, https://intojapanwaraku.com/culture/155244/.

219 **Similar to kajal in kathakali:** "Types of Kumadori Makeup," Japan Arts Council, accessed October 2022, https://www2.ntj.jac.go.jp/dglib/contents/learn/edc25
/en/kumadori-makeup/types.html.

220 **The "genderless" subculture:** Motoko Rich, "With Manicures and Makeup,
Japan's 'Genderless' Blur Line Between Pink and Blue," *The New York Times*, January 5, 2017, https://www.nytimes.com/2017/01/05/world/asia/with-manicures
-and-makeup-japans-genderless-blur-line-between-pink-and-blue.html.

223 **where Eitaro was born:** "Introduction to Hanamachi," About Karyukai, accessed October 2022, https://www.tokyo-geisha.com/html/kagai/ooimachi.php.

CHAPTER EIGHT

240 **But the art form originated:** Mark Edward and Stephen Farrier, eds., *Drag
Histories, Herstories and Hairstories: Drag in a Changing Scene*, vol. 2, Methuen Drama
Engage (London: Methuen Drama, 2021), xxi.

243 **The mythical King Theseus:** Simon Doonan, *Drag: The Complete Story* (London: Laurence King Publishing, 2019), 104.

243 **Romans are depicted in:** Doonan, *Drag*, 109–111.

244 **The various facial makeup patterns:** Hsueh-Fang Liu, "The Art of Facial
Makeup in Chinese Opera" (master's thesis, Rochester Institute of Technology, 1997),
17, https://scholarworks.rit.edu/cgi/viewcontent.cgi?article=4318&context=theses.

245 **Drag activist groups:** Doonan, *Drag*, 213.

245 **Impersonations of starlets:** Doonan, *Drag*, 178–179.

250 **YouTube video by *Cold Cuts*:** Cold Cuts, "COLD CUTS PRESENTS •
ANYA KNEEZ: A Queen in Beirut," streamed on June 26, 2017, YouTube video,
10:53, https://www.youtube.com/watch?v=ZsRBB6NHrRU.

258 **"The world is not ready":** Trey Strange, "Beirut Pride Was Forcibly Can-
celed. Lebanon's LGBTQ Community Remains Undeterred," *HuffPost*, June 11,
2018, https://www.huffpost.com/entry/beirut-pride-cancellation_n_5b1bdc4ee
4b09d7a3d72d7d7.

CHAPTER NINE

265 **Winehouse, twenty-seven:** Author interview with Alex Foden; Naomi Parry,
Amy Winehouse: Beyond Black (New York: Abrams Books, 2021); and Carla AC,
"What Eyeliner Did Amy Winehouse Use," Brand for Beauty, July 11, 2021,
https://brandforbeauty.com/what-eyeliner-did-amy-winehouse-use/.

265 **Tyler James, a close friend:** This and other details on Winehouse in Serbia
are from Tyler James's *My Amy: The Life We Shared* (London: Macmillan, 2021).

266 **Her personal stylist and friend:** Parry, *Amy Winehouse*, 242.

266 **Parry had attempted to style:** James, *My Amy*, 303.

267 **"She's No Good":** Vesna Peric Zimonjic, "They Know That She's No Good . . .
Amy Winehouse Booed Offstage in Serbia," *The Independent*, June 20, 2011,
https://www.independent.co.uk/arts-entertainment/music/news/they-know-that
-shes-no-good-amy-winehouse-booed-off-stage-in-serbia-2299931.html.

267 **"Amy Winehouse Embarrasses Herself":** Meagan Morris, "Amy Wine-house Embarrasses Herself in Belgrade," *SheKnows*, June 19, 2011, https://www.sheknows.com/entertainment/articles/833933/amy-winehouse-embarrasses-herself-in-belgrade/.

267 **Winehouse's team had an inkling:** *Amy*, directed by Asif Kapadia (New York: A24 Films, 2015).

268 **Winehouse was bright:** Janis Winehouse, *Loving Amy: A Mother's Story* (London: Corgi, 2015), 22.

268 **When she was five:** Elizabeth Selby, *Amy Winehouse: A Family Portrait* (London: Jewish Museum London, 2014), 30.

269 **Winehouse especially took to eyeliner:** Mitch Winehouse, *Amy, My Daughter* (London: It Books, 2012), 25.

269 **Her makeup bag:** Janis Winehouse, *Loving Amy*, 76.

272 **The singer was heavily influenced:** Mitch Winehouse, *Amy*, 68; Ben Sisario and Joe Coscarelli, "Ronnie Spector, Who Brought Edge to Girl-Group Sound, Dies at 78," *The New York Times*, January 12, 2022, https://www.nytimes.com/2022/01/12/arts/music/ronnie-spector-dead.html.

272 **Winehouse's look was so reminiscent:** Lynn Yaeger, "Remembering Amy Winehouse," *Vogue*, July 25, 2011, https://www.vogue.com/article/remembering-amy-winehouse.

273 **The diva had even taken:** Mitch Winehouse, *Amy*, 70.

274 **British drag queen Jodie Harsh:** James, *My Amy*, 178.

275 **Winehouse sometimes dressed up in:** Mitch Winehouse, *Amy*, 25.

276 **When Winehouse's makeup artist:** Emma Garland in Parry, *Amy Winehouse*, 33.

276 **"It wouldn't be perfect":** Illamasqua, "ILLAMASQUA X AMY WINE-HOUSE: INTERVIEW WITH STYLIST NAOMI PARRY," streamed on September 30, 2021, YouTube video, 13:44, https://www.youtube.com/watch?v=DSQzE5xMffI.

277 **Winehouse wrote songs:** Cydney Contreras, "Amy Winehouse's Best Friend Claims Her Being 'Hounded' by Paparazzi Led to Her Death," *E! News*, June 11, 2021, https://www.eonline.com/news/1279299/amy-winehouses-best-friend-claims-her-being-hounded-by-paparazzi-led-to-her-death.

277 **the end of her life:** Mitch Winehouse, *Amy*, 279–80.

278 **"Singer Amy Winehouse was photographed":** Alan Cross, "Laugh Lines," *The New York Times*, December 9, 2007, https://archive.nytimes.com/query.nytimes.com/gst/fullpage-9F05E5D7173EF93AA35751C1A9619C8B63.html.

278 **the press itself continued:** Daily Mail Reporter, "Angry Amy Winehouse Loses Her Cool as Fan Tries to Photograph Her at the Supermarket," *Daily Mail*, March 16, 2010, https://www.dailymail.co.uk/tvshowbiz/article-1258428/Angry-Amy-Winehouse-loses-cool-fan-tries-photograph-supermarket.html; Daily Mail Reporter, "Bleary-Eyed Amy Winehouse Falls Back into Her Old Ways at Her Favourite Camden Haunt," *Daily Mail*, April 5, 2010, https://www.dailymail.co.uk/tvshowbiz/article-1263696/Bleary-eyed-Amy-Winehouse-falls-old-ways-favourite-Camden-haunt.html; Jessica Satherley, "Amy Winehouse Stumbles Out of Restaurant Exposing Her Pot Belly," *Daily Mail*, September 11, 2010, https://www.dailymail.co.uk/tvshowbiz/article-1311111/Amy-Winehouse-stumbles-restaurant-exposing-pot-belly.html.

279 **in a restroom:** James, *My Amy*, 248.

280 **she traveled to Saint Lucia:** Blake Wood and Nancy Jo Sales, *Amy Winehouse* (London: Taschen, 2018), 26–27.

282 **"The louder they applauded":** Laura Regensdorf, "Why Statement Black Eyeliner Is a Reigning Makeup Move This Spring," *Vanity Fair*, April 6, 2022, https://www.vanityfair.com/style/2022/04/black-eyeliner-reigning-makeup-move-this-spring.

285 **And a biopic about Winehouse:** Shaad D'Souza, "The Media Exploited Amy Winehouse's Life. A New Biopic Looks Set to Do the Same with Her Death," *The Guardian*, January 24, 2023, https://www.theguardian.com/music/2023/jan/24/back-to-black-new-amy-winehouse-biopic-sam-taylor-johnson-marisa-abela.

285 **She had numerous future:** James, *My Amy*, 271, 310–11.

286 **She was spotted looking happy:** Mitch Winehouse, *Amy*, 287.

286 **started going to the gym:** James, *My Amy*, 247.

286 **tidied up her wardrobe:** Mitch Winehouse, *Amy*, 283.

CHAPTER TEN

291 **Kattan became "obsessed":** This and other details about Kattan's life are from *Huda Boss*, seasons 1 and 2, featuring Mona Monica Kattan and Huda Kattan, aired 2018–2019 on Facebook Watch, https://www.facebook.com/watch/hudabossshow/.

294 **Kattan's personal eyeliner style:** *Huda Boss*, "Episode #2.1."

295 **"If I do something":** Janvi Thanki, "18 Inspiring Huda Kattan Quotes to Channel Your Inner Businesswoman," *Harper's Bazaar Arabia*, October 2, 2019, https://www.harpersbazaararabia.com/culture/people/the-a-list/huda-kattan-quotes.

296 **the "greatest hits" aspect:** Jia Tolentino, "The Age of Instagram Face," *The New Yorker*, December 12, 2019, https://www.newyorker.com/culture/decade-in-review/the-age-of-instagram-face.

298 **"when you can't see":** Bethany Biron, "Masks May Be Causing a Blow to Lipstick Sales, but Eye Makeup Sales Are Booming as Americans Find Creative Ways to Use Cosmetics," *Insider*, August 11, 2020, https://www.businessinsider.com/eye-makeup-sales-rise-lipstick-dips-due-to-mask-wearing-2020-8.

298 **The model has admitted:** Rob Haskell, "Bella from the Heart: On Health Struggles, Happiness, and Everything in Between," *Vogue*, March 15, 2022, https://www.vogue.com/article/bella-hadid-cover-april-2022.

299 **"Instead of luscious lips":** Sangeeta Singh-Kurtz, "The Big Dissolve: They Blew Out Their Faces. Now They're Melting Them Down," *The Cut*, February 1, 2023, https://www.thecut.com/2023/02/buccal-fat-removal-dissolve-fillers-bella-hadid-angular-face.html.

308 **Instagram has played:** Author interview with Holly Dagres of the Atlantic Council in 2022.

308 **Internet platforms have:** Ladan Rahbari, "Duffs and Puffs: Queer Fashion in Iranian Cyberspace," *Middle East Critique* 29, no. 1 (2020): 69–86, https://doi.org/10.1080/19436149.2020.1704503.

308 **Model Elnaz Golrokh:** Heather Saul, "Iranian Model Elnaz Golrokh Leaves Iran with Her Boyfriend After Sharing Photos without Hijab," *The Independent*, May 20, 2016, https://www.independent.co.uk/news/people/iranian-model-elnaz-golrokh-leaves-iran-with-her-boyfriend-after-sharing-photos-without-hijab-a7037801.html.

308 **an image of Marzieh Ebrahimi:** Tehran Correspondent, "Cleric Reopens Scars of Acid Attacks After Threatening Iranian Women," *Al-Monitor*, October 13, 2020, https://www.al-monitor.com/originals/2020/10/iran-cleric-scars-acid-attacks-threat-iran-women-tabatabaee.html.

309 **Iran's cybercrime unit:** Maggie Mallon, "Iran Is Arresting Instagram Models for Copying Kim Kardashian's Style," *Glamour*, May 20, 2016, https://www.glamour.com/story/iran-is-arresting-instagram-models-for-copying-kim-kardashians-style.

310 **a viral TikTok:** Natalie Morris, "Black Woman Uses Eyeliner as Contour on TikTok Video—Proving That the Beauty Industry 'Isn't Inclusive Enough,'" *Metro*, January 22, 2020, https://metro.co.uk/2020/01/22/black-woman-uses-eyeliner-contour-tiktok-video-proving-beauty-industry-isnt-inclusive-enough-12103949/.

314 **The communications company MSL:** MSL, "MSL Study Reveals Racial Pay Gap in Influencer Marketing," Cision PR Newswire, December 6, 2021, https://www.prnewswire.com/news-releases/msl-study-reveals-racial-pay-gap-in-influencer-marketing-301437451.html.